M000209070

Everyday
Sustainability

SUNY series, Praxis: Theory in Action

Nancy A. Naples, editor

Everyday Sustainability

GENDER JUSTICE AND FAIR TRADE TEA IN DARJEELING

Debarati Sen

Back cover image: Woman plantation worker with gloves on. Courtesy of Sue and Jon Hacking.

Published by State University of New York Press, Albany

© 2017 State University of New York

All rights reserved

Printed in the United States of America

No part of this book may be used or reproduced in any manner whatsoever without written permission. No part of this book may be stored in a retrieval system or transmitted in any form or by any means including electronic, electrostatic, magnetic tape, mechanical, photocopying, recording, or otherwise without the prior permission in writing of the publisher.

For information, contact State University of New York Press, Albany, NY
www.sunypress.edu

Production, Eileen Nizer
Marketing, Michael Campochiaro

Library of Congress Cataloging-in-Publication Data

Names: Sen, Debarati, 1976– author.
Title: Everyday sustainability : gender justice and fair trade tea in
 Darjeeling / Debarati Sen.
Description: Albany : State University of New York Press, [2017] |
 Series: Praxis: theory in action | Includes bibliographical references
 and index.
Identifiers: LCCN 2016054530 (print) | LCCN 2017014061 (ebook) |
 ISBN 9781438467153 (ebook) | ISBN 9781438467139 (hardcover : alk.
 paper) | ISBN 9781438467146 (pbk. : alk. paper)
Subjects: LCSH: Women tea plantation workers—India—Darjeeling. |
 Women—India—Darjeeling—Social conditions. | Tea trade—
 Environmental aspects—India—Darjeeling. | Fair trade associations—
 India—Darjeeling.
Classification: LCC HD6073.T182 (ebook) | LCC HD6073.T182 I474 2017
 (print) | DDC 331.4/83372095414—dc23
LC record available at https://lccn.loc.gov/2016054530

10 9 8 7 6 5 4 3 2 1

In memory of my mother Suvasree Sen

Contents

List of Illustrations

Note: I have not included a single close-up picture of any plantation workers as I want to keep their names and identity protected.

List of Tables

Acknowledgments

A book is most definitely a product of an author's labor, but importantly it bears witness to the immense generosity of people near and far, making things possible in a way the author never really imagined. I hope that this acknowledgment makes visible the efforts of numerous people who have believed in me, inspired me, contributed to my growth as a scholar and as a human being, and filled my world with laughter, food, and happy thoughts!

My deepest gratitude is to all my interlocutors in Darjeeling who over a dozen years have shared their stories and their creative vision for social change and educated me about the value of hard work, entrepreneurialism, humility, and creativity despite all odds. I am indebted to them for their trust in me and their insistence on writing their stories. In writing this book I am deeply aware of the uneven field of power that our relationships are embedded in; I hope I have been able to do justice to their spirit of camaraderie and their rich lives.

This book would not have been possible without the friendships that have sustained my many long and short visits to Darjeeling since 2003. Navin Tamang, Sailesh Sharma, Ashesh Rai, and Roshan Rai at DLR Prerana deserve special mention. Others who opened their homes and workplaces to my constant presence with a smile are Binita Rai, Mr. and Mrs. Sunirmal Chakravarty, Rajah Bannerjee, PC Tamang, Shantanu and Aditi Biswas, Shashi Rai, Sushma and Shantanu Ghosh. Mashqura Fareedi, Pasang Lepcha. Chaitali Ghosh and her husband Late Dey-Bapi Ghosh, also extended their hospitality and perspective on many occasions. My fellow travelers in the Darjeeling journey, Sarah Besky, Townsend Middleton, and Sara Shneiderman, continue to inspire me with their work.

At my alma mater (Rutgers University) I have enjoyed the support and encouragement of a fabulous dissertation committee. I thank my chair, Dorothy Hodgson. Do, thanks for being such a positive role model for an aspiring feminist anthropologist. I am grateful to David

Hughes for making me think beyond the dissertation and keeping in mind deep questions about power, resource use, representation, and questions of labor and development. Laura Ahearn—my fellow traveler in Himalayan studies—inspired me to think deeply about women and questions of agency as it pertains to Nepali women and women all over the world. I would like to thank Leela Fernandes for pushing me to think about broader feminist political economic questions that pertain to labor, gender, and transnational social justice in South Asia.

Apart from my committee, I would like to acknowledge the support and friendship of many others at Rutgers, most notably Rick Schroeder, Ana Ramos, Indrani Chatterjee, Ethel Brooks, Nikol Alexander Floyd, and Teresa Delcorso. I would also like to thank Penny Burness and Ginny Caputo for helping me navigate Rutgers bureaucracy and life in the United States. A cohort of students who also graduated from Rutgers deserve special thanks for their time and friendship, most notably Bradley Wilson, Cynthia Gorman, Ariella Rotramel, Chelsea Booth, Chaunetta Jones, Fatimah Williams, Drew Gerkey, Dillon Mahoney, Sharon Baskind, Noelle Mole, Rebecca Etz, Ben Neimark, Madhvi Zutshi, N. Jacob, and Edgar Rivera Colon. Mona Bhan and Mushtaque Ahangar deserve special mention for the marathon discussions, magical meals, and providing the space to relive the Delhi University days in the middle of New Jersey.

I have had the good fortune of finding great feminist mentors who have educated me about everything in academe that is not written in the "books." My deepest gratitude to Srimati Basu for work-shopping my book proposal and many of its ideas over amazing food and drinks. Priti Ramamurthy deserves special thanks for reading my work innumerable times and providing generous comments. Piya Chatterjee deserves a big "thank you" for being there when the book seemed impossible and sharing her amazing vision for social justice, especially as it pertains to *chā-bāgān* ladies. Geraldine Forbes has been a great champion of my book project right from the time of the AIIS book workshop; she has continued to enquire about "the book" over the years and has provided great feedback. I also want to thank Michelle T. Berger, Subhra Gururani, Lamia Karim, Katherine March, Megan Moodie, Shirin Rai, Raka Ray, Srila Roy, Aradhana Sharma, Ashwini Tambe, and Paige West for their valuable engagement with my work. My thinking benefitted from engagements in panels that Susan Andretta, Pallavi Bannerjee, Jessica Johnson, Omotayo Jolaosho, Andrew Flachs, Shaila Galvin, Lipika Kamra, Sarah Lyon, Carl Maida, Tad Mutersbaugh, and Mallarika Sinha Roy invited me to participate in.

My friends at American University, where I taught between 2009 and 2011, were a source of great inspiration. Loubna Skalli Hanna—

thanks for all that you did in those two years. Thank you Gretchen Schafft for opening your heart and home to me. I am grateful also to Geoff Burkhart and Sabiyha Prince for their wisdom and generosity. Thanks also to my dear colleagues Susan Shepler, Carolyn Gallaher, Sue Taylor, Brett Williams, Dolores Koeing, and Nina Shapiro Perl.

I am also lucky to have lifelong friends who are also accomplished editors. Poulomi Chatterjee deserves special mention for the gift of her friendship and her keen editorial attention to book contract jargon. My friend Srirupa Prasad has stood by me in the toughest of times and I thank her and Amit Prasad for providing me with my first home in in the United States. Rachel Watkins, my sister, my friend and mentor, thank you for being there—I am forever indebted to you. I would like to thank Anne Richards for some serious hand-holding and a steady supply of food, wisdom, and laughter. My friends Iraj Omidvar, Heidi Schrer, Jim McCaferty, Catherine Odera, Amanda Richey, and Matthew Mitchelson have cheered me along to the finish line. I would also like to thank Mallarika Sinha Roy, Basantarani Haobam, Rukmini Sen, Pritha DasGupta, and Faizan Ahmed for enquiring about the book over the years.

A book project spanning years is also sustained by resources and I am grateful to the following agencies and programs for their support: Wenner Gren Foundation Individual Research Grant (no. 7495) and NSF DDIG Grant (no. 0612860), for supporting long stretches of ethnographic fieldwork. Princeton University's office of Population Research, the Taraknath Das Foundation of Columbia University's Marion Jemmott grant, and Rutgers University's Seed Grants sponsored shorter stays in Darjeeling. The Kennesaw State CHSS Summer Research Grant and the Manuscript Completion Program made possible some of the unhindered writing time. I would like to thank the American Institute of Indian Studies "Dissertation to Book" workshop for providing initial feedback on my dissertation. I would like to thank my department chairs, Joe Bock and Susan Smith, and the Dean of the College of Humanities and Social Sciences at Kennesaw State University, Robin Dorff, for their support of a jointly appointed junior faculty to complete the colossal task of writing the first single authored book.

Thanks also to Rafael Chaiken, Michael Campochairo, Dan Flynn, Eileen Nizer, and David Prout for everything they did to ensure that my book was on schedule.

Thanks to Nancy Naples at SUNY Press for her enthusiasm and support for this book. Special thanks to Beth Bouloukos for all the support and help along the way. The suggestions from the two anonymous reviewers have made this a much better book, I am grateful to them. Any shortcoming in the book is the author's responsibility.

I am grateful to *Feminist Studies* and *Anthropology in Action* (Berghan Publishing) for granting me permission to reproduce my work from their journal. The same goes for Zed Books for allowing me to use my work published with them. I would like to thank Dustin Gibson, Kirsteen Anderson, and Paola Garcia for editorial assistance at various early stages of the book.

Losing my only parent at twenty-three was life altering in so many ways. My *chotomama* (Arijit Sen) has always been a source of strength ever since my childhood and I thank him for being there at critical moments in my life. My *baromama* (Surojit Sen) helped open many doors in Darjeeling, for which I am grateful. Both my uncles have also shared their love for Darjeeling—their childhood place. My parents-in-law, Manasij and Samita Majumder, deserve my gratitude for taking care of so many loose ends in Kolkata. Panna and Krishanu Chatterjee and Supriyo and Shika Biswas may not share blood ties with me, but they have looked out for me over the years.

My soulmate and partner-in-crime, Jijo/Sarasij Majumder, has seen this project through since its inception, sharing the pleasure and pain that accompany any book project. I am grateful for his love, patience, humor, and constant assurance that I should strive higher than I thought possible.

My two parents, my *ma* (Suvasree Sen) and my *dida* (Ratna Sen), are not alive to see this book come to fruition. For both of them Darjeeling was the best place on earth and I so regret not having the chance to share it with them. Ma, a single parent in India since the 1970s with all its complications, instilled in me a deep respect for learning and being independent and never taking no for an answer just because I am a woman. I thank her for my foundational lessons in feminism, and I dedicate this book to her.

Abbreviations

10YFP	Ten Year Framework of Programs
ABGL	Akhil Bharatiya Gorkha League
CPI	Communist Party of India
CPI (M)	Communist Part of India (Marxist)
CSR	Corporate Social Responsibility
DGHC	Darjeeling Gorkha Hill Council
DPA	Darjeeling Planter's Association
DTA	Darjeeling Tea Association
EFTA	European Fair Trade Association
FLO	Fair Trade Labelling Organizations International
GI	Geographical Indications
GJM	Gorkha Janamukti Morcha
GNLF	Gorkha National Liberation Front
GTA	Gorkhaland Territorial Administration
IC	Internal Control (for organic certification)
ICDS	Integrative Child Development Services (Government of India)
IMO	Institute of Marketecology
MNREGA	Mahatma Gandhi National Rural Employment Guarantee Act [Also referred to as NREGA]
NABARD	National Bank for Agricultural and Rural Development
SCP	Sustainable Consumption and Production

SKS	Sānu Krishak Sansthā
SPO	Small Producer Organizations
UNCSD	United Nation Commission on Sustainable Development
WTO	World Trade Organization

Note on Transliteration

In this book I have used common transliterations of Nepali words and phrases only where it was absolutely necessary to demonstrate nuance, to communicate spontaneity of many conversations and give readers a way to feel what the fieldwork situation was like. I do not make a distinction, while writing, between Darjeeling Nepali and Nepali spoken in Nepal. Instead, I have provided the meaning of each Nepali word in parentheses in text for ease of reading and understanding. I have tried to make some distinction in pronunciation, most common of them is the "a" vs. "ā" distinction.

Introduction

Throughout rural areas of Darjeeling district, sirens ring out from tea plantations at 7:00 a.m. sharp, signaling the beginning of a busy workday not only for plantation workers but also for smallholding tea farmers who belong to a small farmers' cooperative (Sānu Krishak Sansthā).[1] Mostly women, these tea farmers live in villages outside plantation lands and are not formally tied to the state's plantation bureaucracy. The Darjeeling Tea Association (DTA) denies their existence in formal conversations. Yet on hearing the plantation siren, these women begin tending the tea bushes growing alongside other crops in their rocky backyards. The tea that they cultivate fetches ready cash income for their household maintenance if they are able to locate the right networks to send it to Darjeeling town for sale. According to Geeta, one such farmer, the siren had acquired increasing significance over time: "It reminds us that what we do and have done inside our farms for years is also valuable. The tea we women produce is the real organic that plantations want to buy. It is because of our daily task of procurement for our families that small-farmer-grown tea is sold at high prices on the world market."

Geeta's statement signals how new market-based sustainability initiatives such as Fair Trade and organic certification[2] are challenging traditional tea production orthodoxies in Darjeeling—which had been legally and geographically constrained to plantation-based agriculture—producing material and cultural consequences for surrounding villages. For major plantations, the shift from industrial agriculture to sustainable organic production is costly and difficult (see chapter 2), opening spaces for communities and family farmers on the fringes of plantation country to grow organic tea and thereby to dream of a better economic future in a region characterized by economic stagnation, massive unemployment, and consequent out-migration. Yet new practices grounded in philosophies of sustainable development and corporate social responsibility have both positives and negatives: they have given smallholder families

1

some hope for a steady agriculture-based livelihood, while simultaneously trapping them in precarious contracts, as I shall describe throughout this book. In the picture below we see one such farmer standing
proudly displaying his compost while telling me that organic cultivation
will make him as rich as a Punjabi farmer. Ironically, much of the agricultural success in Punjab state is due to high yielding green revolution
technologies. This particular man and his family did not even belong
to any cooperative like SKS. But living on plantation fringes producing
a modest harvest of tea, he nurtured great hopes about having a co-op
in his own area hoping to enjoy agricultural prosperity as promised in
Green Revolution promotions seen in Figure 0.1.

Therefore, it was not only women but also men who realized
the economic potential of working in Darjeeling's informal tea sector.
Men likewise rejoiced in the siren and women's enthusiasm to work.
Biren Rai, who had been seeking a job in the local government and
was an active member of a local political party, now began his day by
checking paperwork in the newly formed Sānu Krishak Sansthā office,
as an office bearer. Biren often told me:

Figure 0.1. Organic Farmer Dreaming about Green Revolution.

Fair Trade and the women have made our cooperative stronger. We have to work like a *panchāyat* [local government body] and preserve the purity of our cooperative since our reputation is growing all over the world. If the cooperative grows, some unemployed men may find jobs here. Maybe one day there will be enough Fair Trade premium money from our tea sales.

Biren's comments allude to the growing popularity of small-farmer-produced tea on the global Fair Trade market, and the hope and excitement this trend has produced among small farmers in remote rural villages or Darjeeling district.

Meanwhile, in the eighty-seven government-supported official "Darjeeling" designated tea plantations—only one-third of which have Fair Trade and Organic certifications—the 7:00 a.m. siren signals the beginning of another day of strictly monitored labor (*thikā*, wagework) for women tea pickers. Whereas women farmers in the villages find new purpose in Fair Trade and organic cultivation, women plantation workers perceive the new Fair Trade and organic certification policies as an additional layer of management intervention and disciplining of their daily work and social lives. These women detest conforming to Fair Trade regulations. Decreased green leaf growth during the first few years of organic conversion (Bisen and Singh 2012) reduced plantation workers' seasonal extra cash income from exceeding their daily quota of collecting leaves. As Sushma explained in 2004:

> Fair Trade has not assisted in our daily job of procuring for our families. For that we women have to play *ghumāuri* [informal savings and mentoring groups within plantations]. We have to keep looking for money to make liquor for local sale, buy rationed rice on the black market, rear chicken and pigs. If the plantation owner favors us then we sometimes get a chance to take out a loan from the fund.[3]

The skepticism about the potential benefits of Fair Trade and organic production stemmed from the inability of this transnational-trade-based sustainable development campaign to challenge the state-controlled wage structure within plantations. The meager wages made women's job of procuring for their families' basic needs extremely difficult, and most turned to various kinds of small but important entrepreneurial ventures to raise their standard of living.

That women have diverging attitudes and aspirations surrounding the new agrarian politics and change in Darjeeling is reflected in the preceding quotations. Women's such deep contemplation of Fair Trade occurred in a context where authorities in the plantation bureaucracy and heads of tea-growing cooperatives in the off-plantation, rural areas of Darjeeling were noticeably celebrating and fetishizing women's labor and expertise. The circulating discourses celebrated the value of smallholder women farmers and wage-earning women plantation workers in terms reminiscent of the global discourses about women's empowerment that are central to Fair Trade propaganda and its acceptance in the West. They portrayed women as loyal, willing to take risks, entrepreneurial, responsible, knowledgeable, and hardworking, as evident from Biren Rai's comments in the earlier part of this introduction.

Organic certification and Fair Trade are distinct: whereas organic certification focuses on geography and soil qualities, Fair Trade, with its emphasis on transparency and inclusion of the marginalized in the production process, valorizes women (Sen and Majumder 2011; Mutersbaugh 2002, 2005; Mutersbaugh et al. 2005; Mutersbaugh and Lyon 2010). On Darjeeling plantations Fair Trade and organic certifications always went hand in hand. Steady flows of visitors and officials of nongovernmental organizations (NGOs) passed through the plantations and cooperatives, filming and recording women, often trying to document their natural and affective connections to tea. The smiling faces of women plantation workers were plastered on billboards all over Darjeeling town. Despite these Corporate Social Responsibility (CSR)-inflected narratives and imagery and the pseudo-feminist propaganda about sustainable development, I encountered both skepticism and creativity in women's engagement with emerging discourses and resources emanating from the global drive for sustainable tea production.

Everyday Sustainability takes readers to ground zero of market-based sustainability initiatives—Darjeeling—where Fair Trade ostensibly promises gender justice to minority women engaged in organic tea production on postcolonial plantations and smallholder farms. These women tea farmers and plantation workers have distinct imaginaries and everyday practices of social justice that at times dovetail with and at other times rub against the tenets of the emerging global morality market. This book enquires why women beneficiaries of transnational justice-making projects remain skeptical about the potential for economic and social empowerment through Fair Trade while simultaneously seeking to use the movement to give voice to their situated desires for economic and social justice. *Everyday Sustain-*

ability illuminates the contradictions and complexities of the gendered ethical selves that emerge at the margins of transnational "conscious capitalism" initiatives designed to empower women. This is the first book-length comparative ethnographic treatment of Fair Trade from a postcolonial transnational feminist framework, a perspective absent from recent studies of Fair Trade.

A focus on women's justice imaginaries (their perceptions of social justice) and related entrepreneurialism is particularly timely in the present moment, when feminists are debating and mobilizing either for or against the privatized political playing field of neoliberalism, with its myriad possibilities and limitations (Prughl 1999; Pulido 1996; Wright 2006). *Everyday Sustainability* underscores how some of the poorest women in Darjeeling have found creative ways to negotiate the "market." Since 1947, they have engaged first with the developmentalist state, then with the transnational market-based justice paradigms that strategically celebrate them as authentic subjects for empowerment because of their "indigenous" organic tea production methods.

The neoliberal market has indeed found its pristine subjects to protect and empower. But how do women tea producers navigate this market-based system? Why do they need to engage in a politics of counter-vigilance against Fair Trade's global imperatives? How do they master different strategies of sometimes shielding themselves from and sometimes engaging with Fair Trade to defend their individual and collective aspirations for economic and social justice? How do these divergent engagements with Fair Trade shape their subjectivities and their community and family lives?

What was amply clear in my eleven years of sustained ethnographic engagement with women on plantations and on surrounding smallholdings was that Fair Trade rarely benefited these women, and it did so only when women developed their own situated pathways of cultural and economic entrepreneurship to make Fair Trade work for them. In their innovative maneuvers they sometimes rejected Fair Trade in the interests of protecting their reputations and sustaining their everyday business enterprises through other means, such as the *ghumāuri* mutual aid groups on plantations. Women members of the smallholder tea cooperative plotted and planned critical engagements with Fair Trade bureaucracy and community patriarchs to ensure "transparent" Fair Trade, ironically. At each step they were building social sustainability (Cruz-Torres and McElwee 2012) on the margins of the hegemonic global Fair Trade movement through creativity and entrepreneurship, which interestingly, went completely unnoticed by the movement's advocates and bureaucrats.

Valorizations about women were double-edged and provided frequent fodder for rumination and reflection among women plantation workers and tea farmers trying to comprehend the changes in their communities and workplaces. Though they encouraged women to see themselves as important, such valorizations were also a ploy to appropriate women's labor and time. There was misrecognition in the strategic recognition of women's expertise, knowledge, and commitment to work in community and global propaganda. Women workers and farmers were simultaneously the targets of both valorization and exploitation by a patriarchal village structure and a male-dominated plantation bureaucracy. Prior to Fair Trade women had been exploited both inside and outside plantations, often in the context of multiple patriarchies (Chatterjee 2001; Grewal and Kaplan 1994) that restricted their ability to leave their village and their accepted activities. Fair Trade transformed traditional patriarchies by thrusting the roles and responsibilities of entrepreneurs, supervisors, and decision makers on women, without granting them rights to resources and recognition in their everyday struggles. This book explores how women tea farmers and plantation workers negotiate with and contest new modes of capitalist exploitation that are couched in deceptive language of agency, freedom, and emancipation.

Geeta, Sushma, and Biren Rai's assertions of value derive from their exposure to the governing practices of Fair Trade, which operate through valorization of rural life and fetishization of women's labor to invent and perpetuate an organic tea tradition in Darjeeling. When local plantation managers interested in trading with small tea farmers would bring Fair Trade officials on tours, or representatives of local NGOs promoting rural development would bring in independent tea buyers, they would often extoll the virtues of women's *maya* (love and care) for tea production. Then the women smallholders would be photographed in stereotyped poses that mirror the images in state marketing materials for Darjeeling tea. For their part, the women tea farmers distinguished themselves as superior to women plantation workers in their everyday cultural discourse; for example, by portraying themselves as indigenous artisanal tea producers. Such fetishisms also mask the everyday appropriation of women's labor and time in the process of bringing Darjeeling's marginal tea producers into the ambit of Fair Trade. Women in these tea-farming households were particularly critical of the periodic demands on their time and labor since they are engaged in the actual harvesting of tea and carrying out Fair Trade and organic training. Women plantation workers, meanwhile, followed a strategic path of avoiding Fair Trade–related activities on the plantations where they worked.

Fair Trade and its emphasis on organic cultivation precipitated a sea change in Darjeeling's postcolonial tea production history, as detailed in chapter 2. A transformation in the preferences of Western consumers has led to significant reorganization of tea production. Though plantations continue to dominate the scene in Darjeeling, the logic of tea production is very gradually shifting from Fordist plantation methods to new contractual arrangements. In the postindependence period and building up to the 1990s plantation agriculture focused on increasing productivity using "green revolution" technologies—mostly chemical fertilizers. Technology carried more importance than specialty branding or perceptions of quality. Plantations aimed to increase efficiency and hence the quantity of tea produced, just as any factory producing commodities for the market would.

After the 1990s, however, tea was reinvented in the West as a health and culture good (Dolan 2001, 2008). This new mindset required a different kind of production regime that plantations were not prepared to implement. Initially, the Fair Trade movement recited the mantra of empowering marginalized producers in the global economy, and even now in the certification process, Fair Trade institutions avoid using the word "plantations" in their publicity materials, instead calling them gardens, large farms, or "hired labor organizations" (Fairtrade India 2013).

International Fair Trade standards banned the use of chemicals. The quality and ecology of the tea leaves became more important than quantity. Heightened consumer demand for sustainable, chemical-free tea challenged the plantations' hegemony as producers of tea for the global market. In this new scenario plantation owners had to employ savvy marketing and strategic CSR campaigns to reinvent themselves as champions for small-farmer-grown tea, often by misrepresenting wage laborers as smallholder farmers. As a result of such practices, Darjeeling, especially the coffee-producing southern region, now has the largest number of plantations with Fair Trade certification of any state in India (Fairtrade India 2013). "Asia leads in the plantation-based Fair Trade. Specifically, this region accounts for 80 percent of the world's Fair Trade tea plantation workers . . . supplies 49 percent of all Fairtrade workers in the world, it accounts for 12 percent of all Fairtrade farmers" (Makita and Tsuruta 2017: 5). "India is Asia's largest supplier of Fairtrade producers within both categories of organizations, comprising small farmers and hired labor respectively. . . . For the category of hired labor organizations, India is the largest supplier of Fairtrade workers globally . . . In Asia 21 percent Fair Trade premium revenue comes from tea, whereas tea constitutes only 5 percent global Fairtrade premium" (Makita and Tsuruta 2017: 6).

At one of the plantations where I conducted research, the manager constantly spewed Gandhian notions of purity and simplicity and declared that he was going to give all the land back to the women in ten years. Other plantations declared themselves leaders of Darjeeling's small farmer movement because they formed strategic alliances with smallholder farmers, who, as I detail later, are not legally entitled to produce or export Darjeeling brand tea, and therefore have no choice but to rely on plantations to market and process their produce resulting in new contracts (see also Watts and Goodman 2004).

Figure 0.2. *Ama* (Mother of the house) Hand-Rolling Green Tea in SKS.

The social and political life of sustainable tea production in Darjeeling is concealed in out-of-the-way places hidden by the aesthetics of plantation landscape reified in popular travel writing (Koehler 2015; Wright 2011). Here is an excerpt, "Coffee in India might have the moment, but Darjeeling tea has romance—not in the colonial vestiges of how a tea estate in structured, but in the green hills, in Darjeeling and its backdrop if majestic, icy Himalayan peaks, in pure mountain air and vintage Raj-era bungalows . . . The romance is also in the tea themselves: struggling artisans in the truest sense . . . using methods and tools that have changed little in a century" (Koehler 2015:227–28). Academic engagements with the tea industry also tend to focus on plantations alone (Sharma and Das 2011). The advent of Fair Trade may generally mean business as usual within plantations, but outside of them Fair Trade has engendered new expectations of emerging from the precariousness of rural life, plagued with massive unemployment and male out-migration and substance abuse. While the tea plantations formally employ about 60,000 workers, informal tea production is common among the rural Darjeeling population of 1,118,860 (Darjeeling Census 2011), especially in the Kurseong and Darjeeling subdivisions. The state categorizes any tea grown outside of its eighty-seven recognized plantations as illegal for sale, but there is a sizable informal tea market that flows through plantations now made possible by the necessities of Fair Trade and organic standards.

Late Capitalism and Fair Trade in Darjeeling

These changes occur in a wider context of global capitalism where there are new articulations between the formal and informal sectors (Sanyal 2007; Goodman and Watts 1997, 10) in the "developing" world. The guiding narrative that sustained tea plantations immediately after India's independence was one of modernization to enable production for a global market in a space that brings together capital, labor, and resources within a formal ambit of wagework. In this framework, non-plantation Darjeeling is a vast stretch of unknown and unacknowledged population and space—a wilderness that contrasted sharply with the uniform, managed, geographically homogenous, monocultural, and manicured aesthetic of the plantations. The two pictures below show the contrast between manicured plantation landscape (figure 0.3) and the unkempt lands of the non-plantation tea growers (figure 0.4).

Figure 0.3. Aesthetic of Plantation Monoculture (*Kaman*).

Figure 0.4. Aesthetic of Non-Plantation Tea Production (*Basti*).

Throughout India planners and policymakers view informal economic spheres as throwbacks to the past (Breman 1996, 2003; Jhabwala et al. 2003). On the assumption that they would progressively be absorbed within the formal sphere of the modernizing Indian economy and agribusiness of plantations, informal sectors rarely have sites of state intervention. But these beliefs are increasingly belied by the dynamism of India's informal sector—which policymakers now call the *jugaad* economy—signifying a site of tremendous entrepreneurship, creativity, and social innovation (Majumder 2015; Sengupta 2015). As the nature of economic development interventions started changing, both within and outside India, the articulation between the formal and the informal sectors became increasingly flexible and engaged in productive tension.

In Darjeeling, Fair Trade ushered in a convergence of these two related yet different global trends. The non-plantation areas came under the umbrella of NGO interventions or of NGO-mediated government interventions, sometimes through microcredit-based rural development under National Bank for Agricultural and Rural Development (NABARD) and later promotion of organic cultivation to tap into global resources promoting sustainable development. Fair Trade regulations, pushed foreign buyers and owners of plantations—where the soil was too contaminated with agrochemicals for organic production—to explore outlying areas to source globally marketable organic tea leaves. Darjeeling, thus, was drawn into a late-capitalist logic of transnational trade that valued heterogeneity in crop production, small farmers, the informal sector, and entrepreneurial women. So, rather than being absorbed into the sphere of wagework, the informal economy is developing intricate connections with transnational circuits of trade and commerce. What we see in Darjeeling is a subtle unfolding of late capitalist logic of heterogeneity, household labor and self-exploitation, and weakening of labor unions in which boundaries between plantation/non-plantation and private-intimate/public become increasingly porous.

All of these transitions were enabled by region-specific gendered social structures and dynamics of tea production. In this book I engage feminist ethnography with the unfolding of emerging global political economic processes to establish the centrality of the informal, clandestine sphere of tea production, the intimate gendered structures (Stephen 2003, 2005; Freeman 2014) that support the trade of Darjeeling tea through gendered small-scale entrepreneurialism, and the cultural lens through which women in rural Darjeeling understand and work within transnational trade and justice regimes. Additionally, I focus on "everyday sustainability"; that is, practices and processes through which women actively learn about emerging market-based sustainability and justice regimes and evaluate their effectiveness in addressing their everyday community-level struggles over resources, representation, and entrepreneurship.

The unfolding of transnational justice regimes (like Fair Trade) in rural Darjeeling remains puzzling to many smallholding women farmers, even as they hope it will improve their future prospects. The advent of such regimes has suddenly lent importance to their views about organics but also burdened them with new demands on their time, such as attending various community training programs. Women find the heightened attention being paid to them upsets their daily schedule of tea production. Instead, they find themselves preparing elaborate meals for mostly white guests in their homes who pester them to share their views about Fair Trade-organic tea. Some are interrupted in the middle of their workday to tidy themselves for photographs they are told will travel far. At other times they find themselves forced to challenge the male leaders of their local cooperative to get Fair Trade funds. Due to these time-consuming activities women often debated skeptically whether Fair Trade advanced their own economic and social projects. Fair Trade and related development ventures in Darjeeling were evaluated from the vantage point of situated gendered projects of value as I elaborate in the next section.

Gendered Projects of Value

Darjeeling, thus, is an important site in which to examine how social reproduction strategies of smallholder women farmers and tea plantation workers play out vis-à-vis new capitalist appropriations of labor and resources—evident in women's new collective entrepreneurial ventures or strengthening existing ones like *ghumāuri*. Social reproduction in the late capitalist context has been the focus of many critical assessments of varying responses to reorganization of production under global capitalism (Harvey 2014; Fraser 2013; Gidwani 2008; Chari 2004, Katz 2001b). In this book I propose that we broaden our understanding of social reproduction from narrow economistic concepts like "need economy" as espoused by economist Kalyan Sanyal (2007; also see Majumder forthcoming) and instead focus on the cultural, economic, political, and affective work involved in social reproduction. Scholars and activists (whether Fair Trade promoters or local development activists) should take note of the reality of gendered everyday entrepreneurialism in rural areas as manifested in the households of both farmers with small landholdings and wage laborers with no formal access to land or other major assets. These everyday entrepreneurialisms sustain livelihood and community in rural areas. Women plantation workers and smallholder farmers are critical actors in Darjeeling's precarious informal economy, as amply demonstrated in the subsequent chapters. What Fair Trade has done is to provide a new context for the poorest segments of India's informal economy to articulate a gendered critique based on their everyday struggles over social reproduction and cultural production.

The symbolic, subjective, and self-making elements in a need economy (that is, reproduction), take on distinct cultural forms that constitute an individual's or group's self-image in the context of situated political economies (see also Freeman 2014; Karim 2011). Therefore social reproduction is not simply about meeting needs, as Sanyal proposed, but also about everyday cultural production, which relies on but is also in tension with the profit-driven corporate economy. Examining the tensions and relations between processes of cultural production, social reproduction, and cultural reproduction, as feminist scholar Priti Ramamurthy (2003, 2010, 2011) proposes, is exponentially more useful for understanding practices and meaning-making around Fair Trade (see also de Certeau 1984). Cultural reproduction thus constitutes the abstract and complex categories that people inhabit as wageworkers, consumers, or entrepreneurs, to use the hegemonic definitions of states and NGOs. For instance, in the context of Andhra, Ramamurthy foregrounds how men and women of lower-caste agricultural families systematically accumulate capital to further identity-based cultural productions in everyday life that redefine their gender and caste-based social positions in the regional cultural and political economic system.

Drawing on Ramamurthy, I view women tea workers' cultural productions as more complex than simple social reproduction in terms of an economic logic that inevitably categorizes them as completely dominated by or completely resistant to Fair Trade. Rather I see them re-articulating global discourses and categories of cultural reproduction available to them for purposes of empowerment. Their goal is not simply sustaining production relations infused with patriarchy, but rather self-making which gives rise to contestations of Fair Trade, patriarchy, and collusions between the two. Their everyday social, cultural, and economic entrepreneurial activities to support their families and their own aspirations become the vantage point from which they understand and engage with global sustainable development policies.

Acknowledging and documenting these nuanced entrepreneurial forms of economic and affective life marks the cutting edge of feminist anthropological work in recent time. *Everyday Sustainability* takes these engagements in a new direction where such entrepreneurialisms become the focal point of gendered engagements with the emerging global "morality market" (Chowdhury 2011). As feminist anthropologist Carla Freeman urges in her recent work on the Caribbean middle class, such an acknowledgment of gendered entrepreneurialism requires us to understand it as dynamic:

> . . . always *in formation*—akin to the processual work of class, gender, race and culture—and inextricably bound up with these dimensions of identity . . . entrepreneurial labors increasingly exceed the formal boundaries of productive enterprise to include everyday facets of social reproduction (i.e., work 'at home' and work 'at work' bleed into one another), they seem to permeate every crevice of conscious and even unconscious life. (Freeman 2014, 2–3, emphasis in original)

Women in Darjeeling present themselves to interlocutors (like me) and to themselves as complex subjects of emerging transnational rights discourses that stretch the static frames of women's agency, without understanding how women navigate global and local power structures in their everyday lives. One can locate these emerging cultural productions in these women's everyday discourses around sustaining their families as well as in their delicate navigation of categories of social reproduction that restrict them to static roles of "housewife," "worker," "daughter," or "mother." Women constantly find these identifications limit their possibilities for sustaining themselves and their families. The new categories of cultural reproduction emanating from Fair Trade/transnational justice discourse—which valorize them as skilled, powerful, and happy—do not enable us to understand the challenging cultural terrain women navigate in terms of their everyday mobilizations and maneuvers around household and community.

The simultaneous valorization and devaluation of women in the emerging discourses and practices of Fair Trade compel women in small tea-farming homes to prioritize their own ambitions in order to challenge the discursive frames and practices through which local and transnational communities interpret their needs and advocate policies for their "empowerment." Women tea producers transform the disciplining tendencies of well-meaning capacity-building initiatives by advancing what I call their own "gendered projects of value"—a key ideological and material threshold of discourses on everyday sustainability. These projects adhere to the distinct gender roles present in Darjeeling's rural areas. Women plantation workers and women farmers are drawn to different strategies of self-making as a result of their navigation of distinct micro-histories of tea production, class formation, and the effects on their intimate lives. These gendered projects of value manifest in new collaborative entrepreneurial initiatives that women in rural Darjeeling undertake based on their mutual experiences of labor and procurement for their families. They are not just born out of simple kin networks, labor unions, or political parties, but out of decades of contesting local developments' individualized and or limited women's empowerment strategies, which collude with male patriarchy and ignore women's grounded micro-strategies. Fair Trade for them seems continuation of patriarchal local development.

In Darjeeling these gendered projects of value are expressed in performative acts that operationalize women's individual and collective aspirations. Sometimes women enthusiastically participate in Fair Trade, accepting and almost enacting the "survival narratives" that Fair Trade publicity materials promote, giving interviews to certifiers, voluntourists and posing for clichéd pictures of "third-world empowered women."

At other times they either strategically withdraw from and mock Fair Trade capacity-building practices, or revitalize their own informal collectives that celebrate their work, body, and creativity. In these shifting strategies of conforming, withdrawing, and informally organizing, one can locate the embryo of counter-hegemony (Sen and Majumder 2015). Women's adherence to gendered projects of value also alerts us to take note of forms of self-governance that question "neoliberal governmentalities" (Karim 2011) hereby expressed in Fair Trade.

In non-plantation areas gendered projects of value manifest in women tea farmers' collective efforts to question patriarchal cultural categories—such as dutiful housewife—that spatially limit their entrepreneurial ventures. Women collectively mobilize to establish themselves as housewife-entrepreneurs, a role that both Fair Trade policies and local patriarchs deny them, exposing them to gendered shaming as "businesswomen." In this process women question why Fair Trade fails to support their efforts to challenge existing practices of social and cultural reproduction that undermine their entrepreneurialism.

On plantations, women workers' gendered projects of value are discernible in their efforts to navigate (a) discipline practices based in shaming, and (b) male envy in the community and their own households over their steady employment. Women plantation workers' everyday work and family lives are organized around "performative obedience" expressed in agentive narratives of their ability to run the plantation from its margins. Women mock Fair Trade's vacuous celebration of their skills that does very little to improve their lives. As I will show later, most women plantation workers avoid Fair Trade initiatives and instead turn to clandestine mentoring spaces like *ghumāuri* groups.

Analyzing these everyday gendered projects of value from an ethnographic perspective was useful for understanding how poor women articulate what they value in the context of their everyday sustainability. It provides a glimpse into their everyday evaluation of emerging sustainability regimes as well as how they prioritize certain economic, political, and cultural projects. Grounded exploration of "gendered projects of value" and its effects on household and community life, as well as on women's individual and collective subjectivities, is critical for understanding existing justice imaginaries. It draws us into the drama of everyday sustainability in the Darjeeling tea industry.

Gender and Sustainability

Analyzing the current state of global engagements on gender and sustainability from the vantage point of "gendered projects of value" holds a distinct benefit. When looked through the prism of women's desires and their micro-entreprenurialisms the current state of sustainability discourse appears to be far removed from acknowledging the creative entrepreneurial work women are doing to sustain their families and communities. Although James Wolfensohn declared at the UN Conference on Women in Beijing the centrality of women to sustainable development and social justice (see Sharma 2008, 19) the policies that were formed inspired by Wolfensohn's motto fall short of sustaining women's creativity in meeting their community's needs since it moves away from the welfare model of women's development. It emphasizes self-sustaining entrepreneurialism, therefore its motto: "trade not aid."

Paul Rice, chairman of Fair Trade USA (previously Transfair USA) remarked in a recent interview that Fair Trade would pay hidden dividends in farmers' and workers' increased self-confidence and pride as they solved their own problems with Fair Trade's support. The message that Rice and the overall Fair Trade establishment broadcast echoes the World Bank's sustainable development paradigm inaugurated in 1997, when Wolfensohn advocated "sustainable development that is people centered and gender-conscious, that seeks equity for all and empowerment of the weak and vulnerable everywhere so that they may be the producers of their own welfare and bounty, not the recipients of charity and aid" (Serageldin 1998, 4). My decade of research leads me to wonder whether the self-appointed foot soldiers of the global sustainability movement are at all ready for the confidence, creativity, and critical entrepreneurial work of women beneficiaries, as I discuss in chapter 3 and 5.

The World Bank's $24.5 million Gender Action Plan, whose motivational force was "gender equality is smart economics," has been severely critiqued by feminist scholars and practitioners because of its inability to address structural inequities (Harcourt and Nelson 2015; Kabeer 1999; Sharma 2008, Cornwall 2014). For instance, Fair Trade—a movement intended to protect the interests of the structurally vulnerable in the postcolonial world—has ended up certifying plantations, the very vestiges of the colonial tea trade, as authentic heritage—rebranding them as "hired labor organizations" or "large farms" to reduce the stigma.

Feminist scholars advocate more attention to the intricate workings of culture and power in keeping women from their own ambitions. In pushing for more attention to social sustainability, feminist scholars foreground that a true commitment to sustainability has to reckon with existing power structures that hinder inclusivity, produce vulnerability, and prevent access to resources for women in their communities (Gezon 2012; Gunewardena and Kingsolver 2008). Current feminist research on sustainability regimes, such as sustainable agriculture, is often "drowned out by research from the natural and sometimes even social sciences that tends to see sustainability as concerning only measurable outcomes" (Pilgeram 2011, 375). Still, feminist political ecologists constantly remind us to consider "gender as a critical variable in shaping resource access and control, interacting with class, caste, race, culture, and ethnicity to shape processes of ecological change, the struggle of men and women to sustain ecologically variable livelihoods, and the prospects of any community for sustainable development" (Rocheleau and Thomas-Slayter 1996, 2). Mainstreamed gender catchwords increasingly appear in policy documents but feminist objectives are rarely incorporated into assessment or implementation of individual projects. In fact what is even more shocking is the disavowal of feminist frameworks in the frenzy of collecting gender related data. This disturbing trend is symptomatic of much research on gender and sustainability, which gloss over difficult questions of community-oriented long-term feasibility of interventions (Bercker et al. 1999).

Despite these assertions, the idea that social sustainability should be an important consideration in sustainable development policy or practice remains on the margins. Maria Cruz-Torres and Pamela McElwee (2012) note that before 2012 only three papers published in the respected journal *Sustainable Development* had focused on women and gender in sustainability initiatives. They also reference a recent citation index search of critical environmental social science journals, in which only 3.9 percent of articles referenced gender, sex, or feminism. Many of the current sustainability indicators (such as ecological footprinting) and market indicators (such as Fair Trade product sales) do not adequately factor in gender equity (Smith 2015) or other indicators of social sustainability (such as racial inequality) in the processes of assessing and modifying current initiatives. Anecdotal survival narratives of women saved by Fair Trade fill YouTube and other websites, but there is little solid research on how women understand emerging sustainability initiatives like Fair Trade. Such research would move us beyond the gender audits that reveal only numbers and not how sustainability is lived, practiced, and dreamed about under tough economic conditions through situated "gendered projects of value." *Everyday Sustainability* is poised to close this gap.

A focus on gendered projects of value (and associated identity-based cultural productions) directs us to an understanding of processes and moments through which rural women actively produce conceptions of sustainability based in the context of their livelihoods (Rocheleau 1995; Rocheleau and Edmunds 1997). Women plantation workers and small farmers participating in Fair Trade–Organic certified institutions create culturally appropriate categories of sustainability practice within the structural limitations on their lives. In this way poor women are not merely passive recipients of sustainability initiatives, they have their own justice imaginaries. Documenting and strengthening these collective efforts would remedy the lack of attention to social issues in the triple bottom-line approach—economy, environment, and society—popularized by Jon Elkington (1997).

Women affected by sustainability policies are constantly assessing the value of these regimes in the specific cultural contexts where vulnerabilities and inequities of resource use emanate and are magnified as global power structures work through them. In beneficiaries' minds issues of social sustainability are primary, since gendered actions on the ground provide the cultural terrain on which sustainability policy and practice takes hold. Because women are in charge of the everyday sustenance of their families, their assessments of the feasibility of sustainability policies is of primary importance. The focus on women has to be non-essentialist—more feminist materialist

(Agarwal 1994, 2010) rather than ecofeminist. In the Indian Himalayan context, Shubhra Gururani (2002a and b) cautions against the empty celebration of women's knowledge of forestry in emerging discourses of sustainable forest management. For her it is of utmost importance that we consider that women's "practical knowledge may be locally specific, but it is not locally bound, as local interests and global discourses of environment and development often inform the contours and substance of such knowledge" (2002, 320). Therefore Liza Gezon (2012, 237) emphasizes, "Women are thus important to sustainability discussions because of their tendency to be on the quiet but cutting edge of change. Women's strategies are critical in defining local adaptations to outside pressures—pressures in conjunction with globalization or the movement of global capital" and associated regulatory regimes. An ethnographic focus on gendered projects of value can assist in the fine-tuning of current sustainability initiatives, whether focused on gender or not (see also Redclift 1994; Schroeder 1999).

Empowerment Lite?

At the heart of current transnational sustainability initiatives is a key contradiction: undermining the significance of social sustainability and the desire to unleash women's entrepreneurial potential through better access to market forces and monetary investments (see also Cornwall and Edwards 2014). To counter the focus on monetary investment in current development policy and practice, some noted scholars of development advocate for designing acceptable value universals. Amartya Sen conceptualized "development as a process of expanding the real freedoms that people enjoy" (2000, 3). Through this formulation he questioned established ways of thinking about human well-being premised on income or commodity use. Expanding on his idea Martha Nussbaum developed a list of certain freedoms that she believes should be at the core of the "capabilities," or "human development approach." Nussbaum defines the capabilities approach as a "comparative quality of life assessment and . . . theorizing about social justice" (2011, 18). It is organized as a set of key questions like:

> What is each person able to do and to be? In other words, the approach *takes each person as an end*, asking not just about the total average well-being but about the opportunities available to each person. It is focused on choice or freedom,

holding that the crucial good societies should be promoting
for their people is a set of opportunities, or substantial
freedoms, which people then may or may not exercise
in action: the choice is theirs. It thus commits itself to
respect for people's powers of self-definition. (Nussbaum
2011, 18)

This model, premised on what Nussbaum calls political liberalism,
emphasizes pluralism and deep concern over entrenched social injustice and inequality that result in capability failures. Nussbaum claims
that her approach is most concerned with the question of human
dignity and that she endorses the contemporary transnational human
rights framework for mitigating issues of indignity in the quest for
well-being. The emphasis on choice and freedoms evident in the preceding quotation also permeates donor-driven NGO interventions in
India, which promote women's rights. However, Nussbaum's conceptualizations suffer from the lack of a feminist intersectional frame, which
is essential to destabilize the one-size-fits-all approach to economic
and social empowerment. She eventually reverts back to individual
women's loan access as a way for women to escape dependence and
structures of violence (2011, 8).

Seeking an alternative to this hegemonic neoliberal frame of
thinking about women's empowerment, some feminists have called
for greater attention to the communal and indigenous ways of being
(see Karim 2011; Gershon 2011). A way out of the neoliberal impasse
should not use the "traditional" and/or "indigenous" as a default tem-
plate for authentic alternatives, since the traditional might not be the
filter through which the poor always think about collective aspirations
for social and economic justice (see Moodie 2015; Freeman 2014).

Everyday economic and social entrepreneurialism paves the way
for situated counter-hegemonies to emerge that simultaneously builds
on and critique development interventions. My focus is on women's
resilience (Katz 2001) and their complex engagements with and desires
surrounding neoliberal economic policies (Klenk 2004; Ramamurthy
2003; Sharma 2008). Women in Darjeeling thus expose the hidden
agendas of well-intentioned transnational justice regimes by enacting
new social subjectivities that derive strength from global and local
ideologies of both development and gender. For instance, women tea
farmers are heavily invested in identifying themselves as housewives,
but they also want to be seen as entrepreneurs. Thus women enact
new roles based on new cultural productions that derive from col-

lective memories of dealing with and navigating successive development regimes. Through skepticism and creative use of Fair Trade ideas, women test the sustainability of Fair Trade in their communities while procuring in a way that protects their dignity—putting an end to housewifesation (Mies 1982; Babb 2005), which is a characteristic feature of labor appropriation in India's economy.

The activities of women smallholders compels one to think more about the significance of women's informal collectives and networks in navigating global capital. Inside and outside plantations women question the efficacy of established development institutions (such as unions, cooperatives, political parties, and *panchāyats*). In pursuing this line of inquiry I join feminist scholars who are investigating women's collectives and their power to create a vision of social change. Such collectives may come about as a result of governmentalization (Sharma 2008), may already exist in some form as a cultural resource, as in the case of *ghumāuri*:[4] (March and Taqqu 1985), or may have come about in the context of navigating existing economic and cultural exigencies (Subramaniam and Purkayastha 2004). These collectives can be envisioned as homogenous spaces that enable capital accumulation or simply provide a space for resistance to such accumulative tendencies. But an ethnographic examination of the nuanced workings of these collectives and the hybrid forms they take—sometimes as a revolving credit group, sometimes as a safe mentoring space, sometimes as a parallel union—reveals that "informal networks involve the community in the process of decision making through the creation of social spaces for sharing experiences that are particularly empowering for participants. Unstructured by the imperatives of large and bureaucratic community based groups . . . [they] rework ideas and themes from the dominant culture in ways which bring forth hidden and potentially subversive dimensions" (Purkayastha and Subramaniam 2004, 8).

In this context women's empowerment through collective action, albeit messy and sometimes ephemeral, "takes on a life of its own; it erupts, interrupts, and exceeds neoliberal regulative logics" (Sharma 2008, 196). In this book I highlight these collective excesses produced through women's collective action in rural Darjeeling. I hope acknowledging the power of these efforts will move us beyond seeing simply how women cope with Fair Trade to how they adopt or reject it in making their collectives more sustainable. Women in rural Darjeeling thus demonstrate social innovation and social entrepreneurship, CSR social work buzzwords—with great finesse and sagacity.

Everyday Gendered Translations of Transnational Justice Regimes

Women's collective mobilizations around and counter to Fair Trade in rural Darjeeling are deeply relevant for feminist scholars interested in the dynamics of the burgeoning global morality market driven by ethical biopolitics (Adelman 2008; Chowdhury 2011; Fernandes 2013). Organizations like the United Nations that formulate rules and regulations based on human rights and gender justice constitute emerging transnational justice regimes (Merry 2006; Goodale and Merry 2007). The work of these justice regimes is advanced by a global bureaucracy and a loose agglomeration of nonelected activists who try to save the poor from their plight through activism and imposition of Western standards of well-being and justice, which in my previous work I have conceptualized as "ethical biopolitics" (Sen and Majumder 2011). Cultural Anthropologist Aihwa Ong (2006) calls them "techno-ethical" regimes. The lessons from rural Darjeeling illustrate how women themselves, through constant negotiation and questioning of the values encoded in these justice regimes, translate global discourses of sustainability and empowerment to the context of their gendered everyday through catachrestic endeavors (Spivak 1993). Poor women can thus measure the success of Fair Trade only in its deconstructed, negated adoption. These micro-translations and actions based upon new meanings of Fair Trade form the core of "everyday sustainability." We must understand these micro-translations if we are to understand how "direct-stakeholders" (Batliwala 2002, 395) work with transnational justice regimes.

It is also important that we rethink our notion of who translates global rights discourses for the beneficiaries and under what circumstances. Women encounter transnational justice regimes in their homes and workplaces, outside of the formal legal realms where processes of gender justice normally unfold. Through their advancement of "gendered projects of value" women strategically expose the inability of transnational justice regimes to limit the appropriation of women's labor and time within existing production systems. Further, their everyday mockery of Fair Trade exposes how transnational justice regimes entrench the power of patriarchal production systems through deceptive language of women's empowerment and inclusion. My book extends Ong's assertion that transnational justice regimes are not encountering merely naked flawed bodies to be saved, but people with specific desires articulated through a determined attachment to situated self-making projects; that is, gendered projects of value and related economic and social entrepreneurialisms.

Feminists also concern themselves with how these new privatized rights discourses are translated in context for their intended beneficiaries, what Sally Merry (2006) calls vernacularization. She claims the translation, or mediation, process is central to the effective working of transnational justice regimes in specific cultural contexts. She writes:

> Those who are most vulnerable, often the subjects of human rights, come to see the relevance of this framework for their lives *only through the mediation of middle level and elite activists who reframe their everyday problems in human rights terms.* . . . Grassroots women adopt this new framework in a limited way. (Merry 2006:219; emphasis mine)

While we can appreciate the role of middle-level activists in translating human rights in vernacular terms, in certain instances the mediators themselves might be agents of power in a patriarchal production system. And if that is so, we need to consider whether women may be doing their own mediation based on their critical commonsense developed in the context of their gendered projects of value. Long after the intervention of mediators ends, women continue to make sense of justice regimes in their own way, and we need to understand how they do so. The translations of smallholder tea farmers differ from those of plantation wage laborers. Women's rights consciousness does not derive only from mediators but also from a place-based history of engagement with forces of power. FLO officials visiting Darjeeling, plantation managers, NGO workers, and cooperative officers all have ideas about what women in Darjeeling should be doing to better their lives, ideas which women often find limiting. Even as Fair Trade officials celebrate the creativity of Darjeeling's women, these women often remind these officials and themselves that emerging discourses of justice might not enable them to become who they want to be in the community and household spheres.

The value of such situated translations is reflected in Rajni's statement about the bustle of Fair Trade training programs in their community: "Women from our villages are famous in other parts of the world. The white people come and make films on us, take our photographs to many countries, but it is here in our villages that no one cares for us." Her rebuke may not reflect a deep understanding of the Fair Trade philosophy as understood in the West, but it reflects a

practical consciousness of the structural limitations in the gendered
social field of her community, where people still do not care about
women the way women would like them to. Rajni is articulating what
postcolonial feminist scholar Gayatri Chakraborty Spivak (2002, 123)
calls the lack of "realistic plans for infrastructural change" even in
well-meaning women's empowerment ventures. I juxtapose women's
own justice ideas with Fair Trade notions of empowerment in chapter 4 to demonstrate how women defend their justice imaginaries by
questioning the directives of Fair Trade certifiers (translators in Merry's
terminology). Translation into context is impossible if the translator
superficially interprets the gendered playing field.

Further, I uphold that women's engagement with transnational
justice regimes often takes an embodied form even if they are not fully
fathoming the principles of liberalism and enlightenment ideals of
which human rights inspired Fair Trade is a part (see chapters 7 and
8). Women often vent their skepticism toward Fair Trade by drawing
attention to the deficient state of their own bodies, and the social body
of which they are an integral part. Once engaged in deep conversation
with smallholder women tea farmers about organic tea an older lady
joked and asked whether her daughter will find an "organic husband."
I detail in chapter 7 how the metaphor of the organic husband was a
way for this woman and many others to express apprehensions about
the precarity of their everyday lives (Peet and Watts 1993). Women
in Darjeeling are acutely affected by the chronic male unemployment
and the massive male out-migration puts a strain on marital relations
making women's daily tasks of social reproduction extremely onerous.
The idea of an "organic husband" was a way to express that despite
much discussion of well-being of tea plants in the discourse of organic
production no one really cared about the everyday sustainability of
families producing tea. Women in Darjeeling find numerous ways of
making meaning/translating of Fair Trade ideas in a situation where
none of this Fair Trade material is easily available in Nepali—the local
language in Darjeeling. Translation is also not a one-time thing; it has
a social life, and translated discourses find new meaning based on
time and context. Women's collective ways of making meaning and
translating Fair Trade organics for themselves somehow never find
voice in these large discourses of saving the poor based on notions
of individual autonomy, homogenized understandings of women and
the reification of the "modern" first world as the agent of change (see
Grewal and Kaplan 1994; Chowdhury 2011; Hyndman 2004). Women
thus never become the imagined subject of governance as proposed
by some scholars (Agrawal 2005).

Making Gendered Sense of Fair Trade

In this book I engage Fair Trade from a transnational feminist and postcolonial feminist frame deeply concerned with the neo-imperialist tone of current activism around women's empowerment (Abu-Lughod 2013; Fernandes 2013; Chowdhury 2011). New Fair Trade solidarity practices that question neoliberal capitalist excesses ironically add sign value to Western consumer capitalism through harnessing the affective labor of liberal consumers and activists (Buttle and Gould 2004). It is thus imperative that we begin to document how "target populations" are making sense of emerging sustainability/justice regimes in the context of their everyday lives. My epistemological foundation lies in recent debates among transnational feminists on how best to engage with and write about the lives of poor women in a non-essentialist mode that celebrates their creative potential. The best way to do so is to uphold the everyday, as feminist anthropologists have always insisted and an idea that postcolonial feminists emphasize: ". . . issues concerning the most 'backward' parts of the world may claim the most advanced understanding of contemporary 'reality' " (Sunder-Rajan and Park 2005, 66).

It is this granular perspective grounded in the gendered everyday that is sadly absent from existing work on market-based sustainable development ventures (Trestappen et al. 2013; Sen 2014). Approaching Fair Trade from the granular vantage point of gendered everyday "meaning making" opens up a space for examining numerous issues. First, how Fair Trade gains legitimacy through mobilizing gendered representational tropes with colonial roots. Through these tropes, Fair Trade bureaucrats and enthusiasts in the West imagine the political lives and "capabilities" of Fair Trade beneficiaries as a gendered postcolonial fantasy. Second, when Fair Trade enthusiasts engage in solidarity visits and Fair Trade–related "voluntourism" (Brondo 2013; Vrasti 2013) in the global South, their discursive and on-site engagement with women workers or farmers is influenced by their gendered representations of producers drawn from images in the media. I argue that the activities of these volunteers and voluntourists govern workers and farmers in informal ways while increasing Fair Trade's acceptance as a development alternative in the global morality market. Third, this approach also reveals counter-political possibilities that emerge when Fair Trade's meaning is decoded and rearticulated with situated desires for social and economic change based on gendered projects of value. Fair Trade is thus as much material practices that reflect unfolding power relations between the global North and the global

South as it is a discursive domain meaningful to both consumers and women producers.

Fair Trade has aptly been described as an "economics of semiology" (Dolan 2008, 2010) since it is not just a process for ethical buying and selling of goods across nations, it is also a way of exchanging meaning between producers and consumers, often mediated by Fair Trade's transnational bureaucracy. According to Keith Brown (2013, 113), "Fair Traders need to frame workers as impoverished, exotic, and needy to compel customers to support their cause." As I show in chapter 3, Fair Trade enthusiasts in Darjeeling's plantation and non-plantation areas operate on the basis of such commodity affects (West 2014). They engage in solidarity practices aimed at promoting Fair Trade and bettering the lives of workers and farmers. These solidarity practices also operate as "soft biopolitics" since they measure, witness, and document Fair Trade's "success" on plantations and farms for cosmopolitan Western and Indian consumers.

Everyday Sustainabilty is an important contribution to the emerging literature on Fair Trade and associated consumer-driven sustainability and social-justice initiatives. It is the first book-length examination of women's subjective understandings and use of sustainable development projects in a comparative framework. Scholars of Fair Trade in different cultural contexts have demonstrated how Western consumers are drawn to new forms of redemptive consumption, and how the biopolitical imperatives of Fair Trade have engendered new forms of privatized bureaucracies that seek to manage workers' livelihoods in accordance with Western ethics of alternative development (Mutersbaugh 2002, 2005; Mutersbaugh and Lyon 2010; Mutersbaugh et al. 2005).

Everyday Sustainabilty categorically demonstrates how and why minority Nepali women tea producers nurture their own justice imaginaries and activities through practicing everyday ethical counter-politics both through and despite Fair Trade. Attitudes, values, imaginaries, and practices that rural poor women bring to the table of Fair Trade– enabled gender justice are largely absent from the recent literature on Fair Trade. In engaging with the Fair Trade movement and associated processes of organic certification from a feminist postcolonial framework, I close a major gap in recent studies of the Fair Trade movement and other market-based sustainability initiatives.

Overview of the Book

Chapter 1 details the methodology of data collection for this book. I use Kamalā Visweswaran's (1994, 1997) concept of "home work" to complicate the circumstances of data collection. In chapter 2, I uphold the everyday anxieties of Darjeeling Nepalis related to their crisis in cultural citizenship within the Indian nation. Here I map the effects of Nepali subnationalism on Darjeeling's plantation and non-plantation areas in terms of the cultural political economy of labor and gendered identity formation. In chapter 3, I detail from both ethnographic and historical perspectives the gendered political-economic realities in Darjeeling's tea industry, with a focus on the Fair Trade, organic-certified tea industry. In addition to introducing the two distinct groups of women (smallholder tea farmers and wage-earning plantation workers), this chapter upholds where and how Fair Trade has affects on Small Producer Organizations (SPOs) like Sānu Krishak Sansthā and large Fair Trade-Organic certified plantations like Sonākheti and Phulbāri.

Chapter 4's ethnographic focus is comparative, drawing on my ethnographic research in tea plantations and non-plantation tea-producing areas. I document the influences of a peculiar form of "voluntourism" related to Fair Trade and its effects on women's place in plantation political life. I show how forces beyond formal bureaucratic regulation, through informal solidarity, further the Fair Trade governance regimes that regulate producers' lives.

In chapter 5, I document the gendered dynamics of Fair Trade as it has unfolded on certified Darjeeling tea plantations. Two contradictory processes are at work here: On one hand women plantation workers' "survival narratives" are receiving increasing visibility in Fair Trade publicity material. On the other hand, women have categorically eschewed existing collective bargaining institutions (that is, labor unions) and new privatized collectives (that is, Joint Bodies or worker-management partnerships) to promote their interests. Women workers instead engage in much more clandestine forms of collective organizing, namely, revolving credit and mentoring groups called *ghumāuri*.

Through ethnography of Fair Trade operations and their effects on a small farmers' tea cooperative in Darjeeling, I describe in chapter 6 how women farmers in the community enact new ethical subject positions as they navigate multiple local and global patriarchies. I contend that Fair Trade interventions can inadvertently strengthen patriarchal/gendered power relations in producer communities, but that women tea farmers also creatively use specific Fair Trade interventions to defend their own priorities and rupture the imbrications between Fair Trade and local patriarchies.

Having devoted ethnographic attention to the specific struggles of women plantation workers (chapter 5) and women tea farmers (chapter 6), in chapter 7, I compare these struggles and map their effects on household discourse and conjugal relationships. Women plantation workers and tea farmers engaged in forms of talk that upheld the communicative and symbolic dimensions of their work, with distinct effects on intra-household relations at the two sites. Fair Trade–related activities produced a new social landscape of community and household relations in the cooperative, which affected not only the "conjugal contract" but also social and economic relations among households of the extended family.

Finally, chapter 8, compares the political subjectivities of women plantation workers and women tea farmers in light of the institutional structures in which each is embedded. On plantations, women rarely challenge Fair Trade, systemic nepotism, or workplace hazards. Women smallholders, on the other hand, actively challenge both hegemonic male domination of the cooperative and adverse conditions at home. This chapter highlights how the different political subjectivities of the two types of women impact the scope of their collectives (*ghumāuri*: versus Women's Wing) and corresponding efforts to force social change and gain a public voice. Women tea farmers and women plantation workers see themselves as very different kinds of ethical actors embedded in distinct institutions.

1

Locations

Homework and Fieldwork

Research on the everyday experience of social sustainability encounters the ordinary pitfalls associated with workings of power, positionality, complicity, and friction between researcher, subjects, and contexts. Since experiencing social sustainability entails direct and indirect submission to various modes of being and becoming, intimate interactions between the researcher and subject are far from being immediate. The researcher's relationship with her respondents and her presence itself is a palimpsest of power and desire steeped in long histories of exploitations, hierarchies, and differences. Caught in the mire of very complex histories of marginality, Indian Nepalis may perceive someone like me as one who holds the position of the mainstream oppressor caste/class. Being a Bengali middle-class and upper-catse *bhadramohila* (respected lady) residing in the United States, I had to engage with the awkwardness of my presence in some of their lives over a decade with my caste and/or class privileges intact. The "data" that fills this book then rests on a layered process of negotiation and positioning with forces in the field and also forces "at home" (in academe).

I also find it paramount to emphasize the importance of grounded feminist ethnographic research for a nuanced engagement with sustainable development discourse and practice. Such an emphasis will enable scholars and practitioners to consider not just the complexity of where the fieldwork is being done, but acknowledge that our academic choices (theoretical and methodological) are also deeply political and may have consequences for our particular ontologies of engaging the sustainable. One needs to be reflexive about such methodological and theoretical selections and contemplate more deeply the perception of such research methods in the fields in which one's book will be read.

Such "locations" often remain under the radar in these days of producing activism and policy friendly research. I believe that the arguments that I have made in this book are possible because of my academic location and the way I approached my field, as a feminist interlocutor deeply mindful of complicities and contours of power.

I begin this chapter detailing factors that shaped my fieldwork experiences; how they affected the minutiae of interactions I had with the participants in the field. This is followed by discussion of this book's methodology which I call a feminist longitudinal ethnography.

Fieldwork: Pressures to be a
"Conventional Anthropologist"

Very early on in my fieldwork, I felt the pressure of being a conventional anthropologist. For instance, even before I had landed in Sonākheti plantation, the owner told me that he had a plan for me. I had already sent him a formal letter explaining my research and its goals so that my intentions would be clear. But he insisted that I study the "cultures and customs among the Gurkhas."[1] He placed another challenge before me stating: "I am not going to give any of this information to you up front. You anthropologists are trained to investigate these cultural things, so please come back after you are done and tell me what I have not found out in my years here." He soon realized that my objectives were different. He was not the only one. Other bureaucrats or officials in Darjeeling town whom I met had similar responses. At social gatherings, they would introduce me as someone who would write a "book on Darjeeling," which was true. At other times the introductory sentence would be "she is here to study the tribal culture of the Gurkhas." I did not object to any of these depictions of my work and my presence out of respect for my hosts' generosity and time. This way I also got access to powerful people's extremely pejorative opinions about plantation workers, tea production, regional politics, and Darjeeling's future. I would frequently find myself in situations where extremely problematic statements would be made, assuming that my caste and class position would make me party to their nuances. Many of these interactions confirmed the existence of popular stereotypes about Nepali/Gurkha men and women, which influenced localized development and Fair Trade interactions as amply documented throughout *Everyday Sustainability*.

There was another reason why I went along with their depictions of my research objectives. Whenever I mentioned to bureaucrats or plantation owners in detail about my comparative work on Fair Trade, they would quiz me on why I was interested in small tea farmers. Most plantation authorities and tea bureaucrats were in denial about the presence of small farmer-grown tea. Some old officers of the Darjeeling Planters' Association (now called Darjeeling Tea Association) worked with local NGOs that had become liaisons for transnational Fair Trade bodies. I soon realized that they had very little idea of Fair Trade's history and association with small farmers even when the state tea board had already begun making inroads into these non-plantation areas for tea farmer training (see chapter 3 for details).

Usually, I handed these people my business card followed by my much-practiced research sound bite. Immediately there would be comments on how local tea farmers were numerically insignificant and yet foreigners (and U.S.-based scholars) were the only ones interested in them. They would ask me the reasons behind this spurt of interest, which had soared between 2004 and 2011 when the bulk of my ethnography was conducted. I would have a tough time convincing them that I was on to something, and the small farmers were not only significant for Western buyers but also for plantations in Darjeeling.

Once the plantation owners realized that I was not studying "Gurkha customs" per se or "tribalism," they made an effort to monitor my interactions within the plantation. Mapping "Fairness" through plantation ethnography was a real test of patience, irony, and every process deeply fraught with classed, gendered, raced assumptions about my leanings as a Bengali, middle-class *bhadromohila* from Kolkata via the United States suddenly speaking good Nepali and eating *gundruk and dalle* (local vegetables)!

People had very little spare time and the workers who were articulate and informative were hesitant to share their views in spite of knowing that I did not intend to put them at risk. This was understandable considering that Bengalis also tend to perceive Nepalis in stereotypical ways, such as they are simple people, they drink a lot, Nepali women are outgoing and wayward, and they are fickle. Nepalis tend to see Bengalis as sharp, privileged, and not as well dressed as them, despite their inherited class privilege of having cushy jobs in the government. These are the dominating representational tropes shaping the friction-laden interactions between two groups. Being a Bengali and discussing politics with Nepalis was tricky. My fluency in Nepali combined with repeated visits without any "project" idea was perplexing for my interlocutors, but they knew I was someone they could eventually trust with their views. I always explained to them that the places and people would be protected with pseudonyms. They knew that I had lived the first five years of my life as an infant in Darjeeling. Once I had stayed in the plantation and cooperative area long enough, the elderly women would refer to me as "*Darjeeling ko Chori*" ("Girl from Darjeeling") when they introduced me to strangers and cracked jokes about town traders mistaking me for a stupid Bengali tourist until I opened my mouth to bargain in Darjeeling Nepali.

In the plantations, the strict discipline of field and factory life was made unbearable by the presence of "*chamchas*" (henchmen of the planter) who literally reported on every aspect of workers' and "visitors'" work and leisure routines. Considering the owners' presumptions about the liberal and left-leaning politics of academics, they consciously discouraged me from "wasting my time with the union goons." I would be surprised when the plantation managers would meet me at some corner of their large (more than 400 or so acre estates) and know the details of my previous day's movements, although we had not met in weeks. They would tease me about becoming too close to Nepalis as if I had transgressed borders of respectability for an upper-caste Bengali woman. In an indirect way a compliment about how well I spoke the local language was always a reminder of their suspicion about my interactions with workers in a setup of intense disciplining of the labor force.

Whenever I asked the planter about collective bargaining, I was directed to closely observe the activities of the Joint Body and was rarely encouraged to talk to key labor union members. The union was not a taboo topic between the plantation administration, and me, but they made a tremendous effort to convince me that the plantation had no "union problems" common in the 1980s and that NGOs were doing such amazing work (see also chapter 4). Some management folks even told me, "Please let me know what you learnt from members of the Joint Body about their feelings about Fair Trade." One planter's standard statement was, "The sustainable revolution has already been unleashed in Sonākheti through organic farming and Fair Trade. It was supposed to produce new energy, prosperity and improve plantation life, but we do not know what good things are in store, and I rely on you for all this emerging information." Apart from politeness, this statement was a reminder that nothing unethical could happen in a Fair Trade–certified sustainable plantation. It was also a reminder of an unspoken expectation of not raising suspicion about this plantation in exchange for the owner's generosity toward me. He still wanted me to follow closely the "tribal culture" of various Nepali groups present in his estate. He considered it natural that as an anthropologist, I would be interested in tribal customs, as we study culture. He even

joked about my lack of excitement about meeting local healers and
shamans (*jhākri*). He told me "All the white researchers and visitors
here get so excited when I invite them to meet *maila baje* (the local
shaman) while you have no interest, you seem to be more interested
in local gossip."

Plantation workers in the beginning were extremely hesitant to
talk to me, even when I had started living in their homes. I took advantage of homestay programs at the plantations and then gradually went
beyond the homestays to interact with other workers and living with
them. Naturally many plantation workers saw me as an acquaintance of
the privileged plantation management since their bosses often spoke to
me in English, Bengali, and Hindi. Some saw me as the owner's *pāonā*
(guest), but they soon realized that I was far more interested in plantation life under the radar, away from the performances workers put on
for other visitors. Compared to how quickly I established rapport with
the members of the tea cooperative, it took longer to break ice in the
plantation because of the intense gendered surveillance. In Phulbāri
the owners were non-resident Marwari, but the resident director was
a Nepali gentleman. We frequently met in his factory office and our
class status and conversations in English often raised suspicion among
workers in Phulbāri as to how much they could trust me. I was an
"other" in a community where Bengalis are seen as outsiders.

I detail the history of these fraught ethnic relations in the next
chapter. Bengalis and Nepalis have deep animosities because the latter feel exploited by Bengalis or *madeshis* plains people. The Nepalis
in Darjeeling consider themselves to be *pāhāDi* or hill people. For
both Bengalis and Nepalis, the perceived differences result in thinking
about each community through stereotypes. Such hostility also exists
between Nepalis, Marwaris, Biharis (other non-Nepali communities
in Darjeeling), and other dominant regional ethnic groups that exist
in Darjeeling. The animosity and ridicule of Bengalis of course has a
particular historical backdrop. Darjeeling is a district in the state of
West Bengal, and the Gorkhaland movement was aimed at separation
from Bengal to form a separate Nepali state within the Indian nation.
Bengalis were thus envisioned as immediate oppressors reflecting the
neglect of the Indian state toward its regional and ethnic minorities.

There was no denial of my class privilege. Although I was upper
caste, being Hindu helped on many occasions considering so many
of my informants were Rais and Chettris. I also got along very well
with people of Buddhist leanings because I did not practice the strict
dietary restrictions like a quintessential Hindu—I was not averse to
eating beef or pork. It should be noted that I rarely had Tibetan (*bhote*)

research subjects since Tibetans are mostly residents of urban areas in the Darjeeling district and are not farmers; they are more active in trading and tourism. Sometimes my open dietary practices were a cause of concern for very orthodox Nepali Hindu families (especially the *Chetri-Bauns*). But soon they realized that I was not exactly invested in being a devout Hindu, and of course, I ate whatever they cooked at home as an exercise in respect for their time and taking care of me. I was, however, forbidden from touching the kitchen *chulā* (cooking fire) in some Hindu homes even though I was upper caste. The fact that I was married to a Hindu man went in my favor, but not without complications. The mark of a married Hindu woman was wearing vermillion, which I did not use. Initially this resulted in some serious doubt about whether I was actually married. I had some wedding pictures in my laptop which came in handy. But being married without children was another serious issue and a trigger for much ridicule. My respondents advised me to have children before I returned to Darjeeling after my dissertation fieldwork. Being a married woman made it easy for me to discuss delicate household matters, and women assumed that I would understand their personal problems. There were many things I learned about these women that they asked me not to write about, especially details of abuse or violence in family life, and I have kept those details out to honor these requests.

Informant, Interlocutor, Researcher, or Activist?

There were times during fieldwork when I found myself to be like an informant and translator, but I would not call myself an activist (even if some see me that way) for reasons that will become evident in this section. Lower-level bureaucrats would try to understand many things about the Fair Trade movement by quizzing me since none of the training material was available in Nepali between 2004 and 2006. The most difficult questions were from tea farmers and some plantation workers who wanted to know why all of a sudden white people were interested in helping them. Many tea farmers initially saw Fair Trade as an NGO aid or government aid program. Some joked, saying that there was an overflow of money they got from selling their tea. They would use the English word "flow" to interpret FLO (the certifier with which they had become familiar). This was a very useful way for me to engage people on how they viewed Fair Trade and if at all they thought they benefited from it.

My assumptions about what women in the plantations and non-plantation areas should do to scale up their political and entrepreneurial ventures were reigned in from time to time by women reminding me that I would not be there after a few months when they would have to carry on their entrepreneurial ventures and associated community-level strategic interventions. Once I had asked Chitra Rai (an active member of the Women's Wing of the local political party Gorkha Janamukti Morcha and resident of Phulbāri plantation) why they do not build alliances with women's wing members of other political parties or activist organizations in New Delhi. She replied with sarcasm:

> You think everyone is like you, leaving your home and husband and spending time with us eating pork, joking in Nepali about our lives. Most other educated Indian women think that we are sexually promiscuous, that we are not interested in education or stupid and that we, Nepali women, are best suited to be servants in their home. We will never join with a mainstream women's organization, this is our fight for dignity of Nepali communities within India.

Sunita, another activist went further to explain why such alliances were not possible. The December 2012 protest against the Delhi rape was the most visible backdrop of her comments. She stated:

> [L]ook at all these women out on the streets of Delhi, our country's capital, fighting for injustice for this young woman who was raped. But every time I think about these protests I cannot forget that Nepali women are killed and abused in Delhi because people think we are outsiders and our girls are prostitutes, sometimes the police refuse to note down FIRs. But we cannot expect anyone to cry out on our behalf, take the streets. Nepali women do not matter. So how can we expect these same NGOs to suddenly support our cause?

The past eleven years of engaging with women in Darjeeling has left me with no option but to engage the "everyday" with the hybridity of an "insider-outsider" (Chowdhury 2011). Women and men have freely critiqued my privilege, at the same time opening up about their intimate lives in ways that I never imagined possible as a fledgling graduate student when I landed in Darjeeling in 2004. The sustained engagement of hybridity has not only shaped what I did while collecting data, but made me conscious about my positioning as a scholar and my representational strategies when I wrote about women in Darjeeling.

In recent years feminist scholars, especially feminist scholars of color (Davis 2013; Chatterjee (2009); and transnational feminists (Alexander and Mohanty 2013; Chowdhury 2011, Nagar and Swarr 2005) have raised rightful concerns over what passes as feminism, gender sensitive research, feminist activism, and, pertinent for this book, feminist ethnography. Such concerns stem from the acknowledgment of highly charged contexts of poverty, violence, marginality, and other gender-based oppression that find their way into research agenda. There is concern with what feminist anthropologists are supposed to do with the "data" they collect and how they manage the desires of their subjects who expect the ethnographer to do something for them in return for their time. There is also unease, bordering on who can call himself or herself a feminist activist ethnographer (Davis 2013, 26–27). These discussions parallel the ones I experience in the inter-disciplinary graduate program where most of my graduate teaching is centered. There is a certain kind of celebration of "practice" (perhaps for good reason) in that space but little reflection on the implications of such emphasis and even less reflection on the playing field in which such "practice" or "activism" will play out.

I am not arguing that practice-oriented, applied, and activist projects are not academic enough, but one must reflect on the playing field of practice where complicities are part of the efforts to engage. The tenuousness of the insider/outsider dilemma cannot be resolved by mere conviction nor by the soundest research design; one's research instead stands on these tensions and informs it. All forms of engagement take place in the context of ethnographer's/researcher's complicities. One must not lose sight of "homework" (Visweswaran 1997) to reflect not only on what one does in the field but how one locates one's research within academic politics and activist practice, in my case this politics of doing. As a way out of this impasse I would like to clarify again that I see myself as an academic, as an interlocutor who is engaged in a feminist ethnographic longitudinal study for rural Darjeeling—not an activist in the sense that has become very popular in U.S. academic feminist circles (see also Fernandes 2013). I still believe that there is a place for academic feminist research that can produce policy or "practice" or "activism" supporting research, as evident from where my work is being cited. Interestingly, I notice that the academic content of this book may fit some contemporary definitions of feminist activist ethnography since the feminist ethnography presented in this book "draws on methodological strategies that embrace the everyday experiences of people—especially those forced to live on the margins" and treats these experiences "as epistemologically valid" (Davis 2013, 26). My approach to fieldwork and writing this book is best expressed in fellow feminist anthropologist Piya Chatterjee's (2009: 132) words:

> Epistemological divides are geopolitical divides, and some bridges between "activisms" and "scholarship" span the incommensurable. It is through these impossibilities, then, that I counterintuitively attempt to build an "imagined bridge." In doing so I make no claims about chasms crossed: incommensurabilities made commensurable; the strange, familiar. Rather through careful ethnographic reflexivities on my own positionalities and knowledge claims, and through careful tracking of difference and power, I seek to build the possibilities of both understanding and solidarity. These require, in the deepest ways, leaps of faith, hope, and tenacious optimism.

Over this decade-long engagement I witnessed small glimpses of such leaps of faith in the friendships that I formed. Here's a picture of a fifty

Figure 1.1. Price of Friendship.

rupee bill that one of my interlocutors asked me to take a picture of a put in my *kitab* (book). She wrote both our names on this bill and the place where we were and then paid the shopkeeper for the stuff she bought from him with this particular bill. When I asked her why she gave it away she told me "maybe one day this note will return and I will remember our friendship that has stood the test of time and the pressures of the world." It is my hope that in writing this book, I would have at least tried to be a true friend, if not totally successful.

Note on Methodology

My impetus to talk about "homework" (Visweswaran 1997) in the last section comes from keen observation of research methods terminology used to describe and slot interpretive and qualitative research found in standard social science classrooms popular in the United States. Since I insist that research on social sustainability must be grounded in the minutiae of everyday gendered existence, it is even more important to engage this issue of "homework." Very early on in my academic training in the U.S. I encountered phrases, such as "backyard research," in methods textbooks (Creswell 2013). While intended as a cautionary exercise in emphasizing research ethics and objectivity, I perceive in the use of this terminology (backyard) a potential to "other" forms of enquiry perceived less objective and with lesser universal appeal. A less pejorative term used for ethnographic work is "exploratory." The rhetorical power of such research terminologies can directly impact the scope of making policy recommendations when it comes to sustainable development as well. The reason why questions of social sustainability have remained in the backwaters of sustainability or sustainable development-related literature is often a result of "homework" related politics. Since feminist methods, let alone feminist anthropological methods, did not figure in my own graduate training or taught in standard research methods classes, I feel the need to situate my work as a certain kind of academic feminist anthropology involving longitudinal ethnographic fieldwork, which is much more complicated than just being in my backyard, i.e., another place in my home country India.

The use of "backyard" has the potential to valorize the research of those who have traveled a distance to do fieldwork and "other" work of those who return to their "native" countries to do research after having lived as a legal alien in a foreign country for more than a decade. The complexities of inhabiting these different worlds of citizen, alien, and research are somewhat lost when one designates certain research as "backyard" work. When I read Kirin Narayan's seminal article "How Native Is a 'Native' Anthropologist?" (1993) I realized, that although these terminologies may be well positioned they do not reflect the complex positionalities of researchers. Not acknowledging such complexity in turn harbors the danger of misrepresentation in this media saturated world. Thus, there is a dire need to develop an intersectional approach (Cho, Crenshaw, and McCall 2013) to deconstruct the use of these terminologies in our academic "home."

To comprehend these "locations" one also needs to attend to the dynamic nature of the "insider"/"outsider" position of any researcher. Nancy Naples calls it the bipolarity of the "insider"/"outsider" status while complicating feminist standpoint epistemology, requesting scholars to tackle issues of power and privilege directly as part of designing and implementing research. An essential part of "homework" then is to recognize these bipolarities and what Narayan calls hybridities in the research process and write about them as part of methodology. Such processes are important since, as Naples notes, "Women and others who are not typically found in positions of power within educational institutions are objectified in academic practices and constructed in ways that distort or render invisible their experiences and their everyday activities" (2003, 52). It is through these experiences of locating oneself, ones work, and ones interlocutors/research subjects voices that data on any topic emerges. Instead of treating these experiences as particular, I posit that for any grounded research, these locations become nodal points of understanding the diversity of sustainability practice and its relations to local and global power play. It helps us understand whether gendered forms of being and becoming articulate (or not) with emerging market based justice regimes like Fair Trade and organics.

It is important that we make these methodological signposts such that more than a decade of grounded reflexive longitudinal ethnography in one of the poorest places in South Asia cannot be easily read off as exploratory "backyard research." As the previous sections in this chapter demonstrated, I had to make a great effort to not become willfully complicit with the hegemonic forces at play in one's field site to collect "data" and engage in negotiations which respect the desires of ones interlocutors. Most importantly college students need to understand the politics of objectivity, witnessing, and evidence when reading our books and encountering their mentors as complex subjects. As Nancy Naples so eloquently points out, ". . . a belief in the value neutrality of social scientific and other intellectual practices, in fact, serves to mask the relations of ruling embedded in the production of knowledge in the academy" (2003: 52; see also Harrison 2007).

Having such nuance will enable everyone to appreciate what research one is about to do, what methodology one is going to use, and how the process and product are going to be evaluated and situated within the academe (anthropology and beyond). While in feminist anthropology, and in anthropology more generally, the post '70s call to being reflexive, acknowledging one's privilege and "outing ones politics" is now considered an exercise in objectivity, such nuance in methodological choice and approach is still lost to colleagues in social sciences who fail to understand that every piece of research is political. People who do quantitative analysis of large data sets in the United States are also "backyard researchers" (and native anthropologists if they are doing research among U.S. populations) since their assumptions about U.S. society might frame their survey tools or choice of subjects. But somehow the labels are reserved about certain kinds of researchers and these terminologies tend to take us back to a time when "natives" like me were thought to be "subjects" and not producers of knowledge. My propositions in this paragraph are to refrain from making any kind of moral claim to innocence, authenticity for "native" anthropology, as I am deeply aware of my class and caste privilege in India as much as I am aware of my marginal status in academe as a nonresident alien woman from the developing world.

The depth of what I describe is not new, but it is not talked about enough outside feminist circles. Someone like me may find it tough to balance a position between that of an "expert/authentic insider" (sort of as culture broker for all things India) or a "native anthropologist" without the objectivity of an outsider. Therefore, Narayan proposed that we embrace and enact hybridity (1993, 679) not only in our understanding of culture (and our subject's lives) but in the scrutiny of ourselves as researchers. I belabor this point about terminological choice since, as most feminist scholars know, language and power are inextricably linked. It shapes how one frames oneself, one's methods, one's choice of subject because people make decisions about what is "data" based on such framings. I teach graduate students in an interdisciplinary field and more so than in anthropology classrooms I feel the need to teach and think about the complexity of research methods and politics of labeling within it. Feminist scholars and feminist anthropologists have for years discussed and written about positionality, bias in research, and ethics without these labels, but they are never cited in standard social science research design books and the de-contextualized caution about "backyard research" continues unchecked.

I see myself as an interlocutor and not an activist speaking for poor women in Darjeeling's rural areas. I cannot find solutions to all their problems, I know they have a good sense of what's best for them (in a non-essentialist way); my task is to produce knowledge that leads to a better understanding of their resilience, entrepreneurialism, creativity, and intelligence through which they *sustain* themselves everyday as development fads ebb and flow through their communities, sometimes as missionary help, sometimes as a gesture of plantation management, sometimes in the form of student volunteers, local NGO projects, Fair Trade certifiers, political party projects. That is what I am best trained to do: write about reality in their terms, knowing that the process is fraught with power, privilege, anger, disgust, but also mutual coexistence and respect. Having an Indian passport makes Darjeeling no less familiar and strange. We all just work with different biases and first principles and operate on hybrid playing fields, both researcher and subjects. Researchers also play "serious games" (Ortner 2005).

This book is based on ethnographic research completed over eleven years, beginning in 2004. Being fluent in multiple languages spoken in this district in India's eastern Himalayas, I was able to collect long-term, grounded data on women's past and present justice imaginaries and related everyday practices. The core of my methodology is a combination of life-history and semi-structured interviews with long-term participant observation. I also conducted content analysis of Fair Trade policy documents and social media stories of women's empowerment in Darjeeling and beyond. I did fieldwork in two Fair Trade–certified plantations (Sonākheti and Phulbāri)[2] and the largest Fair Trade–certified tea cooperative in Darjeeling (Sānu Krishak Sansthā). Among the 147 respondents I interviewed in the plantation sector were ordinary workers, managers, plantation owners, and Fair Trade bureaucrats. In the cooperative area I interviewed about 97 people. Thereby I identified a core sample of 40 women plantation workers and 30 women smallholder tea farmers, whose narratives form the cornerstone of this ethnography.

Everyday Marginality of Nepalis in India

I found myself in a packed TATA Sumo[1] at the New-Jalpaiguri Railway station on a muggy July day in 2006. Like many other middle-class Bengalis who had visited Darjeeling before, I knew that if I could bear the suffocating heat and humidity for about an hour or so I would enjoy the cool moist air of Darjeeling tea country upon reaching the outskirts of Kurseong town. There is a reason the British built sanatoriums there in the days of the Raj (Chatterjee 2001; Koehler 2015).

I was sharing my ride that day with a few Bengali and Marwari men, lower-level government bureaucrats and traders making regular trips to Kolkata from Darjeeling via Siliguri and back. They struck up a conversation with me on this long ride. Their assumptions about me and the very problematic conversation that ensued made the ride to Darjeeling more uncomfortable than usual. The exchange in the car is a peek into the gendered forms of discrimination faced by average Nepali women: the sort of class sexualities accorded by dint of their economic contributions.

> **Passenger 1:** Madam first time in Darjeeling? Did you get a nice hotel? This is off-season, you may not get to see the Kanchenjungha . . . but you will get a nice empty town.

> **Me:** Actually this is not my first time; I have been there before for work.

> **Passenger 2:** You work in Darjeeling? Which office?

> **Me:** I am a researcher . . . I am doing research for my PhD.

> **Passenger 1:** OK, yes that is good, but what are you researching? Coming from North Bengal University?

Me: I am an anthropologist studying for my PhD in the USA and I am very interested in issues of economic development and especially women's roles in Darjeeling's economy.

Passenger 2: OK, so you are going to spend a lot of time on plantations, am I correct? Do you know the joke about the 3Ws of Darjeeling?

Me: Not really, I have never heard this joke.

Passenger 2: One should never trust its weather, its women and the wine. And by wine I mean *raksi*, not foreign liquor.

Collective laughter ensued among the men, strangely the Nepali driver of the car also joined in with a muted laugh, I could see him on the rearview mirror. I was very annoyed at this blatant display of sexism, classism, and regionalism shown in the casual denigration of Nepali women from Darjeeling. I held back my reactions. Sadly, the next ten years taught me that this sort of rebuke of Nepali women was an everyday occurrence that shadows the struggles and creativity of the women behind these colonial—now—post-colonial tropes.

The myth of the "nimble fingered" women also had related sister myths in Darjeeling which shaped the gendered political economy of tea production. The sister myths took on themes of sexual promiscuity, alcoholism, and unpredictability of women, justifying the need to govern, aiding the post-colonial extension of the white man's burden which was now proudly carried over by his brown brothers as evident in this friendly chitchat on the way to Darjeeling. These sister myths had roots in the regions history, politics, culture, and activism, and shaped the terrain of gendered respectability (Sen 2012).

These sexualized, classist, gendered tropes operated at the "grass-roots" of Darjeeling's tea economy. This situation takes us to the heart of the gendered cultural political-economy of Darjeeling's tea production, the contemporary identity struggles of its men and women, the crisis in marginality and respectability that Nepalis in India have to navigate in and outside Darjeeling. In this context, when I met Nepali strangers during fieldwork I was always a face of the mainstream that marginalized them. As I detailed in chapter 1, being Bengali was not an advantage during many research interactions, but opened doors during different ones.

A much stereotyped and ridiculed group, Nepalis in India and their struggles for acceptance as rightful cultural citizens of India (despite formal legal citizenship) have only increased over the past 100 years in response to the neglect and racism of mainstream India—both people and government (Middleton 2015; Sen 2012). Locally the manifestation of this national problem remains deeply gendered as women plantation workers are subject to the toughest stereotypes, augmented by the intense envy about their permanent jobs (in a region plagued with underdevelopment, substance abuse, and lack of employment options). But average Nepali women, along with *Lepchanis* (Lepcha women)[2] and *Bhotenis* (Tibetan women), were designated as outsiders if they phenotypically resembled East Asians, just like my women friends from Manipur, Nagaland, Meghalaya in Delhi University. They could not pass as Indian and had the toughest go. Women outside the market areas and plantations also live under the shadow of the 3Ws; their everyday life is defined by a cultural political economy of distinction through serious mobility games (Ortner 2006) of respectability at the family, community, and personal level. The pride of being housewife entrepreneurs in the non-plantation *basti* (village) areas is a reflection of this politics of distinction. The advent of organic and Fair Trade production furthered this gendered politics of distinction within Nepali men and women, and between women and women, since the display, control, and use of women's labor is at the heart of Fair Trade's success and failures in Darjeeling.

To understand what possibilities women want to further through their gendered projects of value and how their aspirational entrepreneurial ventures are located in a particular context one needs to appreciate the nuances of gendered class formation in Darjeeling's rural areas within and outside plantations. To grasp these changing relations, knowledge about certain aspects of colonial tea production in Darjeeling as well as its postcolonial specifics is important.[3] Also important is an understanding of more recent protracted political mobilizations manifested in the two major subnational political outbursts (Gorkhaland Movement I and II). The latter shaped these gendered rural-class distinctions. One also needs to understand the different kinds of development initiatives that have affected plantation and non-plantation rural areas post-1947, the year India became independent from British rule. I attempt to detail all of the above in the rest of the chapter.

Politics of Recognition

Amidst the colorful happy faces of Nepali tea pluckers on Indian television and the occasional newspaper article about the abuse and trafficking of Nepali women in Delhi, there is a striking paucity of information and research about the political involvements of average Nepali women (especially rural plantation workers or smallholder women farmers) in their community's quest for political autonomy within India. It does not take that much effort to understand that women from rural areas in Darjeeling would play an important role in their communities' struggle for respect and recognition; their confident presence in the market (as traders) and in villages and plantations has given them access to resources which are reflected in stereotypes about the "Darjeeling Girl" (Leichty 2003). Women's engagement with Nepali subnationalism within India shapes how women imagine the political and how they insert themselves or not within political practices (Kandiyoti 1994) affecting their individual and collective practices of social and economic entrepreneurship within and outside plantations. As I will demonstrate in chapters 7 and 8, women's imagination of political possibilities also impacts the tenor or their household relations and community activism.

Feminist philosopher Nancy Fraser's conceptual distinction between "politics of recognition"[4] and "politics of equality" (Fraser 1997, 2000) is useful in framing the specificity of political transformations in Darjeeling. Also important is the need to complicate the dichotomy that Fraser presents in order to understand what she perceives as the downside of contemporary struggles over identity. A move beyond the recognition-redistribution dilemma to locate Nepali women's complex positionalities within Nepali struggles for political and cultural autonomy requires an intersectional feminist approach (Cho, Crenshaw, and McCall 2013) aiding a well-rounded understanding of women's strategic positionalities within Nepali subnationalism.[5] This approach helps us understand the gendered ramifications of subnationalism in India's northeast as well as locate the specificity of Nepali women's subjectivities within discussions of contemporary South Asian feminism.

It is too easy to characterize women plantation workers' participation in subnational politics as a struggle for subnational and ethnic recognition where Nepali males set the political agenda sidelining women laborers' issues of wage bargaining, or as simply a struggle for more labor rights where women encounter male domination in all spheres of their lives, such as household, community, and workplace. The multiple marginalities of Nepali women plantation workers (i.e., their marginalization in their workplaces, in the households, and as Nepalis, since they are a part of minority community in India) make them complex subaltern agents for whom cultural "politics of recognition" has material and affective consequences in their communities and workplaces. The latter articulates a politics of equality, which has symbolic and gendered implications.

For women outside plantations in the *basti* areas where the small-holder women farmers reside, support for subnationalism entailed filling trucks to go to rallies, money collection, food preparation. The changed circumstances in many rural areas after the GNLF came to power in the late eighties was access to *patta* (formal land deeds), the inroad of NGOs and their projects like micro-credit, the *ānganwādi* ICDS programs for women, roads, and eventually electricity, along with government jobs for some influential men loyal to the GNLF. In fact, the plantations were the last bastions of non-GNLF politics until the very end when the Communist Party was overthrown by the GNLF (also in the late eighties) to form the Darjeeling Gorkha Hill Council (DGCH).

The gendered marginalization of women in Darjeeling remains embedded in a political field (Ray 1999) with mutually overlapping social, political, and ethnic terrains that deny women plantation workers both dignity and higher wages at the same time as it paves the way for some of Darjeeling's rural residents to gain landed resources through a reorganization of "fallow" or unregulated land. Hence, it is crucial to apply a feminist intersectional lens and account for ethnicity and gender within a single framework to understand women's cultural struggles in Darjeeling, and its nuances, since there is no single reality called "women of Darjeeling." For that we need to extend and reformulate Fraser's "recognition-redistribution" dichotomy and emphasize their intertwining to take note of women's complex gendered positionalities within Nepali subnationalism. I demonstrate in this book that women's agency within Nepali subnationalism has to be understood in terms of place-based meaning-making that attends to their everyday entrepreneurialism and work within and outside household practices to negotiate patriarchy and its newly emerging benevolent forms.

Meaning-making is as much economic as it is a cultural redefining of oneself in the midst of multiple marginalities and regional political economies. One needs to understand "women of Darjeeling" not only through their roles in economic production and social reproduction, but also through their cultural productions, as I have asserted in the introduction to this book. I contend that meaning-making occurs by an appropriation of the language of subnationalism, i.e., politics of recognition to reinterpret workplace and household situations in bolstering claims for higher wages and other kinds of redistribution of power and resources within the plantation and cooperative[6] hierarchy. The concept of meaning-making helps us discern how women plantation workers code their equality-claims in language of ethnic exceptionalism and recognition (as *pāhāDi*/hill women). It may seem that Nepali women plantation workers and smallholder women farmers are giving in to dominant male hegemonic plans about Darjeeling's future. However, I see such place-based meaning-making practices as interruptions to the suppression and silencing of women's voices within subnationalist politics as revealed to interlocutors like me during critical ethnographic encounters.

Women's narratives point to the evolution of a particular form of gendered historical consciousness through which women plantation workers and smallholder farmers find a way to express how political shifts in Nepali labor and ethnic politics have engendered "interstitial politics"—not apparent to the casual observer (Fraser 1997; Sexsmith 2012; Sen 2012). The post-communist era cultural politics of subnationalism helped women address issues of structural violence by having the freedom to express themselves as proud *pāhāDi*[7] workers or farmers, but such modalities did not question other forms of structural limitations facing the Nepali workforce, such as the absence of regular wage and bonus increases. Nepali women plantation workers, irrespective of their present political affiliations, feel that the Gorkhaland Movement has empowered them in some aspects of their lives as much as it has disempowered them in other arenas. To elucidate my point further, I offer an ethnographic vignette.

One crisp winter morning Lachmi, a tea-plucker, and I set out to meet the other twelve women plantation workers in the tea-plucking group who Lachmi oversaw. Lachmi was in a particularly bad mood that day, lamenting her inability to negotiate a job for her youngest son in the plantation bungalow as a guard. As we walked away from her home into the plantation she pointed me to a Nepali male *Chaprāsi* (field supervisor) and told me "do you see him sister; they are the bane of our existence, those *chamchās*.[8] Here I am, always encouraging the girls in my group to work hard so that our company makes more money and here they are roaming around whole day and misreporting to the manager and owner to prove their efficiency." Upon this comment, I asked Lachmi why there were no women field supervisors—*Chaprāsis*. She replied:

> There is no reason why we women cannot become *Chaprāsis*, but who will fight that battle? Are the unions of any use? They are only interested in Gorkhaland and *partybazi*.[9] Our *sāhib*[10] always listens to the wrong kind of people, the insincere Nepali men, who tell him that women are

untrustworthy and drink too much—worthless. We might
not know how to run the country like Indira Gandhi, but
we know how this plantation works and we are *pāhāDis*;[11]
we work harder than people in the plains.

Encapsulated in Lachmi's words are deep frustrations with the plantation manager and his male henchmen's close surveillance of women
workers. Also notable is anger over the local labor union preoccupied in *partybazi* without engaging any questions of women worker's
empowerment. Her sarcastic comment about India's first female prime
minister has to be contextualized as disgust for the negative sexualized
representations that are part of everyday work and community life,
as evident from my opening vignette in this chapter, and have made
Nepali women become the "other" of mainstream Indian femininity.
Her negotiation of these existing frustrations is articulated through
pride for a *pāhāDi* identity, which many plantation workers used as
a motivational reference for their toil. In doing so they defended the
essentialized image of a hill worker that the male leaders of Gorkha
National Liberation Front (GNLF) and now the Gorkha Janamukti Morcha (GJM) carefully use as a key cultural trope through which the
broader Nepali community maintained their distinction in the local
economy of difference; distinguishing them as people of substance
different from the *adivasis* (indigenous people/sons of the soil) in the
plains and *madeshis* (other plains people). Ethnic pride and loathing
for sexist labor practices perpetuated within Nepali politics marks the
complexity of women's political engagements in Darjeeling. Outside
plantations in the *basti* areas the celebration of *pāhāDi* identity is
reflected in the pride of owning ones land (*mato*), the privilege of
which is not available to the plantation workers.

   Thus, an intersectional feminist understanding of women's
agency in Darjeeling's tea plantations must acknowledge that women
are marginalized in complex ways resulting from "multiple patriarchies" (Chatterjee 2001) and their ethnic, economic, and political
manifestations. In response to such multiple marginalizations, women
use cultural tropes of an essentialized *pāhāDi* identity. These symbolic
tropes hinder the possibility of raising important work-based issues
in the plantation, such as the need for new shoes in the monsoon or
a small loan for their child's education. Yet a job for the male members of the household, the claims of which are couched in languages
of ethnicity and subnationalism, also have material consequences for
these women. Thus, production and reproduction of minority identity,
whether ethnicized or subnationalist, in response to larger political

economic forces, is a deeply gendered and classed process (Alexander Floyd 2001; Kandiyoti 1994).

These gendered everyday material and discursive manifestations of "politics of recognition" are totally absent from the existing literature on subnationalism in India (Kohli 1997; Das Gupta 1997; Middleton 2015). The paucity of information about the creativity of poor women in Darjeeling is perpetuated by the increased media focus and scholarly interest in the struggles of the broader Nepali community within India. The latter focuses on diagnostic moments of ethnic anxiety, decentralized territorial arrangements and forms of violence, and how Nepali people are struggling to find a "tribal slot" (Samanta 1996; Lama 1996; Middleton 2015; Li 2000), in which men are disproportionately represented barring a few instances where women become martyrs. But detailed ethnography of everyday realities helps us move beyond seeing Nepali women either as victims, silent bystanders, or heroes. Instead, it upholds women's complex subjectivities and how, through their labor and affect, women uphold the symbolic economies of struggle, the critical cultural work they do to make the movement meaningful for average people—despite dictatorial and corrupt leaders, and setbacks in the movement (see also chapter 5). The social reproduction of local politics and regional distinctions is intricately tied to the labor of women at work and home.

Struggles of Darjeeling Nepalis

The majority of Darjeeling's population is Nepali, but Nepali people are a minority group in India. The Nepali community in Darjeeling has been engaged in gaining more resources and recognition within the Indian nation-state. After India's independence from British rule in 1947, India maintained an open boundary with Nepal. Citizens of each country could move freely across borders, work, and live in India and Nepal, but they did not have voting rights.[12] Since colonial times, people from Nepal migrated to work in Darjeeling's tea plantations. Nepali men were recruited to fight in the British army and to work as guards and cooks in colonial households. In the early years of plantations men, children and women were employed in tea plantations, but a much more gendered division of labor emerged after WWII when a huge number of Nepali men were recruited in the India army's *Gurkha* Regiment (Dash 1947). When World War II ended a lot of these soldiers returned to Darjeeling, where they faced joblessness. The economic crisis due to the war, which resulted in a food crisis, meant plantations were not expanding to hire more laborers. It was also during this time that the first cries of Gorkhastan (a separate state for Indian Nepalis) were raised by the CPI. Unemployed returning soldiers found new engagements in CPI-dominated plantation unions. Some also joined the Akhil Bharatiya Gorkha League (ABGL) which had less power and was more mainstream nationalist in their affiliation with the Congress Party. The Gorkhastan movement fizzled in the face of militant CPI-led labor organizing but was in the agendas of ABGL and CPI politics.

Darjeeling Nepalis like Maila Baje, a veteran political figure who rose to prominence during the 1940s, provided leadership of the first CPI-affiliated labor union that was established in the region and called the Darjeeling Tea Garden Workers' Union in 1945 (Rai 2000, 28). The demands made by this union under Maila Baje's leadership also laid the groundwork for the Plantation Labor Act (1951). The demands included wage and bonus regulation and adjustment, pension payment, provisions for maternity costs, hospital construction, educational opportunities within plantations, and abolition of child labor.

The years between independence and the first Gorkhaland agitation saw an increase in union activity and a slowdown of plantation growth. But this period also brought about a gradual realization that state-mandated wages and other facilities could not end the everyday marginalization of Nepalis within India who could not claim a secure spot in the country. Because of an open border policy, Nepali migrants, even if they have legal citizenship rights in India, are frequently called outsiders. They experience cultural marginality. During my fieldwork, the main accusations that Nepali youth had toward the rest of India was that Indian citizens of non-Nepali descent treated them as foreigners even though most Nepali families have been in Darjeeling for generations. While Nepali migrants have settled in other parts of India, such as Delhi or Dehra Dun (in North Western India), or Assam, in Darjeeling district, they are the majority. Because of their different language, culture, customs, and their movement back and forth between Nepal and India and their distinct phenotype, there developed a feeling among non-Nepali Indian citizens that Nepalis belong to Nepal. Because of cultural discrimination, Nepali people also felt like outsiders in spite of their legal entitlements.

Contrary to mainstream notions, especially reflected in mainstream private media, that Nepalis are possibly more loyal to their "homeland"—Nepal—than to India, my ethnographic experiences reveal that the relationship between Nepali people in Darjeeling with their original homeland was contested, just like other diasporas. Many even now have a picture of the Royal Family of Nepal in their homes, but through my interviews I learned that they consider themselves part of India because this is where they work and have settled, in spite of visits to Nepal. Visits to Nepal for economic well-being are increasingly rare. Women tea farmers and plantation workers also perceived Nepal to be an underdeveloped country that has lesser prospects than India. Some of my informants would have male family members or neighbors get brides from Nepal. Women tea farmers explained to me that many agricultural households preferred women from Nepal as brides because they were supposedly more simple (*sidhā*), and they were also good at agricultural work. My informants also mentioned that cross-border marriages were now few. Narratives of Nepali men revealed that they wanted to migrate to Mumbai, Goa, Delhi, and Bangalore for work. Nepal was not a viable option for them. In recent years, migration from Nepal to other parts of India, especially Delhi, has increased since the state of West Bengal (where Darjeeling is located) and Eastern India in general are seen as lacking in employment prospects. The complexity of the ties between Nepalis in India to their original country is lost in popular representations of Nepali people.

In post-independence India, a Nepali watchman in a middle-class Indian home was a quintessential representation of the community and its place in the nation. Soon after my return from Darjeeling in September 2007, there was widespread violence in Darjeeling because a radio jockey in Delhi had made sarcastic remarks about a Nepali boy becoming the "Indian Idol."[13] The radio jockey continued his sarcastic remarks, saying that everyone in Delhi would have to guard their own homes and businesses now that there would be no Nepali people to guard homes and communities as Nepali boys were entering talent contests. There would be no roadside *momo*[14] shops in Delhi. Young Nepali men in Darjeeling reacted violently to these insults to their community and Nepali men. GNLF[15] members called for a strike, and the radio station had to go off air for a while. Knowing how much my informants wanted Prashant (the Nepali contestant in Indian Idol) to win in "Indian Idol," I was not surprised by the violence that followed these remarks.

Common literacy around the Nepali community in India is formed through the image of "*bāhādur*," "*kānchā*," or "*kānchi*" (stereotypical names of Nepali people) that appear in numerous Hindi films. Nepalis were accepted as trusted servants, and through their occupation provided security to Indian homes and the nation. In many ways, Nepali people still are taken for granted in these occupations. It is common in India to hear derogatory stereotypes about Nepali men, especially about the work they can perform, their stupidity, and their faithfulness. The owner of Sonākheti frequently used these stereotypes with me in our conversations. Nepali women are seen as hard working, but whimsical and sexually promiscuous.

Nepali people share their marginality with other people from India's northeast.[16] Nepali people believe that Bengalis or Marwaris (other *madeshi* regional groups originating outside Darjeeling) who occupy important offices and dominate business ventures discriminate against them despite benefiting from Nepali labor. They were also of the view that Nepali people suffer disadvantages in social and occupational settings because of these enduring stereotypes about their capabilities. In the places where I did my fieldwork, the standard advice given to a migrating man was, "Please do not end up becoming *bāhādur* or *kānchā* (servant), try to do something better." Such feelings of inferiority have deep historical roots of servitude in colonial labor recruitment and at present are amplified by the poor economic condition of Darjeeling. Nepali women were very anxious about the future of their sons and even if they were in jobs outside Darjeeling women feared the kinds of jobs their male family members were doing. In Darjeeling there were very few employment opportunities for men besides being drivers and some opportunities on the plantation. Women dominated the latter. When men found jobs, they were menial. Nepali people have always had to work under a Bihari, Marwai, Kashmiri, or Bengali business owner in Darjeeling. Even today, in the remotest villages, the main grocery/supply store is owned by a Bihari/Marwari (popularly called a "*kaiya*"). To start small ventures it is common for men and women to approach these traders.

Among Nepalis in India the invocation of *pāhāDi*-ness is pronounced because Nepalis find in this usage an effective way of maintaining their distinctiveness from plains people, whom they perceive as oppressors, as cunning, smart, and privileged. *PāhāDi*-ness simultaneously expresses marginality and pride/difference. Nepali plantation workers and tea farmers took pride in their *pāhāDi* identity. Many Nepali people would say, "*hami pāhāDi majale kām garchu*"/"we *pāhāDis* work with great zest" or "*India lai bachaunu ko lagi pāhāDi lāi chahincha*"/ "to save India you need a *pāhāDi*" (alluding to the presence of Nepalis in the Indian army). Political parties in the hills also used *pāhāDi*-ness strategically to build local party loyalties.

Leaders of the Gorkhaland Movement in the 1980s sought to change this situation of marginality and underdevelopment among Nepali people through the formation of a separate Nepali state. This Nepali state was supposed to represent the interests of the Nepali people. This particular form of recognition politics shaped the regions political developments. The movement for a separate state was violent; 1,200 people were killed, mostly men. In 1988, the dream of a Nepali/Gorkha State was temporarily compromised when the Darjeeling Gorkha Hill Council (DGHC) was formed to oversee the development of Darjeeling, and provide respectable work for more Nepalis in DGHC offices. This was GNLF's promise and a way for them to gain legitimacy in the eyes of Nepali people. Unemployed male Nepali youth were particularly attracted to this new party and the movement because they faced chronic unemployment in Darjeeling. Nepali women were also supportive of the new party because it promised a possible brighter future for their sons, brothers, and husbands. Unions with GNLF affiliation became a male-dominated space.

The negative images of Nepali people were also gendered representations of a minority community. Women were seen as hard working (bolstered by their predominance in the plantations and markets), and men were seen as belligerent, lazy, and prone to alcoholism. The images, along with growing discrimination in the rest of India and the lack of opportunities for Nepali youth (except for the army and police services), have led to a crisis in Nepali masculinity. The demoralization among young Nepali men and the problem of substance abuse was a cause for much alarm in Darjeeling. The culmination of pent-up anxiety was seen during the Gorkhaland agitation of 1986, when Nepali GNLF members killed other Nepalis suspected of having other party loyalties.

The mid-1980s were important times in Darjeeling and had significance for the future of the region's labor unions. Events during this time changed the course of the plantation labor union and party politics. The district prepared for a subnational uprising for separate statehood, which culminated in the late 1980s. Many of my informants reported unrest on the plantations, and even inter-union fighting. Until the mid-1980s, most labor unions were dominated by various communist parties, most notably the Communist Party of India Marxist (CPIM). Nepalis, who wanted a separate state from just being a district in the state of West Bengal in eastern India, also wanted their "local" party and this gave birth to GNLF. Communist loyalists joined the GNLF, at times forcibly, because being a Nepali meant supporting the "local" party, the Gorkha/Nepali party. Some people joined the GNLF and became natural loyalists and others recount stories of being violently forced into joining the GNLF. The thrust of the movement was to have a separate state that would uphold the identity of Nepalis as citizens of India, contesting their popular representation in the mainstream as foreigners. Women also participated in the movement, in covert ways, as will become evident in later chapters.[17]

The negative representations of Nepali males in Indian society have created a crisis in masculinity, exacerbated in household and community politics, because of the continued prevalence of women in the labor force. While women have become important in the household economy, men have been faced with high unemployment in Darjeeling, resulting in a massive migration of Nepali men to other places in India. Working for or networking with the local party (GNLF) thus became a way for Nepali male youth to spend their time. This was not just the case in Darjeeling, but in many other parts of India where unemployment is rampant and male youth ended up working for local political parties. But it was not just about spending time in the party; the formation of the Hill Council meant that party involvement would lead to a possible employment in the Hill Council (DGHC) or the party. These major political developments shifted the tenor of union politics within plantations. GNLF supporters urged their party members to be good *pāhāDi*, work hard, and not engage in unnecessary trouble, like the communist unions in the plains.

After the agitation, plantation unions focused on getting people into DGHC jobs since plantations had very few work opportunities for men and plantation employment was stagnating. Many small farmers (including members of the tea cooperative) in the post-Gorkhaland period got their formal land titles. They were ardent supporters of the GNLF. This ownership of land influenced their identity and, at present, they see themselves as "farmers" and not plantation workers. This ownership of land resulted in the formation of a future coopera- tive (now *sanstha*) and strengthened the small farmers' movement to get government recognition for their tea. Plantation workers, also loyal to GNLF, could not show many tangible benefits of the agitation, as the GNLF could not solve the unemployment problem by increasing plantation recruitment. In fact, the GNLF was so averse to traditional labor activism that plantation workers lost faith in it.

These historical developments shaped the contours of social jus- tice as expressed in Darjeeling. In the early 1980s the GNLF was born out of the collective desire of Nepali people in India to have their own state within India, which would be called "Gorkhaland." Whenever I refer to agitation, it means the Gorkhaland Agitation of 1986–88. Darjeeling also witnessed a 2nd Gorkhaland Agitation because the first Gorkhaland Agitation ended without the formation of the Nepali state/ homeland within India. The leadership of DGHC between 1988 and 2007 had also become dictatorial. In 1988, the DGHC was formed, which just led to more decentralized administrative power for the local state in Darjeeling. Subhash Ghising was its chairman. Ghising was seen as a dictator by many locals and, twenty-two years after his rule began, his closest allies ousted him from power by forming a new party Gorkha Jana Mukti Morcha (GJM). This new party had similar viewpoints as the GNLF led by Ghising, but the new movement promised to be less violent and more Gandhian (peaceful) in its approach and tactics, but still rallied for a separate Gorkha state. From my content analysis of newspaper articles and personal interviews with people, I gather that this new party GJM and its tactics are being questioned by minority political groups in Darjeeling as being non-democratic and coercive, just like the first Gorkhaland Agitation.

While Nepali minorities in India are victims of stereotyping and economic disparities, there are many significant differences among them. These differences are both socioeconomic and cultural, and are deeply gendered. Non-plantation tea producers, like the women tea farmers in my study who engaged in household tea production, were seen as dutiful tradition-bound wives. Ironically, women tea farmers and plantation workers were at most times engaged in the same task of growing and harvesting tea, but the ideologies associated with their work varied significantly. The tea farming households also distinguished themselves from plantation households. Both women plantation workers and market women were seen as *"chuchchi"* (with sharp tongue) and *"bāthi"* (street smart). Tea farmers saw their female relatives as being *"sidhā"* (simple/straight). The ownership of land was a major factor in the tea farmers' self-perception. Male tea farmers took pride in the fact that their women did not have to go to work. Access to family land, no matter how small, motivated women to engage in forms of activism at the family and community level; this stood in sharp contrast to strategies of everyday sustainability in the plantation.

These gendered social distinctions shaped women's practices and subjectivities, as I will describe in the rest of the chapters. Women plantation workers, in the absence of strong unions, would be afraid to get into arguments with their male bosses; they would fear being called *"chuchchi"* (street smart or immodest women) tarnishing their already negative representations. Women tea farmers on the other hand engaged in defying their image as docile housewives, using Fair Trade and seeking recognition for their misrecognized labor.

The continuing marginality and socioeconomic vulnerability of Nepalis also affected my approach to fieldwork as I maneuvered different expectations of people I met in Darjeeling as is evident from the previous chapter and throughout this book.

3

The Reincarnation of Tea

For us, what is conventional tea is organic. When organic and
Fair Trade inspectors ask us about our production practices, at
times they are confused because they think we have no idea
about organic production and we have switched to organic
production recently. They ask us what we used during conventional production; I tell them our convention is organic!

—Secretary of the Tea Farmers Collective
Sānu Krishak Sansthā[1]

I am confident, Ms. Sen, Darjeeling's pride resides in its plantations. There is no tea grown outside it.

—Head of the Darjeeling Planter's Association

The advent of Fair Trade organic tea production in Darjeeling provided an interesting backdrop for the articulation of gendered class
relations in Darjeeling's countryside. Although in the aftermath of the
first Gorkhaland movement many in Darjeeling's rural areas formal-
ized their access to land, it did not result in the formalization of their
tea production. The first epigraph in this section from the secretary
of the Sānu Krishak Sansthā reflects this contradiction. If we recall
Biren Rai's comments in this book's introduction, which reflected his
newfound optimism about the future of organic production for young
men, we can see that the celebration of small-farmer-grown tea in the
Western world and its effects in the backwaters of Darjeeling's tea
industry had raised the hope of formalizing "illegal tea" grown in the
basti. Authorities in Darjeeling's local tea bureaucracy are in constant
denial of the presence of non-plantation tea. What can be traded in
the global market under the "Darjeeling" trademark has to be produced
within the legal limits of the eighty-seven "Darjeeling" plantations.

Even adjacent tea farms on its fringes, under the same microclimatic conditions cannot claim this label.

This contradiction in Darjeeling's tea industry is telling; it reveals the geography of injustice on which organic tea production in the plantation thrives. In a climate where small-farmer-grown tea is still contraband since *hāthe chiā* [Darjeeling tea processed in non-factory settings], plantation owners have appointed themselves as leaders of Darjeeling's small farmer movement (also discussed and demonstrated in chapter 8). Such practices deliberately create terminological confusions to disguise big plantations and their owners as small farmers and small farms. To further obscure the ground realities the FLO has quite ingeniously constructed a nebulous and flexible category—HLO (Hired Labor Organization) that includes small and miniscule farms as well as big plantations, egregiously ignoring the discrepancies on the ground. India, thus, has the highest number of Fair Trade-certified institutions with hired labor (also called Hired Labor Organizations or HLO). In this list plantations get classified as HLOs. Ravi Raman's (2010) recent research on tea production in South India shows that these intentional terminological confusions leave the feudal structure of colonial tea production undisturbed in the postcolonial times. Plantation owners' frequent use of the word garden or farm to designate plantations also leads to faulty perceptions among visitors and general Fair Trade tea consumers.

In the remainder of this chapter I highlight how Fair Trade and organic certification has affected plantations and small producer organizations like SKS.

Plantations and the Reincarnation of Tea

The history of Darjeeling is deeply intertwined with the production of tea. This so-called green gold has given this dreamy Himalayan town and its people global visibility and it forms the backbone of Darjeeling's life and economy. A British planter who brought tea bushes from China in the days of the British Raj planted them in Darjeeling about 200 years ago. Tea is cultivated at altitudes ranging from 600 to 2000 meters. The cool moist climate, sloping mountainous terrains, and sufficient rainfall gave Darjeeling tea its unique muscatel flavor. At present there are about eighty-seven plantations thirty of which are certified organic producers, and the number of organic plantations is growing.[2] At present about 17,500 hectares of land are invested in growing this tea, yielding about 10 to 11 million kilograms annually. Control of tea gardens takes three distinct forms: (1) foreign control through local units of transnational corporations, (2) Indian tea companies (public or private), and (3) joint ventures between foreign or national firms. Plantation owners, however, lease the land from the state and pay revenue from the profits earned (see Koehler 2015 for more details).

While the plantations and tea are a matter of pride for some, others hold tea mono-cropping as a reason for the district's economic impoverishment. They argue that the plantation lobby has prevented any other manufacturing industries to flourish in Darjeeling for the fear of losing their cheap labor (Bhowmik 1981). According to the Indian Tea Board, 80 percent of the tea that is grown in this area is exported to Europe, North America, and Japan. In my interviews with planters, the export figure of individual plantations varied between 90 and 98 percent depending on how much their plantation exported. Darjeeling tea can sell anywhere from Rs100 ($2 approximately) a kilogram to Rs.18,000 ($400) a kilogram, depending upon its quality. Most ordinary people in India do not drink Darjeeling tea because it is unaffordable. Chai which is made of CTC (short for crush, tumble, and curl) tea is more common.

Plantations, which claim to grow Darjeeling tea have to be registered as a Darjeeling brand. This further complicates the issue of authenticity since Darjeeling's tea-growing area does not overlap with the administrative district of the Darjeeling Gorkha Hill Council (DGHC). The latter includes eleven plantations in the plains (*terai*) area, but international buyers do not accept this as orthodox Darjeeling tea. In fact, the tea grown in the plains is of a different quality, considered inferior to Darjeeling tea. In the state of West Bengal, Darjeeling district produces most of its tea for export. The plains tea produced in the foothills of Darjeeling is mostly for domestic consumption and exported to the Middle East and Russia. The tea produced in Darjeeling is known as "orthodox black tea," and the variety produced in the Assam gardens and the foothills of Darjeeling is labeled as "CTC." The market and prices of these two kinds of tea are very different (Koehler 2015).

These confusing distinctions have also created trade problems. About 40 million kilograms of tea sold in the world market were under the label of Darjeeling, but they are not produced in this certified Darjeeling area. In the wake of the World Trade Organization (WTO) regulations to protect intellectual property rights within sovereign domains, the government of India has defined a specific area in which Darjeeling tea can be grown. The government in conjunction with WTO has promulgated a Geographical Indications act that will enforce it.

The Tea Board of India is also pushing for a registered trademark for Darjeeling tea, which will certify its origin in every transaction. The forging of labels in the international market also hints at the huge demand for Darjeeling tea, which amounts to just one percent of the total tea output in India but is remarkable in terms of the money that it can command in the world market.

Darjeeling tea is known for is distinct flavor that its connoisseurs recognize just by touching it to their palette. Darjeeling is a very common ingredient in "English Breakfast" blends. Blends called "Irish Breakfast" contain lower-grade, stronger black teas from Assam (India) or elsewhere. It is the specialty of the Darjeeling brand that makes boundary disputes very strong. Many plantations want to be part of the chosen group that will enjoy a much higher price and prestige in the world of tea.

The fall of the Soviet Union was a dark moment in the Indian tea industry. Plantations of North West Bengal including Darjeeling were no exception to this general downturn in the tea market. Because of political turmoil in the late 1980s and early 1990s, the assured market of the former Soviet Union was no longer available. Together with these political developments, other nontraditional tea-producing countries also offered low prices for similar quality tea. Kenya and Sri Lanka gave stiff competition. According to some plantation owners, the flooding of Indian markets with cheap, aerated drinks reduced domestic consumption of tea, adding to the tea crisis.

Darjeeling in the 1990s was just recovering from the scars of the Gorkhaland movement (discussed in chapter 2), during which a large part of the industry had reduced production. At the end of the movement, the tea industry was faced with this turbulent tea market. Darjeeling tea producers started searching for new markets in the UK and the US. Darjeeling tea was popular in the West, especially the United Kingdom and Europe, and the market was also big in Japan. However, the adversities for plantation owners had not yet ended. The specialty market in tea was the domain of health-conscious consumers who sought a wholesome cup devoid of chemicals/pesticides. This was a time when food scares dominated Western countries, especially Europe (see Friedberg 2004). Consumers were also increasingly concerned about the socioeconomic conditions of the people and communities where this special cup was produced. There was a growing interest in recognizing the rights of producers in third-world nations who toiled in dreadful working conditions and were vulnerable in the turbulent world market.

On one of my early visits to Darjeeling in 2004, the big, bright-red billboard on my way from the airport "shouted" the following phrase, "the reincarnation of Tea." The phrase stuck with me; I saw it being used by plantation managers and publicity personnel in the subsequent months. The reincarnation was essential because of a changed market scenario. The recent shift to organic and biodynamic tea production was a response to this demand. In the mid-1990s, huge shipments of Darjeeling tea were sent back from Europe and Japan because of the high chemical residues found in them. Although the tea produced by chemical intensive methods was of superior quality, the returned shipments made some plantations switch to organic production methods. The decision to switch was not an easy one, as I will explain later.

While plantations still provide the order of reason in Darjeeling's tea economy, they felt the need to form new alliances with the region's "illegal tea producers." In Darjeeling, plantations were recognized as legal spaces for tea production. As indicated earlier, "Geographically Indicated," place-specific branding by the state and confirmed global laws stipulated that Darjeeling tea could only be produced within the eighty-seven recognized tea plantations. Any tea produced outside these boundaries is labeled as illegal. Plantations were and still are forbidden from buying tea from outside Darjeeling, meaning outside these

Figure 3.1. The Reincarnation of Tea. Photo by author.

eighty-seven plantations. The Darjeeling tea logo can only be used for tea produced within these plantations. In the tea world, Darjeeling tea means tea grown in plantations. This is the more publicized history of Darjeeling tea production. But there is also an informal shadow economy of Darjeeling tea, which has been around for many years but has gone unnoticed in the official histories and statistics. Obscured in the dominant representations of the area's geography, which emphasize the orderly colonial plantation aesthetics, this shadow economy has remained outside the tea industry. For instance Jeff Koehler's popular book, *Darjeeling: A History of the World's Greatest Tea*, does not mention anything about Fair Trade, small farmers, tea cooperatives, or women tea plantation workers, at least according to its index. It does discuss organic farming. The book was published in 2015 and perhaps Koehler and I were in Darjeeling talking to very similar people, but the gendered shadow history of the world's greatest tea is absent in his wonderful book.

Clandestine trade between plantations and small growers were rampant during this time. Every now and then there would be news in the papers, or at best planter's gossip, that a particular plantation is buying tea from small growers in India or from Ilam (a district of Nepal that shares its boundaries with Darjeeling). The state-recognized legal boundaries of tea production and ability of the plantations to transgress them illegally have enabled this shadow economy of tea to thrive in Darjeeling for many years. This form of boundary maintenance and subsequent crossing, as I found out, has increased as plantations switched to organic cultivation. Plantations seeking organic and/or Fair Trade labels are finding it hard to keep up with the declining tea production due to organic conversion. Pests are hard to control in the absence of chemical use. Production falls by 30 percent when plantations abandon chemically induced production to adopt organic methods (Bisen and Singh 2012). The production shortfall could be overridden only by buying the so-called illegal tea from small growers. Such critical dependence of the plantations on the small farms to keep up the productivity and maintain quality helps the small growers emerge from the shadows. Combined with the historic (by Darjeeling standards) wage increases in 2011 plantation owners are full of lament about rising costs.

Small tea farmers in Darjeeling's informal economy, who have depended on these illegal circuits and have had no connections with the global market, are now finding new ways to challenge their disenfranchisement within this tea industry by forming their SPOs despite their tenuous contracts with plantations. They are thankful for local NGOs, which are the local face of a new organic movement in the West,

bringing these farmers in touch with transnational agencies and certifiers of organic produce to increase their visibility in the international
tea trade. In this book, I draw attention to some (positive) impacts of
transnational alternative trade campaigns for the regions' small farmers, who are rarely talked about in the Tea Board or tea planter's
community. It brings to light an alternative history of Darjeeling tea
production, which is neglected because very few plantation owners
want to try new ways of producing tea. "While some management
would be open to implementing an entire new system for compensat-
ing workers, they often complain that the mind-set in the Darjeeling
hills is entrenched and not open to large changes" writes Koehler
(2015: 219). He further quotes an executive from the tea industry to
describe the institutional orthodoxy in plantation country—"Those
who rule the tea gardens, rule the hills. . . . They'd rather see eighteen, twenty gardens shut than make any changes," said the executive (Koehler 2015: 2019). He quotes a world-renowned planter, Rajah
Banerjee, who predicts the future of Darjeeling's plantations post-2011
labor negotiations stating—"They take away the rations and there will
be revolution" (Koehler 2015:219).

The new aesthetics of tea consumption in the West, expressed
through a movement for organic Fair Trade–certified tea has impacted
the spatial politics of Darjeeling's tea industry. Marketing of the cultural difference of foods through these transnational alternative trade
movements has engendered a new spatial politics of production in
Darjeeling. The new "politics of recognition" (Fraser 1997), manifested
through an obsession with "small farmers," their "traditional methods
of growing tea," their sustainable lives, and concern about their vulnerability in the global tea market has intensified the struggle over
boundaries of legality, territory, and resources in Darjeeling's organic
tea-producing communities. I will explain the history of Darjeeling's
illegal farmers who exist alongside the plantation in the next section.

In Darjeeling, the switch from conventional to organic tea production due to alternative trade movements has led to the dependence
of the "legal sector," or the plantations, on the "fragile-illegal" spaces
and unrecognized producers, a majority of whom are women. While
the Fair Trade Organic movement gives prominence to the so-called
"illegal farmers," efforts to secure access to land and market among the
"illegal" women tea farmers have gained intensity in the political life
of the villages, so long excluded from the global circuits of tea trade.
Women tea farmers, who claim to have kept alive the production of
illegal—now organic—tea feel disadvantaged as male members in their
community try to dominate the tea business.

The Shadow History of Tea in Darjeeling

When I began my preliminary research in Darjeeling, I was under the impression that I was going to study the effects of Fair Trade/organic policies on plantation workers. The aesthetics of plantations was so binding on my imagination of Darjeeling that I couldn't believe any tea was grown outside plantations. Tea production was synonymous with rolling hillsides dotted with bushes, spreading out uniformly for miles on end, very much an effect of centuries of monoculture and large-scale plantation production. Trapped in the aesthetic tropes, I could not recognize a multicropping arrangement of tea production like we see below. Here tea is grown alongside turmeric, cardamom, ginger, and other produce. As I was getting to know more people in Darjeeling's NGO circle, I heard rumors about "illegal farmers" and their tea cooperative. For me the Darjeeling Planter's Association (DPA)[3] was a natural place to enquire about these new and exciting developments in the history of this region. When I asked the head of DPA, he insisted that there were no tea farmers in Darjeeling. His self-conscious denial stoked my desire to know about the role of farmers in Darjeeling's economy, especially why no one in places of power wanted to talk about them.

My search soon brought me to the right NGO that was involved in development work among such "illegal" farmers and had organized

Figure 3.2. Scene at a SKS Tea Farming Household. Photo by author.

them into an SPO. I detail this NGO's history later in the chapter. It was the thick of the monsoon season when I had planned my trip to the illegal niches. The person who was going to guide me to these villages warned me that the road conditions were going to be terrible because of the recent landslides due to heavy monsoon rains. Through the heavy monsoon mist, we started the journey, which was approximately 20 kilometers from the center of Darjeeling town. On my journey, the plantation aesthetics dominated my imagination, I asked Pravin (an NGO worker), "How far are we from the tea farmer's lands?" He replied "We are there. Soon I will show you the tea cooperative office and you will meet some people." According to Pravin, my reaction to the strikingly unconventional tea landscape was identical to the tea buyers who come here. An American buyer apparently asked him, "Are you sure this is not some wild variety of tea? How can this even be organic tea, this does not look like an average tea plant." Pravin had the IMO (Institute of Marketecology) organic certificates for the co-op ready. He said that he loved this moment when people challenged him, and he would show them the paperwork of organic certification. The contradiction of visual aesthetics and taste is an interesting one and outsiders like me let the visual quickly overtake our minds. Also see figure 0.4, Aesthetics of Non-Plantation Landscape in the introduction, which shows a typical scene in a smallholder tea farm practicing multi-cropping by default instead of monoculture.

The visual aesthetics not only conceal secret tea histories, but also gendered stories of survival, trade and activism. Soon I tasted *hāthe chiā*[4] with a very distinct smoky taste while chatting in the kitchen of a small farmer. I asked Pravin why the tea tasted different. Pravin told me, "When they pluck the leaves and dry it beside the clay ovens, some of the smoke from the oven gets into the tea, which is very sensitive, and the leaves easily take on the flavor of their surroundings. Most people are not used to this smoky taste which happens because of the lack of proper processing units and use of wood-burning or sometimes coal *chulāhs* (ovens)." It was because of these limitations that members of the cooperative have had to depend on a plantation to make their tea market worthy. The situation might appear grim for the farmers are at the mercy of plantations, but plantations also have to depend on these farmers for economic and strategic marketing purposes. Their desperation has linked them to these illegal communities in ways which affected the latter's community dynamics.

For plantations the process of conversion to organic is extremely difficult. Soon after India's independence, chemical-intensive, green revolution technologies were adopted by plantations to boost production; tea was one of India's major exports. Pesticides were used to reduce the effects of pests, which are a perpetual problem in the tea industry even today. When plantations converted to organic pesticides they became less effective in dealing with the pest problem. During conversion yields declined because of the non-use of chemical fertilizers (Bisen and Singh 2012). This is where the small-scale tea farmers grabbed the plantations' attention. Plantations had to wait for three or four years for complete organic certification, but they could expedite the process by buying organic tea from illegal farmers. As I understand from my interviews with plantation owners, organic cultivation methods can never match the volume of productivity achieved through chemical-intensive techniques. Thus, the informal sector tea farmers producing illegal tea suddenly became part of Darjeeling's new economic transformations. They were cultivating illegal tea so far in the margins of plantations in the shadow of national development. There are various reasons why their tea is considered illegal, as I will explain shortly.

Sānu Krishak Sansthā:
The Cooperative of "Illegal" Tea Farmers[5]

Darjeeling's tea farmers own their lands; it is the tea they produce on it which the state, even today, considers illegal despite the Tea Board running programs for them. The picture below is of one such training program conducted in 2015. The tea board logo for Darjeeling GI is present in this poster.

Figure 3.3. Poster from a Recent Small Farmers Training Event Organized by the Tea Board of India in July 2015. Courtesy of Navin Tamang.

Below I have included another picture taken at this event where you see women and men listening to the details of state schemes for small farmers. These are "farmers by default" because they were actually plantation workers during the colonial period and became unemployed when the British owners of the plantations left in 1950 after independence. There are many such cases of abandoned plantations in Darjeeling. Very few scholars and policymakers have documented the history of these communities, except for the local NGO which worked with them.

After the plantation closed, the people in these plantations then arbitrarily divided the land among themselves and continued growing tea. From interviews with community members, it became clear that they uprooted many tea bushes to make space for other agricultural products in the face of unemployment and immense hardships. Because the plantation closed down, workers destroyed the factory out of frustration. At that time, as there were no roads in the community, this forced farmers to make dangerous journeys to Darjeeling town to sell whatever they grew. This area was connected to Lebong with a proper road in the early 2000s.

Due to mono-cropping of tea, these plantation workers did not know how to produce anything else, and almost 100 years of acidic tea mono-cropping had made the land unsuitable for any other forms of agriculture (Tamang 2003). These "farmers" therefore found their way out completely on their own, by selling illegal tea. But due to their marginality these farmers had one advantage. The abandoned plantation was away from the state's attention; there was no use of chemical fertilizers because the farmers simply could not afford it. The people produced superior quality Darjeeling tea through the use of cow dung and compost homemade manure as opposed to the chemical-intensive

Figure 3.4. Men and Women at a Recent Small Farmers Training Event Organized by the Tea Board of India. Courtesy of Navin Tamang.

green revolution technologies. They rolled dried tea leaves beside their *chulās* (clay ovens) in the absence of processing units. They sold this tea in the local market at dirt-cheap prices because it was not legally cultivated; they did not have processing plants to meet government requirements for exporting or selling outside Darjeeling.

The farmers who accidentally practiced "organic" agriculture are now coming to reap some benefits. They have gained international attention from tea buyers in search of an "authentic" cup of Darjeeling tea—just as it was grown during the Raj.[6] The latter has raised hopes among these small farmers who had been selling their organic illegal teas in the local market at give-away prices. They had almost given up tea production to grow other cash crops, which had more value in the local market.

The plantation in which the current co-op members worked closed in 1956 after many turbulent years. This closure was not abrupt but a slow process lasting a decade. The process made the plantation workers jobless, and a period of turmoil ensued. When the tea estate closed down, the people distributed the land among themselves, which gave birth to new "agricultural" settlements. The distribution of the land was done arbitrarily. The people, for the next decade, survived by selling tea leaves illegally in Darjeeling town or to neighboring plantations. At other times, they felled trees in the tea garden reserve forest and sold firewood and charcoal. In 1962 the reserve forest was exhausted and the hope of the tea garden re-opening had receded further; the people, then, began to uproot some of the tea bushes and started to cultivate other crops. They began to grow maize and millet. The production was very low. The lack of knowledge of cultivation and the infertility of the soil were the causes of such low production.

The present cooperative members were mainly fourth- and fifth-generation daily wage laborers in the closed and abandoned British estate. They depended solely on the tea estate for their livelihood and were not engaged in any other productive economic activity. Agriculture was an alien lifestyle for them, at which they failed miserably. The people used to supplement their income by selling milk. Most of the people had bought cows with the loans obtained from the village middlemen at very high interest. The interest rates ranged from 72 percent to 120 percent per annum. The milk was bought by the same middlemen, who then sold it in Darjeeling town.

Through *the Kisān Sabhā* (a leftist farmers' union) in 1977, official measurement and distribution of land among the people were initiated, which, as I understand from my interviews, was completed after the GNLF came to power in the late 1980s. Informants in the cooperative area attribute their getting land titles to the GNLF. In 1973, the first NGO intervention was made in this area. This was a Jesuit NGO run by Catholic missionaries. This NGO helped establish a dairy union and sponsored medical outreach programs. The dairy union ceased to function once this Jesuit NGO withdrew in the mid-1980s. In 1996, with the intervention of secular branch of the same NGO, the small tea farmers were organized into a cooperative, with milk as its first product. The tea cooperative started functioning in 1997 and filed its official registration paperwork in early 2007. There were many hurdles to this registration, although plans had been in the pipeline since its inception in 1997. The main impediment was the legal battle to ensure that these lands fell within the geographically indicated Darjeeling tea-growing area. Although the area of this now-abandoned plantation was at the heart of the "Darjeeling Tea" growing area, the Darjeeling tea bureaucrats have still not responded favorably to registration efforts or to including these farmers within in the designated Darjeeling tea-growing areas.

In 1996 the NGO conducted a survey among the villagers to find out the development needs of this crisis-ridden community. At that time there were a total of 307 homes and the population was close to 1,469 (male 663, female 806). The area also had high illiteracy, women had even lower literacy compared to men. Total land calculated in this survey was 401.92 acres. Animal husbandry and agriculture were the main occupations of the community. The people of this community are mostly *Rais*[7] and *Chettris* with a few *Mukhiās*, *Biswakarmas*, *Gurungs*, *and Tamangs*, ethnic/caste groups who are all members of the Nepali community with Nepali being the common and binding language.

They practice agriculture and most have small land holdings; the average of all the villages being a mere 1.48 acres, and the average per family income (annual) being Rs.11822.76 (according to the 1996 Survey, $237 at present exchange rates). Another baseline survey of the co-op area was conducted by an NGO during the months of August and September 2004. Table 3.1 shows the results:

Table 3.1. 2004 Demography of the Cooperative

2004 NGO Survey		
1. No. of Houses	:	455
2. Population	:	2457
(a) Female	:	1033
(b) Male	:	1424
3. Total Land		775.91 acres

The formation of the informal cooperative was seen as beneficial and more people from the abandoned plantation joined in. This is why we see an increase in the co-op's total area and number of households between 1996 and 2004. At present, the cooperative is apprehensive about including new members because they suspect that new members might not have organic soil in their lands.

The people grew a variety of crops apart from tea, the most common being corn, vegetables and millet in the lower elevations of the cooperative area. When possible, vegetables were taken to the market (ethnographic details are provided in later chapters). The most important cash crops apart from tea were ginger, cardamom, turmeric, and in lower elevations, oranges. Before the cooperative was formed in 1997, tea farmers harvested tea leaves, hand-rolled and dried them, and sold the dried tea leaves in Darjeeling town. After the cooperative was formed, tea farmers sold their green leaf tea to the plantation through the cooperative and did not have to dry most of the tea leaves. A very small amount is dried today and kept for home consumption or sale in the Lebong, Pulbazar, or relatives in Darjeeling town.

The inaccessibility to the Darjeeling markets due to lack of reliable and cheap communication facilities severely limited the earning capacity of the people. In 1996 the first road was built, but certain neighbourhoods within the cooperative area had no roads until early 2000s. For all marketing and selling needs the villagers relied on middlemen, either from the village or outside. Most of these middlemen were also shop owners. The people took loans from these middlemen and paid them off by giving them their agricultural produce at the middlemen's rate. Thus, the people were completely at the mercy of these middlemen who dictated rates of interest and prices of agricultural produce. Middlemen sold dry, illegal tealeaf for Rs.130 to 150 per kg to tea shops in Darjeeling town. They paid Rupees 65 per kilogram in the village. This disparity was true for every commodity. Therefore, the middlemen, leaving the people with a meagre income, maximized a major part of the profit. These middlemen spoke about their own woes to me, stating there were not enough government jobs in Darjeeling and sometimes it was not possible to migrate to Delhi or Bangalore.

In 1998 the cooperative sold tea to the plantation at Rs. 16 per 1 kilo of green leaf tea which increased to Rs. 30 per kg of green leaf tea in 2006–2007 and stood at Rs. 52 in 2016. The Institute of Marketecology (IMO), Switzerland gave a "Producer Organic Certificate" to co-op members maintaining organic farm standards under ECC 2092/91, Naturland, Bio-Swiss (EU Standards), National Organic Program (USA Standards), and National Program for Organic Production (Indian Standards). This is a unique program in the Darjeeling Hills with implications for tea internationally. It is the only small-farmers' project where the community owns the land, has developed a system of organic farming, and shares profits with a corporate/plantation tie up.

In 2004–2005, Fair Trade Labeling Organization International included this cooperative as a partner member. FLO labeling ensured that the products sold under the label were ethically produced and marketed. A percentage of the profit was provided to the primary producers, which was invested by the cooperative to buy an office space, build small bridges and tea weighing sheds, and repair the water tanks, which were built through the NGO help earlier. The cooperative and its recent achievements and publicity as the first small-farmer organic Fair Trade certified multicrop cooperative has raised a great deal of hope among members and their families. During the tea season, there is a great deal of activity in the households for harvesting tea and making sure that they are selling more tea to the cooperative. People are much more motivated about producing tea. The FLO premium was just Rupees 75,000 in 2004–2005 financial year, and in 2008 it had increased to Rs. 440,000 (I explain the concept of FLO premium in the next section). FLO regulates the contract between the cooperative and the plantation to which they sell their tea leaves.[8]

The cooperative has an elected governing body whose members were mostly male. Each household within the designated cooperative area is a member. Male household heads have the membership. In rare cases, when there is no male household member present, women are made members. Every two years the households vote to change the governing board. Within the cooperative area there are eleven clusters of households, which co-op members call *gāon* (village). These cluster settlements vary in size. Some have just seventeen households, whereas others have close to seventy households. These clusters were numbered by the NGO when they began work in this area for administrative efficiency. The cooperative used to have a Women's Wing consisting of female relatives of the male cooperative members. I detail their activities below.

My interviews and participant observations among women have been instructive in understanding that women have fulfilled the major subsistence needs of this community through farming at home and engaging in all kinds of trade in agricultural and other commodities through informal networks. They call this process *sakaunu*—to make do—in Darjeeling Nepali. In subsequent chapters I detail their gendered history of struggle within the community and their present economic and political activities in the community, contrasting them with the activities of the women plantation workers. This section is an overview of what the women's groups have done over the years, to provide a historical backdrop of their present pursuits as they unfold in subsequent chapters.

Figure 3.5. Women's Wing Meeting at SKS.

While the NGO provided logistical support for all activities in the community, their effort to foster gender equity is not the centerpiece of their development and capacity building initiatives. Some efforts were made between 2006 and 2008 to help the Women's Wing start an organic fresh vegetable business under a local label, but sharing the same principles of FLO (as per an interview with the NGO's director). Women still rely on agricultural product sales and seek credit to invest in their farms. The Women's Wing of Sānu Krishak Sansthā started their Credit Union in February 1999 with over 100 women members from cooperative registered families. The credit was made available through the Indian Bank, Darjeeling Branch, under the Self Help Group Scheme. The table below shows the extent of money borrowed by Women's Wing members over the years and the amount of money they saved in five years. They got loans from the bank based on the amount they saved in the bank. The NGO handled the distribution of the loans since many women were illiterate; there was also much stigma associated with going to town and general unease with banks. The NGO, working with Sānu Krishak Sansthā, also helped with accounting to make sure that the Women's Wing members were returning the money to the bank and that their accounts remained updated. Unlike many of the cooperative's male members, the NGO members were more sympathetic to women's needs and desires. Women also consulted the NGO members for ideas and logistical support for their various entrepreneurial ventures. In more recent years women have opted out of loan-induced Self Help Groups and reliance on NGOs. I detail some of this in the chapters to follow.

While the governing body of the cooperative was male dominated, members of the Women's Wing were frequently present at important meetings. The Women's Wing held their separate meeting on the eighth day of every month where the president and secretary of the Women's Wing discussed the activities of the cooperative and how the Women's Wing could benefit from them. Women cooperative members felt that the Women's Wing should receive a separate share of the Fair Trade premium money each year. Women tea farmers accordingly devised a plan to start their own business to sell other organic commodities that they produce apart from tea. They wanted to do it as a group so that they could reduce their dependence on middlemen for selling such products. Women tea farmers in 2006–2007 felt that their business ventures were in tune with the larger concern over equity within the Fair

Table 3.2. Total Amount of Loans and Savings of Women's Wing Members

Year	Credit/Loan (in Rupees)	Savings (in Rupees)
1999–2000	60,000.00	17,270.00
2000–2001	175,000.00	26,670.00
2001–2002	214,620.00	71,090.00
2002–2003	272,400.00	92,250.00
2003–2004	573,000.00	143,050.00

Trade movement. They did not play *ghumāuri*, although they knew about its ubiquity among women plantation workers. At one savings group meeting one women tea farmer even compared "inter-lending" of money that they wanted to engage in with *ghumāuri*. In recent years, due to the Women's Wing's run-ins with SKS, each cooperative member village sends two women as *Mahilā Pratinidhi* to the cooperative to increase women's participation. Women tea farmers also play a key role at the time of IC inspections (Internal Control tests for organic farming) and are paid modest stipends to assist with the process.

Fair Trade in Darjeeling's Tea Sector

Amidst this long and complex history of gendered struggles for resources and recognition and associated economic development processes, Fair Trade and accompanying practices of organic certification in Darjeeling provided a new threshold for some institutional rearrangements in plantations and tea-growing *basti* areas. Seen from the vantage point of plantation management, as expressed by one of the assistant managers of Sonākheti, it led to greater inroad of NGOs stepping in with resources, which mimicked what the state was supposed to do for them anyway. More insidious was this manager's celebration of NGOs as institutions that could bring real change in plantations. I elaborate on such processes in the next chapter.

In the small producer organizations like SKS, where NGOs already had established presence as harbingers of development, Fair Trade and organic combined certification ended up strengthening the power and privilege of educated and landed men and their families—powerful male middlemen, compromising one of its goals of moving intermediaries for better return to producers. These middlemen have to be placed in context. They were by no means as middle class as Nepali families in Darjeeling town or plantation officials, but they held relatively more wealth, power, and social networks than the average smallholder farmer.

Fair Trade's operation with small producer organizations in Darjeeling also resulted in new informal contractual agreements between plantations and small producers that are not sustainable in any way. However, because of the institutional context, the community's history with development and especially women's specific actions and social position, Fair Trade realized its potential goals by default. It did so by giving a legitimate presence to a large group of contraband tea producers (who are still not lawful Darjeeling tea makers since the Geographical

Indications do not cover them). What is evident from the trajectory of
Fair Trade–based sustainable development in Darjeeling is the disconnect from existing struggles for recognition, redistribution, and situated
entrepreneurialisms. What is more disconcerting is not really so much
the failure to address needs, but the hubris of privatized "Fair Trade"
completely in denial of its blind spots when it comes to addressing
structural issues pertaining to women's empowerment and the structural
violence of established ways of producing "Fair Trade" tea.

Overall, the goals of the Fair Trade movement are the following:[8]

> Fair Trade is a trading partnership, based on dialogue,
> transparency and respect that seeks greater equity in inter-
> national trade. It contributes to sustainable development by
> offering better trading conditions to, and securing the rights
> of, marginalized producers and workers—especially in the
> South. Fair Trade organizations (backed by consumers) are
> engaged actively in supporting producers, awareness raising
> and in campaigning for changes in the rules and practice
> of conventional international trade. (European Fair Trade
> Association)

Within the Fair Trade movement, there is great concern over what
kinds of producer organizations FLO should certify. Recently, Fair
Trade affiliated marketers have become conscious about whether plantations should be certified Fair Trade at all. They found inconsisten-
cies in plantation reality and certification. On January 6, 2009, Phyllis
Robinson wrote on the Equal Exchange website:

> Equal Exchange and others believe that no matter how
> "benevolent" a plantation owner is, a joint labor-management
> council and social premiums cannot in and of themselves
> correct the huge imbalance of power that exists on a plan-
> tation. We just don't believe that deep, structural goals
> oriented to change the playing field for small farmers can
> be achieved in a plantation setting. For these reasons, we
> are committed to building market access for small farmer
> tea organizations. . . . (http://smallfarmersbigchange.coop/.
> Accessed January 12, 2009)

Ms. Robinson, who authored the above article, further wrote that Fair
Trade should go back to its roots and attempt to form empowering
partnerships with small farmers, recognizing their rights and struggles.

The Fair Trade movement has engendered a diversity of opinions and expectations in its short history and there have been major fissures, like the formation of Fair Trade USA, which many academics and activists alike perceive as a sellout and full compromise of the goals of Fair Trade as noted in Robinson's comments made at a very different time. The diversity of institutions is a result of the varied ethics and conceptualizations of fairness. Starbucks very recently, at least as evident from field operations in Darjeeling, maintained its own rules and used its own labels through creating its own NGO and rules of operation. In the market for fairness, advocates self-select themselves and do as they please as long as the story and reports sound good. There have been concerted efforts by activists and the Fair Trade bureaucracy to standardize rules and certification requirements. I would like to share the basic certification standards that I saw being used in participant observation and interviews by FLO certifiers:

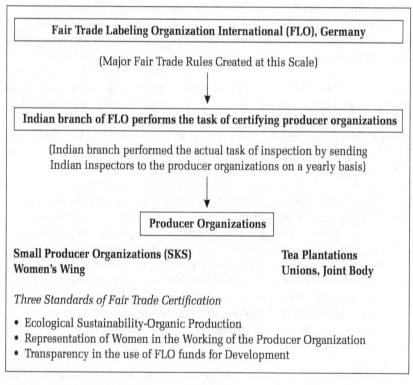

Fair Trade Labeling Organization International (FLO), Germany

(Major Fair Trade Rules Created at this Scale)

Indian branch of FLO performs the task of certifying producer organizations

(Indian branch performed the actual task of inspection by sending Indian inspectors to the producer organizations on a yearly basis)

Producer Organizations

Small Producer Organizations (SKS)   **Tea Plantations**
Women's Wing   **Unions, Joint Body**

Three Standards of Fair Trade Certification

• Ecological Sustainability-Organic Production
• Representation of Women in the Working of the Producer Organization
• Transparency in the use of FLO funds for Development

Figure 3.6. Flowchart of Fair Trade Labeling Organization International (FLO) Operations in Darjeeling.

Fair Trade and Plantations

The plantations in which I did my fieldwork, which I call Sonākheti and Phulbāri were both Fair Trade and organic certified. Both had 60 to 65 percent women workers who did the grueling tasks of plucking, pruning, sorting, and planting new bushes in the nursery and were involved in every stage of the manufacturing process. An additional workforce was hired during the peak season (March to October), especially during June to August when the monsoon rains necessitate quick plucking of rapidly increasing tea tips. It is extremely hard to assess the actual numbers of the informal workers/casual workers. Their wages also varying and are much lower than the regular formal plantation workers. As evident from recent interviews that Jeff Koehler conducted with managers in Darjeeling's plantations, "unauthorized worker absenteeism has become acute. In summer . . . it was 30 percent on the estate." This particular manager in Koehler's interview states further that the absenteeism has increased from 5 to 10 percent around 2003 to 25 to 30 percent in 2013. Koehler quotes other plantations managers who claim that the worker's movement in 2011 (in conjunction with the regional agitation) forced them increase the minimum wage by 34 percent, the largest increase in Darjeeling's tea history. Managers believed that worker absenteeism could be contained through this increase in wage but, on the contrary, absenteeism continued. Koehler quotes a worker from the famous Makaibari estate who explains the continued absenteeism this way, "Life is too expensive. You can buy nothing with ninety rupees" (2015: 156–57). My long stays in similar plantations made evident the daily entrepreneurialism of women as a way to stretch this low wage.

Each plantation worker's day begins at 7:30 a.m. and continues until 4:30 p.m. with an hour-long break for lunch. The plantation system is hierarchical, with the owner/planter in control of every aspect of production and marketing. Field supervisors, group leaders, and ordinary workers/pluckers are mostly Nepali. Other ethnic groups dominate the management and ownership. The ownership is mostly Marwari, with a few owners being Bengali. The management is a mix of Bengali, Marwari, and well-to-do Nepali men. Women mostly occupy the lowest strata of the hierarchy, with a few female group supervisors. Office workers consist of a few women who work as typists and accountants. These women are Nepalis, belonging to comparatively wealthy families in the plantation, who could afford a college degree for their children. After the Second Gorkhaland Agitation put wage increase for plantation workers on their agenda for struggle, the daily wage of an ordinary plantation worker increased from 53.90 to Rs, 67, with a cumulative Rs, 13.10 increase spread over three years" (Koehler 2015: 156). Since 60 to 70 percent of costs in tea production goes toward labor upkeep and wages, these increases were challenging for plantations to accept. It is important to note that none of this wage increase was due to Fair Trade/FLO interventions. It was enabled by regional political mobilization.

Plantation hierarchies were also spatially represented. Most plantation workers are provided with housing. The owner and management live in big bungalows with an entourage of maids, cooks, guards, and drivers. Ordinary workers live in designated housing areas. Clerical staff (office workers, *Chaprāsi*, and *Kāmdhāri*) have better housing provisions than ordinary pluckers. Most plantation workers complained that their housing conditions were a serious issue. Most homes had water leakage, and sanitation was also a major problem. There is a small dispensary in the plantation's main office premises for basic health check-ups. Most plantation homes now have electricity, but some homes that are located far off from the main office still do not have electricity. Plantation workers' families have lived and worked in the same plantation for generations. Upon retirement, a family mem-

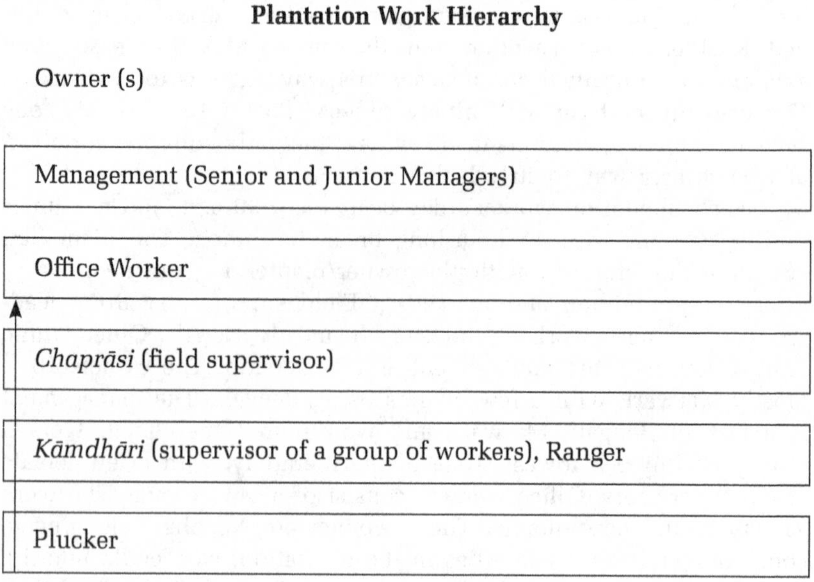

Plantation Work Hierarchy

Owner (s)

Management (Senior and Junior Managers)

Office Worker

Chaprāsi (field supervisor)

Kāmdhāri (supervisor of a group of workers), Ranger

Plucker

Figure 3.7. Organizational Chart of Plantation Hierarchy.

ber can retain each worker's job and his/her housing allocation. This system is seen as a challenge by many plantation owners, evidence of which is found in Koehler's recent book where he writes, "because of the live-in system and the convoluted laws about firing workers, gardens continue to pay periodically absent workers and cannot easily replace them" (Koehler 2015: 157).

Unions, Joint Body, and Fair Trade

All plantation workers in Darjeeling are represented by a union, stipulated by the Plantation Labor Act of 1951. Like elsewhere in India, union activities in Darjeeling are closely tied to the aims and ideologies of the political party with which the union is affiliated (see also Fernandes 1997, Chatterjee 2001, Basu 1992). The union's leadership is loyal to the party. In Darjeeling pre-1984 most labor unions were of communist leanings. After the first Gorkhaland Agitation, the majority of unions became affiliated with the GNLF, the local ethnic party. Communist- or Congress Party-affiliated unions were few and weak. In Sonākheti, every worker is a union member, but there was no major union activity realated to living wages until the Second Gorkhaland Agitation that began in 2007. My interviews with retired and active tea bureaucrats revealed that plantation unions are much less militant now than twenty years ago. A point of comparison was the plains tea garden unions that in the 1980s and 1990s were mostly non-GNLF and affiliated with Center of Indian Trade Unions [CITU, Communist Party of India (Marxist)] or Indian National Trade Union Congress [INTUC (Congress)], the major political parties in the rest of the state of West Bengal. At present plains unions at the Darjeeling foothills are also affiliating with Trainamool Congress, the ruling party of West Bengal state.

Today most plantations also have an organization called a Joint Body. The formation of this group was necessitated by Fair Trade certification. All Fair Trade–certified plantations are required to have a Joint Body to make democratic decisions about the disposal of Fair Trade premium money. According to the Fair Trade certification handbook, the Joint Body is supposed to be a democratic space consisting of a mix of workers, union members, and management staff. My informants have repeatedly told me that the Joint Body has union members who are not greatly involved with the union. They do not include the leadership of the union or union representatives who are brave enough to challenge the owner or the management. The owner handpicked worker representatives, and the presence of senior management staff made this space lack any form of democratic decision-making. Plantation Joint Body meetings were abrupt and irregular. A senior woman office worker in the plantation told me that Joint Body meetings were organized when inspectors, researchers or important tea buyers were visiting. When I first visited the plantation, I was invited to attend the meeting where a FLO official was also present at a Joint Body meeting. When I interviewed past and present union office holders, they had no idea about what Fair Trade was and said that they were never involved in disbursing Fair Trade funds.

In my participant observation of certification dynamics and interviews with Fair Trade certifiers, I have seen them check for involvement of workers in the disbursal of Fair Trade premium. However, since the Joint Body was organized by the management workers' viewpoints about what the premium amount should be spent on rarely made it to the negotiating table. To implement rules, FLO had two specific operations through two departments: FLO-EV, responsible for providing Fair Trade training to member producer communities; and FLO-CERT, which finds out whether producer organizations are indeed carrying out their operations according to Fair Trade standards. To get the Fair Trade label, producer organizations have to undergo yearly inspections by a representative of FLO-CERT.

When producer organizations decide to sell their Darjeeling tea in the Fair Trade market, they send their produce to the retailers in the West. For every kilogram of Darjeeling tea sold in the Fair Trade market, producer organizations get a premium over and above the regular market price of that kilogram of dry tea. For instance, if the tea cooperative sold 5,000 kilograms of black tea in the Fair Trade market in one year, they would get one Euro for every kilogram of tea sold over and above the market price for cost of production. FLO would monitor that the cooperative is indeed getting back 5,000 Euros as Fair Trade premium. My interviews with cooperative governing body members revealed that they were getting their premiums regularly. FLO tried to ensure that this money was being used for community development in producer organizations. FLO officials also ensured that plantations, which processed and exported small-farmer-grown tea, were being transparent in their operations with the co-op.

It is really difficult to trace when exactly Fair Trade projects began in Darjeeling since no one has recorded its history. Plantations try to stretch their Fair Trade legacy as far back as possible for marketing dividends. There is tough competition among the big plantations on how old their organic and Fair Trade operations are, and each has a different story of pioneering these costly changes in the plantation sector. From my interviews with plantation authorities and local NGOs, I gathered that plantations that had a good marketing team were ahead in the Fair Trade game. From their frequent visits to Europe and United Kingdom, particular plantation owners and their managers discovered that they could get their Fair Trade tea certification along with organic branding. The owner of *Sonākheti* claimed that he has been doing Fair Trade since the early 1990s. Other plantation authorities mentioned that they started their Fair Trade affiliations in the new millennium. Small tea farmers' affiliation with Fair Trade was much more recent, since 2004.

It is also important to understand how Fair Trade works in Darjeeling. I noticed some patterns. Plantations who are members of FLO carry out their own Fair Trade–related awareness or development work. The management oversees how Fair Trade funds are disbursed. FLO also grants Darjeeling plantations some special opportunities regarding the use of Fair Trade premium monies. In plantations in other parts of the world, Fair Trade premium must be spent for the enhancement of workers' socioeconomic conditions beyond what they get as wages and fringe benefits. In these plantations, for instance, FLO would not allow wage supplementing or paying a bonus. Keeping in mind the severe under-development of Darjeeling, FLO states, "An exception is made in case of Darjeeling where basic needs for workers (e.g., housing, water, and sanitation) may be partly financed through Fair Trade premium. This is due to the critical economic situation in the Darjeeling region" (FLO 2011). Plantation owners of course have turned this special provision to their advantage by covering 30 to 50 percent of facilities maintenance and worker provisions costs, which they have to provide to workers as per the Plantation Labor Act. What is even more interesting is that these funds are frequently loaned out to workers and the plantation earns interest.

Small farmers' organizations usually work with NGOs to carry out Fair Trade awareness campaigns and plan development. The reason why local NGOs get involved is because these small farmers' communities have depended on NGOs for previous development work. The NGOs now act as consultants and explain Fair Trade rules and regulations to small farmer communities in the local language (Nepali) and assists the cooperative governing board in making the best use of Fair Trade premium money. One NGO member told me, "We are so happy that Fair Trade money has begun flowing into these developmentally deprived communities. Our resources as an NGO are limited for perennial supply of development money to these communities."

NGOs also monitor the relationship between the small farmer co-op and the plantation which processes their tea and sends it to Western retailers. Not all Fair Trade work in Darjeeling happens according to FLO rules. Large beverage giants run their own Fair Trade–related NGOs. Plantations that sold their tea to these large beverage giants involved their own NGOs to carry out welfare work in the plantations. In such instances, these NGOs also provided funds and logistics for welfare work in the plantations.

Conclusion

This partial privatization of state actions through Fair Trade, alongside the celebration of NGOs within plantations indicates the steady emergence of private transnational regimes of governance (Mutersbaugh 2005). The logic of these privatized transnational governing practices is similar to the ones of the state that rule over a national society. Michel Foucault (1990: 13) identifies the logic of the modern state's ruling practices as biopolitical, since administrative and political practices of the state derive their legitimacy by fostering self-disciplining of its citizens by regulating "bio"—the ordinary and existential life of individuals or citizens. These individuals and citizens constitute a national society where individuals and groups depend on each other and impersonal bureaucratic rules for their basic existence. Thus, biopolitics operates by regulating society through the self-regulation of individual citizens (Sen and Majumder 2011).

In the era of globalization, mutual dependence extends beyond the borders of nations. Hence, transnational governance mechanisms like Fair Trade have emerged to govern trade relationships that traverse continents. The Fair Trade model and its practice of certifying and labeling food and agricultural commodities are means of nurturing ecological and equitable life on a transnational scale. Fair Trade practices also operate as a regulating, disciplining, and governing mechanism that is both restrictive and productive. It entails technical interventions in producer communities by monitoring and inspecting farms and farming techniques, checking the conditions of on-farm labor relations, and tracking the use of Fair Trade premium by farming communities to approve Fair Trade labeling of agricultural products. In this sense, Fair Trade fosters individual and collective self-regulation among producer communities and is a transnational biopolitical regime.

Moreover, the effects of Fair Trade as a biopolitical regime are similar to the effects of bureaucratic and governing practices of the state in instructive ways. A contradiction between a bureaucratically inclusive national society and exclusions that curtail rights of minorities characterizes state-centric biopolitics (Ong and Collier 2005: 15). This incessant clash between inclusive ideals and actual facts of exclusion is also the emerging trait of Fair Trade, which promises equality and justice for marginalized producers. Incidents of exclusion of marginalized farmers, who find meeting Fair Trade standards costly, are very common as corporations are appropriating the Fair Trade model or making use of certification practices. Thus the Fair Trade label, whose primary purpose is to convey on-the-ground situations in producer and farmer communities, is displaced to give a false sense of moral choice to consumers buying labeled products. Consequently, the goal of defetishizing the commodity is defeated by further fetishizing the imagined moral relationship that the consumer strikes with the producer. This has lead Mark Moberg and Sarah Lyon (2010: 8) to see Fair Trade as "shaped advantage" that enables "a limited number of producers to enter the global market under more favorable terms, utilizing enhanced institutional capacity and marketing skills to tap into a growing niche market."

However, the resemblance of state-centric biopolitics and Fair Trade extends beyond simply being a mechanism of domination. Disenfranchisement and exclusion notwithstanding, the idea of inclusiveness of state practices nurture expectations among citizens. These expectations make people aware of their rights and give rise to counterpolitics. Similarly, Fair Trade and its certification practices cultivate certain kinds of expectations in producer communities, even among the excluded groups (Lyon 2008; Sen 2009). These expectations serve as a launching pad for critical counterpolitics that tend to challenge and contest national and transnational political economic relationships undergirding Fair Trade, conventional trade, and state practices, as well as various kinds of inequalities within the producer communities, such as class and gender inequalities, that keep the poorest or the most disadvantaged groups from accessing the benefits of Fair Trade or trade in general (Renard and Pérez-Grovas 2007; Sen 2009). This aspect of Fair Trade is relatively unexamined and is highlighted in this book through ethnographic attention to the effects of Fair Trade certification in producer communities. Fair Trade has set in motion a process that helps global market relations to penetrate the remotest corners of the world for resources, but it also creates potentials and possibilities for a global counterpolitics.

The trajectory of Fair Trade is best understood as an interaction between Fair Trade as a social movement (Jaffee 2007) with commitment to ethical and environmental issues, and Fair Trade as a transnational biopolitical regime. Its movement through place and time is marked by shifts, displacement of goals, reassertion of activist values, and uneven impacts on the ground. I argue that Fair Trade blurs the distinction between market-based exchanges of agricultural commodities that extract resources from the Global South, and the global counter-politics that challenge inequities of market-based exchange. This blurring sometimes engenders new possibilities for producers to articulate their situated demands for social justice, but it is also a new system of disciplining producers. Fair Trade's mixed trajectory unfolds in the next chapters of this book.

4

Fair Trade and Women Without History

The Consequences of
Transnational Affective Solidarity

> When we were young it was the age of unions; now it is the
> age of NGOs, they are the ones who can bring real reform to
> these plantations with their new ideas and projects. See how
> they have involved all these young people from the West to
> improve our worker's lives.

These celebratory comments about the effectiveness of NGOs to involve
volunteers and visitors from Western countries for plantation reform
were made by Mr. Pradhan, the manager of a Fair Trade certified tea
plantation—Sonākheti—in Darjeeling district. Mr. Pradhan's observations validate the increase in voluntourism—a combination of aid-
work and tourism. Voluntourism exemplifies cosmopolitan sustainable
tourism also reflected in corporate social responsibility and ethical
consumption initiatives (Vrasti 2013, 9). As a feminist researcher interested in women's political lives within Fair Trade certified plantations
I was naturally drawn to explore the effects of Fair Trade–related
voluntourism on women's everyday political and work lives. More so
since plantation authorities urged me to observe the activities of these
volunteers much more than the workings of traditional labor unions
that had recently negotiated a wage increase for plantation workers
across the board. Some voluntourists I met in Darjeeling contacted
me after I returned to the United States to share their class projects,
photographs, and on a rare instance an amateur documentary available on YouTube,[1] through which I realized how cooperatives were
being understood and represented by voluntourists in documentaries
and websites. I was also able to see the roots of informal ways of
maintaining Fair Trade's public image, a kind of soft biopolitics, unfold

alongside the formal enumeration and documentation of Fair Trade's effects in official documents.

As I spent more time in Darjeeling's Fair Trade certified plantations I realized that the popularity of market-based sustainability and social justice initiatives like Fair Trade had engendered new possibilities for consumer citizens in the global North to demonstrate solidarity with producers in the global South. Self-selected Fair Trade voluntourists extended their affective solidarity by visiting certified production sites to participate in and witness the effects of Fair Trade on workers' livelihoods. Their acts of participating in, witnessing, recollecting, and documenting the effects of Fair Trade in turn produced new kinds of knowledge about plantations while affecting the plantation public sphere. Voluntourism also failed to recognize the inequity of new contract farming arrangements that small producer cooperatives like Sānu Krishak Sansthā had to navigate, sometimes confusing small farms with plantations. In existing studies of Fair Trade, the activities of voluntourists in the global South are unexamined and this chapter will address this important gap in the literature. *Everyday Sustainability* contributes to this growing body of voluntourism-related research to specifically identify Fair Trade enabled voluntourism and its different forms of community engagement.

The potential these voluntary acts of solidarity and related transnational praxis hold for increasing the bargaining power of producer citizens (plantation workers) vis-à-vis the state becomes salient since in India the state regulates wages and other plantation benefits via the plantation labor act (for details see Besky 2014; Koehler 2015). Fair Trade as an empowering venture must address the issue of bargaining power of producers since wages and benefits are baseline determinants of quality of life for plantation workers. What I witnessed was that Fair Trade–engendered solidarity practices erase the complex history of workers' struggle with the state and established systems of power through collective bargaining. Fair Trade enthusiasts operate on a limited understanding of the political lives of women plantation workers and women tea farmers. As I argue in this chapter, in Darjeeling's tea plantations, Fair Trade as transnational praxis has inadvertently pushed justice-seeking and delivery to a non-state sphere that is not accountable to the workers in terms of citizenship rights. Further, this privatization of justice indirectly undermines the possibility of strengthening collective bargaining institutions though Fair Trade and inadvertently decreases the state's accountability to workers or farmers. This chapter contributes to the new line of enquiry in sustainability research where the place of meaning-making around sustainability practice and its relation to new forms of value creation is central (West 2012; Brown 2013).

In the rest of this chapter I provide ethnographic evidence of the growing disconnect between these new kinds solidarity-based transnational praxis—voluntourism—and its effects on plantation associational life concluding with some theoretical reflections on these affective solidarity practices and their effects. These findings are based on research with Fair Trade enthusiasts visiting Darjeeling district between 2004 and 2011. I conducted participant observation and semi-structured interviews with forty-seven Fair Trade enthusiasts who visited two tea plantations, Sonākheti and Phulbāri, where I conducted most of my research for this chapter. The Fair Trade enthusiasts I observed and interviewed fell into three groups: tea buyers (six), student visitors (thirty-one), and student NGO volunteers (ten). I also interviewed seven student visitors traveling through the Fair Trade–certified cooperative (Sānu Krishak Sansthā) area trying to document Fair Trade projects. One of them interviewed me extensively on her visit and later made a documentary but left out my opinions and the footage she shot with me.[2] Since plantations had more structured arrangements hosting voluntourists, it was easier for me contact them and systematically recruit voluntourists there.

Encounters

When these student visitors ask me what my life is like, what I know about Fair Trade and what problems I face, I really don't know where to begin. To tell you the truth, we have been struggling within this plantation system for so long, why have these visitors come now? What can they change with a project or two, they are the owner's guests, and we just want them to enjoy their stay; that is our job.

—Prema Rai (female plantation worker hosting students)

I feel so connected to this planation and its workers already. I have been talking to so many people in the Joint Body and see that Fair Trade has made this plantation sustainable. Isn't that remarkable?

—Hayden Zichne (female student visiting Darjeeling)

The disconnect in expectations around solidarity between student volunteers like Hayden Zichne and their plantation-worker-turned-host like Prema Rai is common in Darjeeling's Fair Trade–Organic Certified tea plantation sector. As a consumption driven transnational solidarity initiative Fair Trade's global regulations are designed to promote greater solidarity between Fair Trade commodity producers and their consumers by providing a meaningful transnational field of praxis so that consumers not only enjoy high quality commodities but empower workers in the global South through meaningful activities to witness justice on the ground. These emerging acts of redemptive consumption (Igoe 2013; Vrasti 2013; Brondo 2013; Brown 2013) are accompanied by a progress-reality-check for worker empowerment—typical within the playing field of commodified social justice movements—not without its ironies and contradictions.

The fault lines within the Fair Trade movement gained much attention in the Spring of 2012 when a key North American stakeholder (Paul Rice, now director of Fair Trade USA) disagreed with the functioning and objectives of the international Fair Trade movement resulting in a high-profile rupture in solidarity between regulatory organizations of the Fair Trade movement. In this chapter I offer a different picture of the tenuousness of the solidarity idea and practice by highlighting a trajectory of faultlines that has received much less attention from the Fair Trade practitioners and academics. The present moment is ripe for foregrounding a different face of the solidarity crisis that laces the subjective aspirations of the weakest stakeholders in the Fair Trade chain, the average Western consumer, and Fair Trade's purported beneficiaries in the margins of a Fair Trade economy.

The Fair Trade movement has enabled "small acts" (Brown 2013) of transnational solidarity building that advance a fetish of what Jim Igoe (2013) identifies as the "redemptive spectacle" of green and socially just capitalism. I argue that these new forms of just-in-time transnational solidarity practices of Fair Trade enthusiasts—consisting of onsite observations of "Fair Trade," informal witnessing, and reporting of justice in social media—transform and shape the lives of producers in small farmers cooperatives and plantation public life in important ways through this new kind of soft-biopolotics. Operating outside the formal purview of Fair Trade certification (which defines and measures the effectiveness of "Fair Trade" production), the transnational praxis of Fair Trade enthusiasts demarcate the success and/or failure of Fair Trade in ways that are central to legitimacy of Fair Trade in the global morality market. An ethnographic exploration of Fair Trade enthusiasts and their voluntary transnational solidarity projects among beneficiaries of Fair Trade (in this case Darjeeling's tea plantation workers) demonstrates the centrality of certain forms of justice voluntourism (Brondo 2013, 115) to the workings around Fair Trade.

These "small acts" (Brown 2013) that unfold in postcolonial space and time are central to the movement in many ways: it secures a market, makes the movement real for its consumer participants—Fair Trade enthusiasts/voluntourists—by providing opportunities to volunteer for Fair Trade (see also Goodman 2004; Brondo 2013) to identify and work toward meeting the "needs" of the disenfranchised, and draws consumers into everyday acts of redemptive consumer behavior (Igoe 2013). These visits as acts of solidarity create a particular kind of gendered postcolonial intersubjective space where new truths about the lives of postcolonial women plantation workers in eastern India are written over a palimpsest of colonial forms of labor management and "native" forms of worker organizing strategies developed in response to such practices. The ironies of solidarity tourism enabled by Fair Trade enthusiasts is that it produces partial truths about associational life in postcolonial Fair Trade certified places. These truths circulating in virtual and real space in turn sustain relationships of material and discursive dominance of the North over the South (see also Gajjala 2014).

Sadly, the exercise in defetishization that the Fair Trade movement promises to its supporters and beneficiaries is fraught with contradictions that often render postcolonial plantation workers as "people without history." These practices knowingly or unknowingly alienate plantation workers from their productive political engagements with the plantation management and also from institutions of collective bargaining and negotiations (via Trade Unions) that emerged within the democratic space of the nation-state. Instead, these rituals of transnational praxis—through "voluntourism"—disproportionally valorize forms of bureaucratic management of justice through Joint Bodies. As new worker-management conglomerates the Joint Bodies are outside the purview of state monitoring and lack any institutionalized transparent means of operation. Fair Trade enthusiasts see the Joint Body as an important node in transnational social justice operations deemphasizing forms of collective bargaining indigenous to specific locales. Thereby, they establish a new set of standards for witnessing, experiencing, and measuring Fair Trade's success in which the significance of labor unions and workers' citizenship rights vis-à-vis unions and the state become progressively less relevant.

In describing the nature of these engagements, I take heed from scholars of postcolonial transnational feminism, (Alexander and

Mohanty 2013, 971) who remind us that in neoliberal times social inclusion and justice take queer forms:

> . . . [R]adical ideas can in fact become a commodity to be consumed . . . no longer seen as . . . connected to emancipatory knowledge . . . Neoliberal governmentalities discursively construct a public domain denuded of power and histories of oppression, where market rationalities redefine democracy and collective responsibility is collapsed into individual characteristics. . . . Such normative understandings of the public domain, where only the personal and the individual are recognizable and the political is no longer a contested domain.

My decade-long research in Darjeeling, India, enables me to witness these contradictions and their consequences for the economic and social justice aspirations of average Nepali tea plantation workers and smallholder women farmers who perform the harshest labor in producing "Fair Trade" tea.

In the following sections I set the ethnographic context for this chapter and its findings, followed by detailed data analysis on the everyday life of Fair Trade enthusiasts and their "transnational" Fair Trade practices.

Rituals of Witnessing

My analysis of the Fair Trade enthusiasts' interviews revealed certain key phrases they used to describe their purpose in visiting Fair Trade–certified plantations. Most frequent reasons cited were "to connect with workers," "to help in Fair Trade projects," and sometimes "to learn about workers' lives," "understand them," "show our support for workers."

The enthusiasts were Europeans and North Americans of diverse backgrounds. The students, who worked as interns in local NGOs, were between eighteen and thirty years old and had some involvement with Fair Trade–related activities or alternative sustainability initiatives in Western countries. The independent tea buyers and NGO volunteers were slightly older, ranging from their late twenties to fifty years of age. Most were consumers of Fair Trade products in their home countries. A few were traveling on their own and spent a week or two on a sustainable farm. Some of them searched online for places where they could participate in Fair Trade initiatives. They were interested in organic agriculture in the global South and came to experience it on plantations, very rarely finding themselves in non-plantation areas like Sānu Krishak Sansthā.

Their first point of entry for Fair Trade was the plantation management. Upon their arrival they were assigned to a "host," usually a plantation worker placed fairly high in the plantation hierarchy. Between the two plantations there were a total of 769 registered plantation workers and about 45 of them hosted Fair Trade enthusiasts in home stays. These "hosts" were the best paid and well-connected among plantation workers. They usually had good housing infrastructure with proper toilets and had some knowledge of English. The home stays enabled them to earn some extra money since visitors paid for these stays. During my fieldwork I found the expenses at home stays to be Rs. 250 to 400 per night including three meals. A student or NGO volunteer could choose to reside in a home stay or an addition to the plantation owner's residence complex called the "eco-house" (in Sonākheti) or "visitor's lodge" (in Phulbāri). The independent tea buyers rarely participated in home stays, usually being housed in the eco-house or visitor's lodge and meeting plantation workers only when the management would assign them a worker-guide during their field visit. Many visitors would start with home stays then move into the eco-house or visitor's lodge because they had televisions, modern restrooms with running hot water, and were close to the managers residences and main roads.

These living arrangements spatially limited the interactional possibilities for Fair Trade enthusiasts. They were exposed only to a certain class of plantation workers, usually better off ones, and were inundated with practiced Fair Trade propaganda. The only way they could learn about Fair Trade or participate in actual "Fair Trade" processes was through participating in Joint Body–managed projects. The two plantations I researched had more frequent Joint Body meetings when the concentration of Fair Trade enthusiasts was high. If visitors wanted to interview workers, their hosts picked the interviewees and also served as interpreters. Those enthusiasts who walked about the plantation on their own would always be surprised at how the owner kept tabs on where each visitor went on such excursions. This monitoring was explained as an exercise in safety.

These arrangements framed how Fair Trade enthusiasts experienced the plantation and learned about its people. The typical daily schedule for student visitors and NGO volunteers was to eat breakfast at the home stay, visit the plantation to see workers (typically tea pluckers) in action under the guidance of the "host" worker, then eat lunch with the host family before visiting the tea-processing factory. Visitors would often strike up conversations with the pluckers, asking questions in English about their family and work. The host-interpreter would try to translate the exchanges. The tea pluckers welcomed the visitors with words of appreciation they had been taught by the plantation managers or host, thanking visitors for buying the tea they produced. Workers would never complain about anything and would appear very happy working at the plantation and receiving visitors at their workplace. Usually the groups of workers would stop their work and ongoing conversation to attend to a visitor. The host selected one or two women from the group, who recited their appreciation with a very artificial demeanor. They would also show the Fair Trade enthusiasts how to pluck tea and pose for photographs or videos. The visitors came with books, brochures, or newspaper clippings bearing iconic images of smiling women tea pickers. The plantation office or local NGOs also supplied these.

The hosts appointed by the management played a key role in mediating what visitors would see and with whom they would speak. For example, Fair Trade tea is marketed using images of smiling women with bare, nimble fingers plucking soft budding tea leaves. In reality, pickers usually use gloves because the rough, stalky tea shrubs scrape their hands and make their fingers bleed (see figure 8.1 in chapter 8). This practice of using gloves contravenes a strict management directive to use uncovered fingers. The host would alert the tea-pluckers to present themselves with bare hands in front of the visitor, who is seen as the plantation owner's guest. Many pluckers would also wear their best clothes and shoes when visitors were expected.

At the tea-processing factory visitors were usually greeted by smiling female workers, who sorted and graded tea leaves, and male managerial office workers. In the factory the visitors tasted tea and observed organic manure being made. The host would also take them to several Fair Trade–related projects, such as biogas production initiatives or schemes to improve the plantation crèche. The visitors played with children in the crèche and often had their photos taken holding them. Such photographs signifying solidarity between producers and consumers were displayed in the management office in the visitor's lodge to create a welcoming atmosphere for future visitors.

Visitors would spend their evenings on their own or with others like them, or be entertained by their host family. Plantation workers would often organize cultural performances based on Nepali folk songs and dances even though such traditional entertainment was not very popular in the plantation community, especially among the younger generation. Yet the traditional songs and performances were presented to Fair Trade enthusiasts to show how the plantation's sustainability initiatives also extend to preserving cultural forms.

Fair Trade enthusiasts might also spend the evening having cocktails at the owners' bungalows, learning about plantation history from the managers or owner. These closely guided visits rarely provided scope for talking to average workers. As a result Fair Trade enthusiasts learned mostly about the formal production process and certain Fair Trade projects and knew very little about the actual circumstances of the workers. Below are brief descriptions of some typical visitors I met and interviewed.

Denis came from the United Kingdom. He was twenty-one and attending college. He visited Sonākheti, where his host was Phulrani, a nurse from the plantation dispensary and member of the Joint Body. Denis stayed in the eco-house and Phulrani met him every morning to escort him around. Denis was very impressed with Phulrani since she took him to the fields and introduced him to other members of the Joint Body. For many Fair Trade enthusiasts, learning about organic agriculture was a way to connect with the local people.

At Phulbāri I met Ellie and Andy. They apparently participated in community farms in rural Pennsylvania and were taking a break from college to travel around Southeast Asia, living in "Fair Trade–certified sustainable communities," as Ellie explained. They were in Darjeeling for a short visit to learn how Fair Trade supported organic agriculture. Ellie reported she found out about Phulbāri from a local travel agent in Darjeeling, who had then arranged the trip. Ellie and Andy were excited to be able to participate in organic farming by living in farming households. They, too, hoped to "connect with" and "learn from" farmers. Like many other Fair Trade enthusiasts, they did not understand the difference between a plantation worker practicing organics and a farmer.

Visitors were also invited to attend Joint Body meetings, which were posed as sites of critical dialogue and discussion between workers and management. The Joint Body was presented as an organic and democratic partnership between workers and management. In contrast, the trade unions were portrayed as troublemakers—organizations of violent outsiders who disturbed the peace in plantation communities by politicizing simple workers trying to maintain their traditional ways of life. Joint Body meetings were usually convened by a junior manager whom Fair Trade enthusiasts assumed was an average worker (see Kamalā's discussion later). The worker-representatives were treated respectfully in front of the visitors.

In a typical meeting the manager would begin with a long list of projects being planned or undertaken with the Fair Trade premium. The manager questioned the workers, who usually responded by describing the ways they benefited from these projects. Workers seldom brought up any grievances about the projects or the general condition of the plantation in these meetings. Even though complaints about the Joint Body were very common, workers never discussed them in front of Fair Trade enthusiasts, who were equated with management. There was absolute silence on the issues of wages, overtime work, casualization of workers, water shortages, and inadequate medical facilities that workers would otherwise discuss.

I have described these rituals of solidarity-building to show the framed encounters between the visitors and workers who are the supposed beneficiaries of Fair Trade. The frame constitutes of the ways in which the local host and the management make critical selections about how visitors experience life in a plantation community. These selections form the contours of a reality that the Fair Trade enthusiasts deeply engage with and believe that they can continue to influence by buying Fair Trade tea (see also Moberg and Lyon 2010). I now turn to how recollecting and documenting such experiences helps to maintain the reality created through these framed encounters.

Recollections and Documentation of Witnessing Fair Trade

Fair Trade enthusiasts were kept busy engaging in meetings and myriad projects during their short visits. Only during my interviews with them did I have opportunities to see how they understood the everyday reality of Darjeeling's plantations and the agency they gave Fair Trade in shaping it. As an interlocutor and interviewer, I came to know about the picture taking shape in the visitors' minds. They would eventually transmit their views of the plantation community and production locales to sites of consumption through narrating their eyewitness stories and experiences online.

I asked Denis what he found out about the plantation and the effects of Fair Trade from his visit. He replied:

> Thanks to Phulrani, I could attend a Joint Body meeting. I know that the children could now access the newly stocked library because of Fair Trade. She told me about organic agriculture. I had heard that plantations are really harsh

on their workers, but it seems that is not true for the Fair
Trade–certified ones. There seems to be a lot of projects
going on. I even helped the local children to pick plastic
on Sunday.

Knowing that Denis had also mentioned wanting to connect with average workers and learning about their struggles, I probed further. I asked
what else he knew about Phulrani's life besides her engagement with
the Joint Body. At this, Denis looked completely puzzled and we ended
our conversation there.

As I reflected on my interactions with Denis and many other Fair
Trade enthusiasts like him I realized how certain institutional arrangements framed their orientation to and experience of plantation life.
Coupled with this dynamic, their interest in learning about plantation
life post–Fair Trade was a barrier since they had already summed up
pre–Fair Trade plantation life as a case of one-sided worker exploitation.
While they were not mistaken about worker exploitation in the postcolonial plantation system in India (Chatterjee 2001), the fact that they
gave an inordinate amount of agency to Fair Trade for rectifying such
exploitation was remarkable since it foreclosed possibilities of seeing
plantation workers as having active political lives beyond Fair Trade.
Voluntourists focused on projects they could initiate and had no interest
in learning about gendered projects of values women cherished.

Therefore, Denis and his like never found out that Phulrani was
also a very active member of the leftist labor union until 1985 and
was planning to terminate her Joint Body membership very soon after
being refused a loan for her husband's medical treatment. Phulrani
told me she was tired of the Joint Body and its projects. I asked why
she wanted to leave the Joint Body since she had been a longtime
member. I asked, "Don't you like taking visitors around?" Phulrani
replied sarcastically:

> They are nice people, they are our *pāonā* (guests), but they
> are only interested in Fair Trade and not in us. They want
> to know more about what the Joint Body is doing than
> what we are doing. That is why I do not want to tell them
> anything about myself. Badmouthing the Joint Body is out
> of the question; I will lose my job then.

Thus, the stories workers shared with Fair Trade enthusiasts were
always incomplete.

Denis's and Phulrani's respective descriptions of their encounter point to a typical disconnect in exchanges between Fair Trade enthusiasts and plantation workers: just like the encounter between Hayden Zichne and Prema Rai in the previous section of this chapter. Workers like Phulrani, who are otherwise active in improving their lives through local initiatives, did not value the Joint Body. Hence Phulrani's comment that Fair Trade enthusiasts are "not interested in us." They perceived the Joint Body to belong to the management and that they had scripted roles in it: Phulrani and other workers compared the Joint Body with a king's court. Workers considered it their duty to tell Fair Trade enthusiasts about the patent Fair Trade projects since that is what a lot of visitors wanted to participate in. Fair Trade enthusiasts wanted to participate in Fair Trade–related projects as a way "to connect" with producers. As I mentioned earlier, the most common purpose with which Fair Trade enthusiasts identified was the need to connect with local initiatives. The process of connection, as we see here, is fraught with irony since the interactions follow a defined pattern, always within a certain frame.

Ellie told me that she approached the Joint Body at Phulbāri to introduce Andy and herself to "indigenous organic methods." I asked how they found out that the organic methods were indigenous. Andy explained that he had had long conversations with the plantation managers, who told him about local shamanic traditions and their effects on the practice of organic agriculture. Andy said, "I am so glad that Fair Trade certification is also reviving these local shamanic traditions." When I asked what they learned, Ellie said, "We met the local shaman and he told us that Fair Trade and organics had improved the air, which surrounded the plantation, and it improved the average worker's health." I knew that the local shaman had given them his stock narrative about Fair Trade improving workers' health. He told me the same thing when I first met him. The same shaman, in other contexts not involving visitors, constantly complained about the acute water shortage on the plantation that was producing various kinds of ailments. He complained to me, "We might breathe fresh air, but cannot control what we eat and drink." He implied that average workers couldn't access good nutrition because of all the chemical-induced conventional food that formed their staple diet and was also supplied by plantation's food system. He often joked saying "the tea plant is better cared for than us." The form of storytelling about their lives that workers engaged in was limited by their scripted roles within Fair Trade–certified plantations.

Unlike students and volunteers, the tea buyers perhaps had the most deprecatory views about the workers whom they were ultimately aiming to support. I was able to meet and interview seven independent tea buyers who came to live in the two plantations. Overall their stated purpose for visiting was to understand how workers lived and worked in Fair Trade–certified organic plantations in Darjeeling. As mentioned, the tea buyers were almost always housed in the plantation guesthouse, which is how they maximized their interactions with the plantation owner to negotiate good buying deals. Among Fair Trade enthusiasts with whom I interacted, the tea buyers spent the least amount of time with average workers.

A Fair Trade tea buyer proudly commented to me, "At least Fair Trade is doing something good for these illiterate workers, or they would create so much union trouble." Later, when I searched another independent buyer on the Internet, I found an online interview about the status of a Fair Trade–certified plantation this buyer had visited in Darjeeling in which she proclaimed that ". . . plantation workers never go on strike, while strikes by the local militant Gurkha population are rife at other plantations."[3] She seemed to be unaware that all plantations in Darjeeling have unions and all plantation workers receive similar benefits through a uniform wage structure mandated by the federal government. But missing in this tea buyer's analysis was the fact that union activity for workers' rights has taken many critical turns in Darjeeling over the last two or three decades because of situated historical and political developments related to ethnic subnationalism. What was most alarming was the subtle celebration of the plantation owner's ability to quell agitating Gurkhas through Fair Trade—repeating the age-old colonial and orientalist representational trope of Nepalis as a martial race with a streak of useless rebelliousness. Although the tea buyers were enthusiastic about connecting with workers, their image of plantation workers in Darjeeling contrasted with their desire to understand workers' actual lives in Fair Trade–certified plantations.

Similarly, many American volunteers who returned from Darjeeling would phone to tell me about the presentations they made at their college or church about the benefits of Fair Trade in Darjeeling. Through site visits and narratives, these enthusiasts cultivated a sense of themselves as activist consumers participating in real change. However, their visits and the publicity they gave to plantations had an effect that can be understood only by seeing how the management and workers felt about the changes brought about by Fair Trade in the years since 1990.

Fair Trade and Privatized Political Fields

I have already written about plantation manager Mr. Pradhan's celebration of NGO projects in plantations earlier in this chapter. The
age of NGOs marks what I call the era of privatized justice, which I
elaborate later. The involvement of NGOs in plantations began with
Fair Trade, which indirectly facilitated the sidelining of unions and
political questions of wage and other benefits. In the following account
based on both historical sketches and interviews I track these changes.

As I reflected on Mr. Pradhan's comments, I came to realize that
these new solidarity practices advanced a very important, albeit unspoken, mission of many plantations: to find new niche markets and more
importantly, to keep the unions at bay by making the Joint Body a
critical node for solidarity practices. Fair Trade enthusiasts who came
with a great desire to participate in and witness Fair Trade were often
co-opted into projects that gave them a sense of purpose, but ironically
furthered the existing inequities in the plantation.

The significance and effects of witnessing practices created by
these peculiar solidarity initiatives can be best understood by locating
these practices as a continuation of the longer history of sidelining
unions prevalent in Darjeeling's plantations since the 1980s. Such practices began with the decline in power of labor-focused leftist unions or
ABGL. Through my interviews with plantation owners, members of the
tea trade bureaucracy, I discovered that the timing of Fair Trade's entry
into plantation life in the early to mid-1990s coincided with a period
of union busting peculiar to Darjeeling district. It became apparent that
Fair Trade inadvertently provided a necessary cover for the gradual
creation of a privatized political field within plantations. The building
of Fair Trade–related institutions within plantations—like the Joint
Body—only furthered this process. The Joint Body gradually became
the face of plantation public life and a poor proxy for elected collective organizing bodies. It gradually replaced institutions like labor
unions as a point of introduction for Fair Trade enthusiasts seeking to
learn about the region and plantation life. Outside visitors could rarely
independently engage with workers and learn about their homegrown
efforts to improve their livelihoods and their struggles for justice.

The effects of these political shifts and the creation of a privatized political field were apparent in my interviews with workers. I
begin by detailing a common-worker-narrated history of associational
life within plantations, as laid out for me by Kamalā in Sonākheti.
Many workers in both plantations where I conducted this research
echoed the logic of Kamalā's explanations. Kamalā, unlike the other

illiterate or semiliterate women plantation workers I interviewed, had a bachelor's degree and worked in the plantation's accounting department. She was the most visible face of the Fair Trade empowerment initiatives on this plantation. She handled major tasks of the Joint Body operations, which also oversaw the emerging home stay program.

Kamalā once asked me whether Joint Body members could directly complain to Fair Trade Labelling Organizations International (FLO) about the plantation's problems, which they could not communicate to FLO inspectors or liaison officers during the scripted Joint Body meetings. She continued, "Sometimes when Fair Trade inspectors are around, I feel like pulling them aside and telling them the real situation. How can they understand the problems here if they do not speak to common people and do not understand Nepali?" Kamalā agreed that I should not use the real name of the plantation in my publications to protect her identity, but somewhat regretted this since she badly wanted to expose the planter, but was afraid of doing it herself because she had small kids and needed her job.

Educated plantation employees like Kamalā were not the only ones who questioned the politics of knowledge production about Sonākheti. Women tea-pluckers without formal education frequently criticized the strategic use of their images and talents for the pursuit of Fair Trade certification. Lachmi told me that whenever the *kuires* (white visitors) come to the plantation she takes them around, which is extremely stressful for her because it entails more walking, and often missing lunch and returning home late. She continued:

> We do not know each other's language. We are called to the meeting of the Joint Body where nothing substantial is discussed. We are shown in a way that says nothing about our lives and frustrations. I know the real story; I know what our lives are like. The tourists and other whites take photographs, and I hate it because we are all supposed to smile and they never send the photos back.

Lachmi continued that people made films about the workers that she never got to see. She never understood why foreigners had so much interest in showing a poor worker in a film.

Both Kamalā and Lachmi constantly pointed to a major gap in their interaction with Fair Trade enthusiasts: the disconnect between what visitors could witness about the life of an average worker within a frame and what women workers actually experienced in the plantations. Kamalā underscored in our many conversations that the Joint

Body could exist because "no one cares about real labor issues, it's all a drama." Probing her further I learned why she made this comment and why workers found the Joint Body ineffective. Kamalā explained to me that the changing dynamics of unions in the plantations came in handy for the plantation management to discipline workers. According to Kamalā, the union was strong in the 1980s, but after the rise of a regionalist party—Gorkha National Liberation Front (GNLF)—plantation authorities bribed the strongest leftist leader. Part of his bribe was a trip abroad. I found out later from interviewing this leftist union leader that the trip was an opportunity to participate in a FLO-sponsored conference in Europe. Kalama mentioned that after his return from Europe this particular leader refused to take part in union activities. My interviews with present and past union members in Sonākheti and Phulbāri revealed to me how plantation authorities used resources from the Fair Trade movement for strategic purposes that furthered their control over labor.

Kamalā further explained that during the 1980s there had been great union leaders whom the workers revered and the management feared. If the union leaders called for a strike or the house arrest of managers, the workers (both men and women) from the farthest neighborhoods within Sonākheti would march up to the factory. According to Kamalā, who did not support the leftists, the bribery was very strategic for breaking up union solidarity, destroying people's trust in collective action and the labor-focused leftist parties.

It is important to note that breaking workers' trust in the leftist party and its focus on raising awareness about labor issues was a strategic move by the owner and a common practice in cases where a plantation owner could support Gorkha political parties like GNLF. Through this act he indirectly signaled his support for the new regional politics between the 19902 and 2000s, for which labor issues were low priority. Post-agitation these strategic activities helped the owner forge profitable relations with new union leaders who now devoted more time to regional politics, which involved making the Nepali plantation workers more conscious of their cultural identity. The intensity of this ethnic turn is detailed in Townsend Middleton's work.

Despite the plantation owner's strategic support of regional Nepali politics, his treatment of average workers was questionable to say the least. Even during my research the plantation management was quick to make contributions for building temples and promoting the cultural projects of Nepali workers. The owner consciously supported the "ethnic" needs of his workers, though he frequently invoked ethnic stereotypes of "childishness," "rebelliousness," and "immaturity" toward the Nepali men, even in front of outsiders. These stereotypes then found their way onto websites where tea buyers wrote about Fair Trade's ability to quell troublesome unions. Some plantation worker hosts at Sonāhketi were deeply perturbed when they found out that a voluntourist from New York had complained to the management about being served the same food three days in a row. For me the irony of this complaint was unbelievable. A volunteer comes to get the experience of living in a plantation house but cannot stand the same Nepali meal two or three times in a row. Knowing that the nearest market to buy vegetables was hard to get to would have perhaps helped set her expectation of meals in an average plantation home.

Via plantation documents and online information I discovered that the first Joint Bodies were formed in Sonākheti in 1994 and in Phulbāri in 1996, when Fair Trade activities started increasing in this region and the first efforts to grow organic tea began. The plantation management took advantage of these new sustainability initiatives and shifts in regional politics to ensure that difficult questions about better health care, increasing casualization of labor, housing improvement, nepotism, verbal abuse of workers, and promotion of women workers would not be raised, while they posted lofty claims about women's empowerment and women supervisors on the plantation website. Beginning at that time, the Joint Body—supposedly formed of union representatives, ordinary workers, and managers—became and continues to be dominated by the management and the workers it hand-picks (like Kamalā) who rarely raise such difficult structural issues in meetings. The particularities of union busting and Joint Body creation might be peculiar to the Sonāhketi plantation, but my interviews with older workers in Phulbāri and local researchers revealed that during the mid-1990s plantations came up with many strategies to delegitimize leftist unions, since any sustained movement for wage or benefits reform would hurt the profits of planters who were facing declining yields. Many workers also mentioned that the plantation owners resisted complying with the standards of the Indian Plantation Labor Act of 1951 that was supposed to guarantee forms of worker well-being within plantations and associated reform.

The trajectory of Fair Trade's entry into Darjeeling plantations coincided with and at times facilitated a particular form of neglecting labor issues. This was ironic since it went against a core principle of the Fair Trade movement: strengthening of collective bargaining institutions. Unlike other industries in India, where union busting continues on a regular basis, in Darjeeling it took hold and continued with the rise of "sustainable" tea production and regeneration of the area through Fair Trade. The solidarity initiatives I have described throughout this chapter continue to further this pattern.

Conclusion

Western political consumerism's foot soldiers have possibly never had so many options for promoting social justice in the global South, beginning with their morning cup of Fair Trade tea or coffee. As I have shown, the tide of political consumerism has transformed Fair Trade and its associated practices into a new kind of transnational praxis that involves particular forms of framed engagements with workers and knowledge production about producer communities in the global South. New rituals of transnational praxis involving observing, reporting, recollecting, and witnessing justice delivery by Fair Trade enthusiasts conjures up a world that can be changed through buying and selling goods under the Fair Trade label (Tsing 2000). These practices inadvertently compromise Fair Trade's mission of promoting better worker-management partnerships through creating new institutions like the Joint Body that are not accountable to local communities in the same way as labor unions. It also leads to a simplistic celebration of small farmer organizations like SKS without attending associated contracts with plantations.

In Darjeeling's tea plantations, Fair Trade experts (plantation managers, Fair Trade enthusiasts, NGOs, certifiers) talk of justice and highlight that individual workers can be empowered through a loan, a cow, or "self-help." Although new privately managed institutions like the Joint Body check for and prevent child labor abuse or lessen the use of plastic in production, there is a deafening silence on structural issues like daily wages—the single most important factor shaping worker empowerment and economic justice fought for by local labor unions. The recent wage increase in Darjeeling plantations took place without any intervention from Fair Trade experts, plantation owners, or the Joint Body. The change became possible when regional political parties adopted a wage hike for workers as one of its core agendas in fighting for greater citizenship rights for Nepali minorities within India via Gorkhaland Movement 2. The need for increased wages has been a topic of common concern among workers ever since I began research, but I never witnessed it being discussed in Joint Body meetings.

While activist consumers continue to play a key role in raising awareness about fair labor practices and broader issues of inequity in global trade (Doane 2010; Goodman 2010), certain aspects of their engagements in Fair Trade–certified production niches have not been explored in detail. My observation of the activities of Fair Trade enthusiasts in this chapter is to help begin that discussion. This group is involved in powerful forms of witnessing that could determine the legitimacy of the social justice claims of Fair Trade products in the face of increased mainstreaming of the social justice goals of Fair Trade (Raynolds 2009). These Fair Trade enthusiasts not only visit and experience, but also disseminate information about their eyewitness experiences of the benefits of Fair Trade–certified workplaces in creative ways on their return to their home countries. They advance an affective soft-biopolitics that assesses Fair Trade's success on just-in-time parameters and produces virtualities about worker life.

Such actions potentially may influence future consumer-citizens' support for Fair Trade products. While student activists in the global North caution against the increased mainstreaming of Fair Trade's goals (see Wilson and Curnow 2013), the witnessing practices of Fair Trade enthusiasts could help Fair Trade maintain its legitimacy as a consumer-based movement that promises to improve the lives of average plantation.

I urge students, consumer activists, and practitioners of Fair Trade who want to demonstrate solidarity with producers and workers in the global South to invest more time in learning about regional histories and situated struggles of producer communities. Such learning might not necessarily be enabled by involvement in Fair Trade–related projects or institutions. Learning about the complex political lives of subjects of injustice will enable them to understand: (a) where their own solidarity related efforts could make the most difference in the lives of workers and farmers; and (b) prevent cooptation of their well-meaning solidarity building efforts.

5

Ghumāuri

Interstitial Sustainability in India's
Fair Trade–Organic Certified Tea Plantations

In Darjeeling's Fair Trade and organic-certified tea plantations the path to gender justice is riddled with ironies. In chapter 3, I described the terminological confusions sustained by Fair Trade's transnational bureaucracy for building more legitimacy and consumer confidence. In this chapter I uphold two contradictory processes at work inside these "certified" plantations. On one hand women plantation workers' "survival narratives" and leadership skills are receiving increasing visibility in Fair Trade publicity material. On the other hand, women have categorically eschewed existing collective bargaining institutions (i.e., labor unions, despite card-holding union members) and new privatized collectives instituted by the Fair Trade certification standards (i.e., Joint Bodies or worker-management partnerships) to promote their interests. Women workers instead engage in much more clandestine forms of collective organizing, namely, revolving credit groups called *ghumāuri*. The prevalence of *ghumāuri* in rural areas in Nepal and Darjeeling is evident from my life history interviews with women plantation workers who claim to have inherited this group practice from their foremothers who migrated from rural Nepal. There is evidence of such practices among women in rural Nepal as demonstrated in Katherine March's work on women's economic activities in rural Nepal (see March and Taqqu 1986). While women's informal activism and resource pooling is common in many other parts of the world, they are rarely discussed or supported by formal development interventions (Subramaniam and Purkayastha 2004). Their success and sustainability can perhaps be attributed to durable invisible paths through which they sustain livelihoods, social relations, and in my case postcolonial Fair Trade–certified plantations.

At present, *ghumāuri* help workers cope with their abysmally low wages through group savings and small entrepreneurial ventures, like pooling in cheap ration rice to make *raksi* (local beer) and selling eggs and vegetables through family networks. But, more importantly, it provides critical mentoring for women, young and old, on labor dynamics, Fair Trade, and daily survival that they cannot access in the male-dominated public sphere, although they actively participate in regional political movements. Women workers try their best to conceal their *ghumāuri*-related activities from plantation authorities, union organizers, Fair Trade certifiers, and male family members through practicing measured invisibility. In this chapter I elucidate why such measured invisibility is necessary in Fair Trade–certified plantations producing sustainable tea and flaunting the success of women leaders.

More ironical is the fact that the new Fair Trade projects in plantations involve starting Self Help Groups (SHGs) mimicking the famous micro-credit programs in various countries in South Asia. The loans from these projects, which come from Fair Trade promoting NGOs and plantation management, are available through nepotistic channels to certain women and their families. Everyday sustainability for average women workers is rooted in the past and present entrepreneurialism through *ghumāuri*.

Survival Narratives

While women do much of the work on small farms and plantations, they often still face unequal treatment, discrimination, and harassment in many rural areas and in factories which have reputations for abuses. Fair Trade strives to help women realize their full potential and to get the respect in their communities that they deserve. Women hired on Fair Trade farms and plantations are guaranteed access to health care, certain job rights, and freedom from harassment so that women are able to play a strong role in their families and in their coops. Fair Trade certified farms have empowered women through opportunities for education, leadership roles, and scholarships so that girls can imagine a future where they can be their own boss.

(From Fair Trade USA website under the entry "What is Fair Trade Impact: Empowering Women")

Our union leaders tell us that for the Nepali community "Gorkhaland" is the biggest issue. Yes, we have learnt the significance of demanding our land, but the miseries of the poor people have not reduced. Our *ghumāuri* group is like a small union where we women can openly discuss issues about our livelihood and work. We can give each other confidence.

—Chhāyā (Plantation worker and supervisor)

The Joint Body is like a *"raja ko durbar"* [king's court]. Any sensible person needing the favors of the king knows that the Joint Body is not a place for honest discussions, it is all about making the king and his *chamchas* [coterie] feel good.

—Sulekha (Plantation worker)

This section emphasizes the contrast in survival narratives of women plantation workers as expressed to me—their interlocutor—and the celebration of women's leadership and guaranteed success in Fair Trade propaganda. The plantation owners mimicked this idea of women becoming bosses in plantations and the few that had women in supervisory positions flaunted it for the greater dividends in the transnational morality market.

Note that that comment about *ghumāuri* being like a small union is made by Chhāyā, who has been active in local politics and labor unions, and has worked as a *Kāmdhāri* (group supervisor) for many years. But even someone like her, with moderately more power and respect compared to other women workers in plantations, remains deeply skeptical about the Gorkhaland movement, local politics and its potential for improving anything significant for women on *thikā* (daily wage). The social wage in Darjeeling is very low and even with recent improvement still stands at less than two dollars per day. The awful food supplements that they get with their weekly ration are not nourishing enough for maintaining their families. That's when *ghumāuri* comes in handy. Therefore, Sulekha and many like her find the activities of the Joint Body useless since it has no connection with existing labor struggles and regional political mobilizations, let alone any real value for women.

Chhāyā and Sulekha's views also reflect women plantation workers' skepticism about individualized strategies of improving women workers' livelihoods promoted by Fair Trade. They seem ineffective in the face of women's everyday practices of self-care and its extension to community-care that are based on informal collectives that have provided a continual space of trust and mentoring in the harsh climate of gendered plantation disciplining.

Therefore, why women cherish there interstitial spaces (Springer 2005; Sexsmith 2012) within plantation communities can only be understood if we understand the gendered effects of regional politics with its specific ramifications for women's rights and desires within tea plantations. Their agency lies in concealing these interstitial spaces of politics from becoming another story told to visitors, which will end up in some Fair Trade documentary and/or photograph. In this way they resisted Fair Trade's appropriation of progressive politics and providing plantation women subject positions that valorize them without giving them any real power or access to resources in their everyday work and community lives for creating a more respectful existence. Rebuke, sarcasm, and *ghumāuri khelnu* (playing ghumāuri) are the only survival options and anchor their gendered projects of value.

Therefore, in the rest of this chapter I uphold aspects of regional labor politics which are relevant for understanding how ghumāuri groups operate and why they continue to be necessary in Fair Trade–certified plantations.

Gendered Transitions in Regional Labor Politics

In Darjeeling's plantation communities, there has been a shift in trade union politics from Marxist ideas of workplace justice to a union politics intended for building consensus about the desirability of a separate Nepali state within India. This shift radically changed the justice-seeking practices and desires of women tea workers in the plantations, which is overlooked by global ethical regimes, such as Fair Trade. Fair Trade, which aims to empower women workers within Darjeeling's plantations, fetishizes local institutions, such as the labor unions, as vehicles for women's empowerment. Fair Trade directives, however, turn a blind eye to the fact that male, ethnic subnational politics silences the voices of female workers in male-dominated labor union politics. This chapter argues that understanding the gendered shifts within local labor unions is important in order to locate women's complex desires and political agency in Darjeeling. This chapter shows that the latter is manifested through the formation of informal savings groups (*ghumāuri*) run by women plantation workers. It provides a space for women to discuss their daily economic and social problems away from the attention of plantation owners and Fair Trade certifiers.

Scholars studying transnational protest movements have often pointed out the limited scope of these movements: the ambivalence within these movements about "local struggles" for justice (Brooks 2006). Such instances of boundedness are more pronounced in plantations that retain old colonial structures of labor domination. This chapter analyzes why such ambivalence can persist (Collins 2002) and its effects on particular sites within a Fair Trade production chain.

Feminists and labor historians of South Asia have tried to theorize and understand the marginalization of women workers within formal labor union politics. Feminist scholars have documented the myriad ways in which women's voices are silenced in union protests (Fernandes 1997) due to "multiple patriarchies" (Chatterjee 2001, 275). Kabeer argues that liberalization has further undermined the possibility of women's mobilization in the postcolonial era, which remains "sporadic, limited and uneven" (Kabeer 2004, 186), and concluded that the process of commodity production is debilitating for women's political futures (Collins 2002; Sen 2002; but see Mills 2002; Ramamurthy 2003 as exceptions). Piya Chatterjee writes that investigations of women's public political participation within plantation production systems have to explore the "informal," i.e., "small protests, usually excised from discussions of what are deemed 'political' activities" (1995, 265). This chapter demonstrates why such small protests become necessary. Such marginalization of women's voices when occurring within the space of a Fair Trade–certified plantation should become an object of greater scrutiny, especially since Fair Trade aims to strengthen women's power within unions and other collective bargaining institutions.

As the focus of oppositional politics within plantation communities in Darjeeling shifted over time, so did the scope and nature of women's organizing and activism within the plantation community. Within the plantation community, the shift in trade union politics based on communist notions of workplace justice to union politics based on giving shape to a more concrete Nepali identity in India, through the creation of a Nepali homeland, has affected women's perception about the effectiveness of unions in their lives. The plantation wages are insufficient (approximately \$1.23 a day in 2006–7 and now stands at little over \$2), and there is a crisis in drinking water and health care measures (Fareedi and Lepcha 2003).

Yet the focus of the union priorities was invested elsewhere. Women had turned their attention away from unions to *ghumāuri* groups, which they found more meaningful in the backdrop of a more male-dominated union. It helped them develop a collective shield of protection against the envy and rebuke they faced in their communities. *Ghumāuri* was an informal savings group run by women plantation workers. It provided a space for women to discuss their daily economic and social problems. In this chapter I establish why such activities were necessary in spite of a Joint Body and FLO funds.

Women's participation and evaluation of Fair Trade policies was influenced by their engagement with the changing landscape of labor politics in Darjeeling. In such a scenario women felt that Fair Trade had little effectiveness because it bypassed structural issues within systems of collective bargaining. Few of the plantation workers knew about Fair Trade. For them the Joint Body meetings were like any other work-related affair where they had to be present. As I mentioned in chapter 3, the Joint Body was not a democratic space; the management controlled every conversation. While much has been written about reasons for the rise of ethnic politics in Darjeeling, little research has been conducted on the gendered community dynamics of such politics and how they are affected by new transnational justice-promoting initiatives.

Foregrounding women plantation workers' narratives, I try to underscore the gendered effects of this ethnic movement on plantation workplace politics and the limits it places on Fair Trade's scope within a plantation at present. Justice within plantations has been elusive. I begin this chapter by describing the effects of ethnic subnationalism on plantation labor politics. This is followed by an analysis of the importance of competing communities within Sonākheti for plantation workers. The chapter also presents worker vignettes to show the effects of these political shifts on workers' identities.

Ethnicized Subnationalism and Plantation Labor Politics

It is important to understand the specific effects of subnational politics on gendered labor politics. Whenever I asked my informants about their involvement with unions, I was often told, "You will not find the union now, but they will not let you sleep during election time." This statement was a way of expressing frustrations with the union and its inability to address issues related to plantation work.

The dissociation of workers' rights and union politics has a long history in Darjeeling's "Nepali Community." In the mid-1980s when the GNLF was slowly gaining importance, plantation unions were still dominated by the local branches of the Communist Party.[1] However, from 1986 onward Subhash Ghising (the leader of GNLF and the chairman of the Hill Council) had already started his campaign for Gorkhaland. He took full advantage of the existing insecurity of Nepali youth (which I detailed in chapter 1) in the region, which finally made the movement extremely violent. Male youth were used as foot soldiers in the Gorkhaland movement. Ghising reinterpreted the clauses of the

Indo Nepal Friendship Treaty[2] (see Samanta 1996) to emphasize that Nepali migrants were unable to vote in India, and therefore, the treaty should be scrapped, and Nepali people should have their separate state within India. His comments found great support among people, especially since a huge number of Nepali people were ousted from the state of Assam and Meghalaya at that time. In reality, a majority of the Nepali people in India was voting, since their children and grand-children were Indian citizens, having been born in India. However, Ghising made judicious use of these insecurities to convince average people to join the GNLF, thereby leaving the Communist Party.

At this time there was also a massive stagnation in Darjeeling's tea industry. Exports suffered as other countries were gaining a foothold in the international tea market. Plantations delayed worker payment and bonuses. GNLF used this opportunity to show that the communist unions were ineffective in fighting the battles for common people in Darjeeling, especially since they were an outside political party. Culturally, the GNLF argued, they were not like the Gurkhas, so they could not understand the real problems of the region and were not well-versed in local problems. Other scholars, like Amiya K. Samanta, write that Ghising distributed anti-communist speeches in audiotape cassettes saying that communists were atheists and they did not want Nepali people to have their own state because their loyalty was toward West Bengal. In reality, most leaders of the CPIM in Darjeeling were Nepali.

In the post-Gorkhaland period, the local state and labor unions in Darjeeling were dominated by the GNLF. During 2005–7 (before the 2nd movement),[3] the focus of the GNLF was to get the Nepali people in Darjeeling recognized as "tribal" so that they could get special ben-efits from the federal government. This involved the "reinvention" of Nepali "tribal" tradition, although the majority of the Nepali people adhered to the Hindu caste system and had various religious and cul-tural practices depending on caste affiliations. However, preoccupation with this new cultural turn defined the focus of the party (GNLF) and the local state in the late 1990s and early 2000s (see Middleton 2005).

Since its inception, the GNLF positioned itself as different from the plains people's parties, especially the red parties (like CPIM). CPIM was seen as serving the interest of the state of West Bengal (in which Darjeeling is a district) and the people of the plains. The non-orthodox tea-producing districts bordering Darjeeling, after long-CPIM-dominated labor unions, at present are slowly affiliating with Trinamool Congress and its allies after the left's historic defeat in West Bengal a few years back. Making people conscious about the stigma of the red party and its principles was a deliberate move to engender a new politics of difference. Adherence to any of the principles of the "red" party was considered incongruous with the political demands of the emerging Nepali state within India. Therefore, the worker-centric policy of the communist unions did not receive priority in the GNLF agenda.

One of the offshoots of this differentiation was that the GNLF encouraged plantation workers to work hard and not engage in militant trade unionism, which was a marked feature of unions in the plains. In my interviews, workers expressed this pride. Expressing pride was a positive motivation for average Nepalis who had to suffer the consequences of negative stereotypes about them, as outlined in chapter 1. Many workers told me that they understood the value of work because this was the only way they could survive. Workers in Darjeeling distinguished themselves from non-Nepali workers in the plains, who, according to my informants, were communists and did not want factories to survive. As proof of this claim they cited the numerous plantation closures in the plains. It seemed from their narratives as though the unions in the plains tea plantations were uselessly conducting a movement to stop work, just because of their party affiliation.

In regular conversation workers always related their hard work with the quality of the tea produced, as if their labor was of a different kind, like their ethnicity, climate, and environment. Workers knew about the high price of Darjeeling tea since they were almost forbidden to consume this green gold. Factory supervisors checked on whether women from the sorting department were stealing tea. One of the male workers once told me, "You know, sister, the British were very clever, and they taught us Nepalis everything about tea except for its taste. We learned how to produce tea, but we never learnt to appreciate the goodness of Darjeeling tea. This was probably good, otherwise our plantation would have stopped by now." He made this last statement with great sarcasm. Other workers in the sorting department complained about the long hours and the low pay. This pride in work was always laced with complaints about the lack of water, the undemocratic plantation practices, and union busting. However, the hegemonic ideology of GNLF's current vision became meaningful for average workers in these self-proclamations about being hard-working *pāhāḍi* workers. These contradictions and ambiguities expressed by workers became beneficial for the GNLF in putting labor issues on the backburner until the second Gorkhaland movement re-prioritized development and employment generation as part of their ruling agenda.

Male GNLF members were constantly engaged in making the "Nepali Community" more conscious about their ethnicity. Being equal citizens of India and gaining respect became the priority, not improving the existing conditions of laborers within Darjeeling. A survey of documents at the time of the formation of the Darjeeling Gorkha Hill Council reveals that the demand for Gorkhaland was accompanied by a request to increase the quota for Nepali men in the army, the dismissal of the Indo Nepal Friendship Treaty, and more direct funds from the central government in Delhi for general development of Darjeeling. The central government, which also regulates the wages of plantation workers through the Tea Board of India, was never requested to increase the wages for plantation workers. Gorkhaland became a panacea for all the evils that existed within Darjeeling. The consequences of hegemonic subnational politics are evident in the following interviews and vignettes.

Chhāyā

Chhāyā and I were neighbors in one of the plantation villages. She was illiterate and could barely sign her name. She was among the most talked about women in the plantation because of her past labor activism work in the Women's Wing of the communist-dominated unions in the 1980s. She was the leader of the Communist Party's Women's Wing, *Mahilā Samity* (Women's Organization). She kept insisting from the beginning that she did not know much about Fair Trade, but she knew about organic agriculture because she supervised in the field. Chhāyā was also a *Kāmdhāri* (group leader). But I had other intentions for meeting her. I wanted to know about women's past activism in plantations in order to understand why active women like Chhāyā had such little interest/knowledge about Fair Trade and current labor union politics.

Chhāyā, forty-eight in 2007, started as a child laborer in Sonākheti when she was ten years old. She was an active union member, and she changed parties (from the CPIM to GNLF) in 1984 when GNLF started dominating the labor unions. Though she shared the subnationalistic urge of Gorkhaland with other members of her plantation community and was a proud *pāhāDi*, she somehow found the preoccupation with Gorkhaland in Darjeeling's "Nepali Community" stifling.[4] Chhāyā told me that she used to hide and go to the CPIM meetings in Siliguiri and Darjeeling when the 1986 Agitation was brewing. Once the GNLF had started the movement, no other party or political opinion was tolerated.[5] In fact, the situation in Darjeeling continues to be that way, where many of my informants feel pressured to join the 2nd Gorkhaland movement because of the fear of violence and of becoming unpopular in their communities.[6]

Chhāyā was one of the six female "field supervisors" known locally as *Kāmdhāri*. Chhāyā was a member of the Fair Trade–funded Joint Body,[7] but I rarely saw her at Joint Body meetings. When I asked her the reason for her absence, she told me she was not aware that the Joint Body had any real benefit for the workers. I then urged her to talk more about why she thought that the Joint Body was not as effective as the union. Chhāyā told me that there were problems in the present GNLF-dominated union. Chhāyā liked unions because she expected them to provide a sense of community, a fellowship of concerned people who shared their ideas and understood each other's problems. But she did not get that from the present GNLF union. She told me that from the beginning she was committed to the CPIM's ideology. She liked the way CPIM trained them to understand workplace politics. I urged Chhāyā to talk more about her activism. From the interview I found out about her version of what the managers in daily conversation referred to as the "union problem." Here are excerpts from Chhāyā's interview:

> **Chhāyā:** In the beginning there was no politics. But slowly problems began with our bonus and other benefits and a union was formed. Every plantation should have a union; it is an absolute necessity for our daily problems. Earlier we consulted the union in the smallest of disputes. This is why the union was important. But now there are no regular union meetings to discuss our issues. Now you see no one; they are all busy in Kurseong or Darjeeling town. Come election time, they will not let you rest in peace because they want our votes. I feel like our small *ghumāuri*[8] group is like a union. We have unity and we care about each other. We try to solve our daily problems. We give each other hope and older sisters guide the younger ones. We teach them how to take care of themselves. We discuss how to save money and not waste it on alcohol. Even some men have started these groups, learning from us. They also have small kids and they know that mutual support is required at difficult times because our wage is not enough.

Me: What did you learn from your experiences in the union when you were active?

Chhāyā: I used to meet women who were elder than me in Kurseong. Women in important positions in the Women's Wing of the Communist Party urged me to head the *Mahilā Samity* (Women's Organization) in the plantation. I listened to them and learnt a lot. I used to travel to all the units in Sonākheti with some other women; we listened to each other's experiences and problems; tried to find solutions to each other's problems. I even went to Calcutta to consult senior members of the party. There was a lot of sharing and planning and a great sense of camaraderie. The party and the union worked out a system for dealing with the management.

Me: You say that the union is a necessity. So what is the state of the present union at Sonākheti?

Chhāyā: I was in CPIM. During the Agitation time, the older men in our locality came and explained to me that I should join the GNLF. As a Nepali, it was my duty to join our local party, so I joined. But I used to hide and go to all the CPIM meetings in Siliguri, Kalimpong, Kurseong, and Darjeeling town. I almost did not survive once as our vehicle was pelted on our way to Darjeeling to attend the CPIM meetings. Those were troubled times, but in my heart I always liked what CPIM taught us.

The GNLF always talked about "Gorkhaland." CPIM on the other hand emphasized rights and entitlements of the average poor workers who are not looked after well in the plantation system. GNLF is not interested in the issues of workers; they are only interested in making us understand the significance of our land and making us conscious of our identity as Nepali. Yes, I understand the significance of the land we live in; we have lived here for so long, and our forefathers toiled here. There was no doubt that "Gorkhaland" was important for us because we needed a place in India which we could call our land. Technically, it was my duty to support the party of the hills which championed this cause. But that is not enough. There are other very important issues besides land. When I look deep into my heart I do not like the principles on which GNLF operates. I think the issue of workers' rights has taken a backseat in the plantation. Before, we used to think how to take these issues up with the management; we used to strategize. Our party (CPIM) used to teach us how to negotiate and talk to big people in difficult situations. As small people, illiterate people, it was important for us to learn these strategies. We had friends in different plantations, we used to have important meetings and share information about how we small people could fight and negotiate with the management. Our leaders in the CPIM used to ask us to think about the most important things for our life as workers and then teach us how to place it before the management. If the management did not agree then we would have to let the leaders know and they would have a meeting with the planter *sāhib*. We had to choose our issues well. Our "company," our "sāhib" is like a parent; you cannot fight with them on any old issue, and you have to be judicious to further our cause. One has to learn to strategize.

Within GNLF the preoccupation with Gorkhaland stood in the way of placing workers' concerns before the management. This preoccupation with the issue of Gorkhaland is the source of all problems in Darjeeling. It has been twenty years since GNLF gained power. There are no jobs, and the youth do not know what to hope for. But I don't feel motivated to attend the present union meetings because they are not concerned about workers' rights. That is why I feel that the *ghumāuri* groups are important.

In 2007, more than twenty years after development of the first Gorkhaland movement in 1986, lives of women in Sonākheti—like Chhāyā's—help us contextualize what the search for a local identity and state within the larger "Nepali community" has meant for labor rights for women workers within the plantation community. The frustration with unions was not just limited to women; male union members also shared these complaints. Knowing that Devilal was an active union person, I asked him how effective the union was in Sonākheti. As usual, he told me that it was not very active. Devilal was very forthcoming about helping me learn the names of other union members. I asked him why there was no union agitation here in Darjeeling, in spite of all the problems. He told me that whatever problems the union was having were on minor issues, nothing major. Usually, when a worker got warnings from the management about wrongdoings, he went with his people to negotiate with the management. If there were payment delays, then too, there was trouble, but the union did not push for any major changes.

The most interesting thing that Devilal told me was that union members were apparently not aware of the true terms of the Plantation Labor Act of 1951. Describing the union further he said, "They make demands just like that and they really have no teeth." Moving on to the question of union issues in Darjeeling, Devilal mentioned that after the Agitation people ceased to be that active in politics. In his words, "People have lost interest in politics." On a philosophical note, Devilal mentioned that people look for direction in their lives. Either it was politics, religion, or something else, and people in Darjeeling were now more into religion. People really "slacked" (he actually used the English word "slack") after the Agitation, and of course this was used to describe the political inactivity of the people.[9] It almost seemed that Devilal was referring to some kind of loss of interest and disillusionment with the current political situation, which impacted union politics in a negative way. He mentioned further that the unions were now more concerned with matters outside the plantation, not inside it. The unemployed male youth from the plantations were recruited to the party by union leaders to work for the GNLF. They were promised jobs in the local state and party offices around Darjeeling.

Competing Communities, Interstitial Spaces

The ineffectiveness of unions had compelled women to make alternative spaces for trying to meet some of their daily needs, and is evident from Chhāyā's other comment documented in chapter 2: "Our *ghumāuri* group is like a small union where we women can openly discuss issues about our livelihood and work. We can give each other confidence." In Chhāyā's comments we can locate the different communities that exist within a Fair Trade–certified plantation. It brings to light the complex social matrix which an average plantation worker has to negotiate in his/her daily life—the Nepali Community, the Union, the *ghumāuri* group. These communities are in friction, and the dialectics among them are influenced by the changing politics of the region. Chhāyā's comments take us to the heart of community and labor politics in Sonahketi and Phulbāri, where GNLF-led labor unions in the post-Agitation[10] period gradually devoted more time and energy to further the demand for a separate Gorkha state or Gorkhaland. Until 2011 there was no categorical struggle for plantation reform or wage increases within regional political mobilizations. Chhāyā's comments are deeply relevant to contextualize the interstitial politics (Springer 2006) within a Fair Trade–certified community of workers. It brings to attention larger structural issues that always remain outside the purview of Fair Trade. Academic criticism of these campaigns advances the idea that these ethical transnational initiatives after all, "advance a project of neoliberalism" (Blowfield and Dolan 2008:1); that they are bounded in a way that gives more agency to consumers-citizens in the first world rather than producers in the third world (Brooks 2006, xxi).

Chhāyā's comments also uphold a peculiar scenario for feminist scholars studying the effects of globalization on women's workplace politics. For feminist scholars, the idea of community remains central to understanding the limits and possibilities of women's consciousness and agency in the context of globalization (Collins 2002). Such scholars identify community as a medium through which factory disciplining is enabled; it also provides women workers with an opportunity to navigate the strictures of factory or household disciplining (Ong 1987). However, when community dynamics become enabling for women to voice their grievances against perceived oppositional/inimical forces, and when they act as a barrier, requires closer attention. One has to explore the constant becoming of the community in question (Li 2001) and emerging forms of "workable sisterhoods (Berger 2006).

The multiple tendencies within a single community[11] need to be acknowledged to understand the gendered consequences of articulation between these tendencies and political forces in the wider environment in which the community is enmeshed. In Darjeeling one has to look at how the change in local politics, from trade union–based to ethnicity-based, creates community dynamics with gendered effects. Below, I further outline the effects of the constant friction between the "plantation community" and the larger "Nepali/Gorkha Community." The latter is the imagined community (Anderson 1991) that Nepali politicians want to convert to a separate state. The former or "plantation community" is the community in which my informants live and work; they have had kith and kin ties here for generations. A less-talked-about feature of plantation life is the ghumāuri[12] group, which I discovered, after much difficulty, during my long-term fieldwork. Ghumāuri, as a community of women plantation workers, is not visible in the plantation public space.

I found out about ghumāuri through careful participant observation. Āshā and I met at a designated spot on January 12, 2007, to join her tea-plucking group. As we walked down the narrow pony road she met Sunita, another plantation worker. Āshā quickly went over to her, leaving me alone in the company of some local youth. From the corner of my eye I could see that she gave Sunita some money and whispered something to her. I could only grasp the last line of the conversation, "let's talk about it some other time; how about tomorrow evening when we return."

As soon as Āshā came to me, I asked her who Sunita was and why she gave her money. She said that she owed Sunita some money. I probed her, asking why she did not return it to her in front of me. Āshā did not answer in the beginning and avoided eye contact with me. She desperately tried to avoid the conversation, as if her whole communication with Sunita was insignificant. I tried to push further. Sensing my persistence Āshā told me that she cannot talk about it on the road where there were so many people. When we reached the designated spot in the plantation where Āshā was going to pluck tea leaves with her other group members, she told me about *ghumāuri*.

Women saved money through *ghumāuri*. In my sample of forty women plantation workers, thirty-seven were members of different *ghumāuri* groups. The meetings took place every two to three months. Women workers had these meetings during their lunch break or after work. They held these meetings during work break because at that time no field supervisors or managers would be doing rounds. Each woman saved between Rs. 50 and Rs. 100 per month. Each group had between eight and fifteen members revolving the pot of money.

A few weeks later, after the incident with Āshā, I attended their *ghumāuri* meeting. In this meeting, a woman plantation worker spoke at length about the financial problems she was having because her husband had to have a surgery, and there was no money in the house. Women in this *ghumāuri* group then started discussing from where they would collect money for her because the savings in their group was not enough. This woman also said that she was scared of the manager because she was not sure whether he liked her. Conversations continued about different possibilities for helping her. I had never witnessed this kind of a close interaction in the plantation before.

The next day, when I met Āshā, she told me how much she trusts me, that I was like her sister; therefore, that I was not allowed to tell anyone connected to the plantation management details about this group practice of *ghumāuri*, especially the plantation owner, his managers, and other workers.[13] She feared that specific knowledge about women's secret activities would raise the curiosity of managers and might result in a delay in her bonus payment.[14] She said she was concerned about my knowledge about the women's lives in the plantation. Because I knew that women wore gloves when picking tea leaves, a serious infraction of the way women are taught to pick when starting the job; I should not know that kind of thing. Women did this to protect their hands from abrasion and staining (see chapter 8 for more details on the politics of clean hands). She also made fun of me because I was so curious; she told me that she had never met any other visitor who was so interested in the activities of pluckers, so much so that she had decided to stay away from her husband for a year to spend time with "coolies."[15]

As I gained more understanding of the political life of my interlocutors within Fair Trade–certified plantations, it was evident why women cherished these alternate collective spaces. *Ghumāuri* was an everyday secret, a therapeutic space for mitigating the unsustainability of wage work. Āshā, Chhāyā, and Lakshmi *didi* (discussed later) were active in various activities of labor unions. They were members of the Communist-leaning parties, especially their Women's Wing, before GNLF came to power in the late 1980s. Now why did women plantation workers need an informal intimate space to survive plantations and Fair Trade? This incident proved to me how much women cherished these alternate spaces. In later interactions I understood that *ghumāuri* was a secret, a perceived therapy for many of their daily problems. Āshā, Chhāyā, and Lachmi *didi* (who I talk about later) were part of women's union politics before, as I detail later in the chapter. When the CPIM was present, they were all members of the women's wing of the CPIM. But why did women need these groups for sustenance in a Fair Trade–certified plantation?

In Darjeeling, women could not rely on the plantation community ties to take care of their workplace needs because of certain shifting party politics within the plantation community. The average daily pay was about $1.28 for a tea-plucker in Darjeeling, one of the lowest wage rates in the formal economy, according to the Indian Labor Bureau.[16] Instead, women entered *ghumāuri* groups in large numbers. Women did not just identify male domination as the cause of their disillusionment (see also Dutta 2008, 220) with union politics. They pointed to something more complex in the politics of the region which had affected their communities and debilitated the power of collective bargaining institutions, leading to increased masculinization of union concerns. As I mentioned before, the union leaders were more interested in recruiting Nepali male youth to work for the GNLF.

The groups have been around in plantations for many years. My interlocutors could not trace their exact history, nor could other scholars in the region. But it was a regular feature in most plantations and was dominated by women. It was significant that women in Sonākheti and Phulbāri constantly upheld this group as an alternate space for them to mentor each other. But at one point in history there was a possibility of articulation between women's issues in their small groups and the broader trade union movement that dominated the plantation community. As Chhāyā told me, now that the *Mahilā Samity* (the Women's Wing of the Communist Party) was not there, the *ghumāuri* group became the only place where workplace politics and family issues could be discussed together without fear. She also mentioned that the Women's Wing of the GNLF was useless.

Monmaya told me that before they used to play *ghumāuri* just for learning how to save money, but they gradually realized that the group had other benefits for women. Communist-dominated trade unions in Darjeeling (pre-1984) were largely dependent on the support of women because they formed the majority of Darjeeling's workforce. The plantations were also the toughest places for the GNLF to influence until the Gorkhaland movement had turned violent (Samanta 1996, Madan Tamang quote from *Telegraph*, July 28, 2008).

My life history interviews with older plantation workers establish that *Mahilā Samity* networks had close ties with these localized women's groups. But when the GNLF leaders started mobilizing the community to rally around the issue of Gorkhaland, they did not just have to depend on women. There were plenty of unemployed local male youth to lend themselves to a cause, to please the local party bosses. When Gorkhaland become the priority within local parties and labor unions, neglect of localized women's efforts to organize became routine.[17] Since every household had its sons or brothers in the GNLF, women felt that their needs were not considered a priority, although they backed the efforts of the GNLF by keeping their silence on labor issues. Women still hope that the young men in the plantation might eventually get some employment. Women's issues gradually receded from the public realm, but came to occupy center stage in *ghumāuri*.

Feminist scholars who study the politics of women's activism rightly propose that there is no straightforward explanation of why women actively participate in labor politics and why not (Fernandes 1997; Mills 2005). Feminists anthropologists have also cautioned against hasty conclusions about the meanings of women's absence or presence in so-called public domain (Mahmood 2001). What becomes a political realm (Berger 2004) and where women's activism and mobilization can manifest itself is an emerging question. There cannot be any a priori assumption about women's power. Producing situated place-based knowledge about why women protest (Baldez 2002), and the conditions that make putatively docile, "nimble-fingered" women belie their powerless images marks the cutting edge of research on women's political activities (See Mills 2005, 119). Building on these works, *Everyday Sustainability* proposes a closer look at the changing nature of labor union politics within plantation communities where women live and work.

Many scholars see community as a hegemonic space (Ong 1987; Collins 2002). However, it is important to note the nature of women's activism and its imbrication with the political becoming of the local community in which women's aspirations take hold. Analysis of women's participation in labor struggles presents two scenarios. In one scenario off-shoring of manufacturing jobs and global patterns of production erode the possibility for women to use the "moral" face-to-face ties through which they had earlier voiced their workplace grievances. Collins (2002) calls this loss of community, "deterritorialization." The other scenario is a little bit different where nimble-fingered third-world docile workers are able to voice their concerns in unions through "cultural struggle" within patriarchal societies (Ong 1987; Mills 1999). Here, patriarchy presents women with a different situation where women articulate their anxieties and displeasures by invoking community relations of paternalism and/or religious or kinship ties, by using discursive strategies so that they are not accused of violating cultural norms (see also Mills 2005; Lynch 2007; Jamal 2005). The general conclusion is that women in the global workplace face adversities at various levels that make it difficult for them to join formal labor organizing in spite of many oppressive labor management practices that otherwise plague them as workers and as women. Community dynamics become pivotal for women's inactivity/activity in political battles.

Close observation of the political activities of women plantation workers presents an interesting caveat in existing feminist debates about women's activism within transnational production systems. Plantation workers in Darjeeling do not have to fear deterritorialization, or loss of community, in the same way as the women workers of the maquiladoras. Darjeeling tea can only be grown in Darjeeling, thereby enjoying the benefits of place-specific branding. Maquiladoras can move across borders, because garments can be manufactured anywhere in the world as long as the raw materials can be supplied "just in time." Any threats from workers about unionizing or of unions raising questions about worker abuse or pay propel companies to move to a new location that can offer "safer" production zones. In Darjeeling, capital becomes spatially fixed, so why does that not enable workers who produce "Fair trade" to raise their voices for a wage increase or better work conditions in formal production spaces?

Women plantation workers in Darjeeling had lived and worked in the same communities where their ancestors grew up and worked. Male supervisors, union leaders, factory clerks, and average plantation workers have shared kinship ties or were at least neighbors for a long time. Like the women workers in Malaysia (Ong 1987), women plantation workers could have used extended family ties (especially with men who are used by the management to discipline workers) to voice some of their grievances about poor salary or nepotism. But my interviews reveal that kin-community ties were not mobilized because women did not want to become unpopular in their communities and households by asking men to change the priority within the current unions. Women workers in the plantation found that participation in the unions was useless. However, they silently hoped that the union would do something for their sons, brothers, or husbands.

It was interesting to note that in the mid-1980s, some of the same women were active in the labor union politics. Even now women plantation workers joined their male counterparts at important political party events and public demonstrations as a show of solidarity. If women plantation workers in Darjeeling did not have to bear the brunt of "deterritorialization" like their counterparts in Bangladesh or Mexico, they had other reasons for being sidelined in the union. Women's current frustrations with unions were even more striking because their plantations were Fair Trade–certified. Instead of unions, women found solace in *ghumāuri* groups to take care of some of their economic and workplace needs.

Conclusion

Union-busting was a common feature in India, and prominent South Asian scholars have tried to theorize why the trade unions have become ineffective in a climate where neoliberal economic policies have gained ground (Bannerjee 1991), but the lack of effective collective bargaining had deeper roots. What was remarkable in the case of Darjeeling was that a shift in union politics from a "politics of redistribution" (workers' equality) to a "politics of recognition" (ethnicized minority politics) intensified the neglect of workers' needs and rights, especially women workers' rights. Men envied their wives' salaries and regular employment (as I will show in chapter 7), and male youth were seen as more vulnerable. The Fair Trade efforts were perceived as a sham since plantations had not raised the minimum wage for a long time. In short, my ethnographic findings reveal that the peculiar tactic of the dominant political party in its drive to raise ethnic consciousness among Nepali people had weakened the movement for workers' rights within the workplace. Workers interviews and their reflections on life are a testimony to this reality. Further voluntourism contributed to privatizing the plantation public sphere by not engaging with unions at all.

Lachmi *didi*, Chhāyā, Kamalā (from chapter 4), and Āshā's subjectivities and comments were important reflections on how everyday women plantation workers understood their place in unions and workplaces. Workplace frustrations have not subsided with the change in union politics, but were expressed in *ghumāuri* groups. Workers wanted more people to know about these inadequacies, especially Fair Trade–certifying institutions, but they feared retribution from employers and male relatives. Illiterate women like Lachmi *didi* and Chhāyā frequently criticized the strategic use of their images and their talents at the present moment. Lachmi *didi* told me that whenever the "*kuires*" (whites) come to the plantation she takes them around. She further added:

> We do not know each other's language. We are called to the meeting of the Joint Body where nothing substantial is discussed. We are shown in a way that says nothing about our lives and frustrations. I know the real story; I know what our lives are like. The tourists and other whites take photographs, and I hate it because we are all supposed to smile and they never send them back.

Lachmi *didi* continued that there were people from both Indian and Western NGOs/ *Sansthās* who made films of them. She never understood why foreigners had so much interest in showing a "coolie" in a "picture" (film).

My interactions revealed to me women's very subjective interpretations of political ideology, work, and hegemony. Sherry Ortner urges anthropologists to explore "how the condition of subjection is subjectively constructed and experienced, as well as the creative ways in which it is—if only episodically overcome" (2005, 34). For Ortner, subjects are not just culturally or religiously produced and not simply defined by a particular position in a social economic matrix. They are not just an effect of power but are subjects defined by a complex set of feelings, anxieties, and hope in a given historical moment (see also Ahearn 2001). Women plantation workers like Chhāyā and Lachmi's stories, and their involvement in gendered projects of value through *ghumāuri* groups demonstrates women's efforts to navigate multiple structures of domination that coalesce together to make their voices fade to the background in a Fair Trade plantation extolling the virtues of women's leadership.

6

Fair Trade vs. *Swachcha Vyāpār*

Ethical Counter-Politics of Women's Empowerment in a Fair Trade–Certified Small Farmers' Cooperative

During my ethnographic work among women organic tea producers in rural Darjeeling, India, I frequently faced difficult questions about the meaning and materiality of Fair Trade. Women smallholder tea farmers were gradually becoming conscious about the global popularity of the organic tea they produced. Whenever I showed Prema, one of the farmers, examples of Fair Trade publicity materials with smiling faces of women tea producers just like her, she always offered comments such as:

> Another one! You know that smiling woman on that tea package is not us. It's nice to know people around the world care about us so much, but why now? Where were these people when we had no roads, when no one gave us loans, when we ate only stale rice? What can they do for us if they do not care about what we women want?

Prema's sarcastic response is a powerful critique of the moral basis of the Fair Trade movement's empowerment directives—directives that govern tea cooperatives in producer communities and that have specific consequences for smallholder women tea farmers' political lives. It is also a rebuke of the virtual environment in which Fair Trade maintains its legitimacy as described in chapter 4 (see also Moodie 2013, Gajjala 2014).

Similar pointed reflections on "Fair Trade" gradually revealed to me how intended beneficiaries of the global Fair Trade movement understood the value of Fair Trade in the context of their situated

identity struggles and their everyday entrepreneurialism to gain social
and economic justice. As a trade-based, transnational, social-justice
movement, the key tenets of Fair Trade are to empower marginalized
producers, in part by ensuring their participation in key decision-
making institutions in their communities, and to promote social justice
in general, with a core focus on women's empowerment (Dolan 2010;
Smith 2015).

Fair Trade is also an alternative economic system, distinguished
from so-called free trade by its biopolitical imperative to measure and
manage the global unfolding of social justice through its trading system
(Sen and Majumder 2011; Mutersbaugh 2002). Fair Trade promoters
and activist consumers believe that the ethical buying and selling of
Fair Trade goods across nations can fulfill these overt goals by chan-
neling new resources and governance mechanisms to producer communities. The Fair Trade product label stands as a proof and promise
of trade-based justice work.

What remains unexplored within this abstract global discourse on
Fair Trade is how subjects of transnational justice regimes understand,
translate, and mobilize around the governance practices of the ostensibly ethical transnational justice regimes of Fair Trade. In this chapter, I
examine how smallholder women tea farmers in rural Darjeeling, Sānu
Krishak Sansthā, negotiate such regimes in the context of their specific
identities (as housewives and savvy entrepreneurs) and histories of
conflict over gendered access to resources in their own communities.
Through long-term ethnography of Fair Trade operations and their
effects on a smallholder tea farmers' cooperative in rural Darjeeling,
I contend that Fair Trade interventions can inadvertently strengthen
gendered and patriarchal power relations in producer communities but
that smallholder women tea farmers also make creative use of specific
Fair Trade interventions to defend their own entrepreneurial ventures
and rupture Fair Trade's imbrications with local patriarchies.

As I will demonstrate ethnographically, the women farmers'
repeated juxtaposition in regular conversation of Fair Trade with
swachcha vyāpār, a distinct Nepali iteration of Fair Trade that incorporates awareness of gender hierarchies, allowed them to articulate the
shortcomings of Fair Trade. In particular, this rhetorical strategy highlighted Fair Trade's inability to promote their specific economic pursuits through entrepreneurial ambitions, some of which were nurtured
during previous participation in other transnational economic-justice
regimes such as micro-lending. Strikingly, women's situated reading
of the "fair" in Fair Trade was filtered through a localized, gendered
political and symbolic economy in which they had to struggle to gain

respect and recognition for their daily labor and the entrepreneurial ventures that were critical for their families' and communities' survival in a context of shrinking economic opportunities for men in Darjeeling. In many of the households in Sānu Krishak Sansthā women are farmers and many conduct major household operations and local labor recruitment depending on the size of farms and financial stability (see also Lahiri Dutta 2014). As I detailed in chapter 3, women's entrepreneurial ventures involve the illegal sale of tea and sale of alcohol, milk, and other produce from their farms, ventures they financed through microcredit loans. For them "Fair Trade" could become *swachcha vyāpār* only to the extent that it could assist them in meeting the needs of their families with dignity through their women-only business ventures. It was *swachcha vyāpār* when it could mitigate the domination of local middlemen who became virtual brokers of transnational market-based justice regimes in their communities while controlling women's reputations.

In recent years feminist scholars have nurtured a healthy skepticism about liberal empowerment strategies (Naples and Desai 2002; Kabeer 1999; Rankin 2004; Spivak 1993; Karim 2011; Cornwall et al. 2007; Kudva and Mishra 2008). More worthy of critical feminist examination is how rural women who contest gendered resource inequities in their own communities strategically mobilize around transnational justice regimes such as Fair Trade. These women critique Fair Trade based on how it uses their images to sell tea in Western markets while their labor and struggles remain unrecognized internationally. Therefore, the images on tea packaging and posters that show women happily plucking tea obscure the male domination of the actual execution of Fair Trade practices. To challenge this opaqueness, women use the phrase *swachcha vyāpār*, which at least rhetorically foregrounds their work and challenges the male domination that devalues their labor and entrepreneurship. To contest how they are represented, they seek to represent themselves. The rhetoric of *swachcha vyāpār* connects the discursive contestation with the actual conflicts by linking women's struggles for recognition and respect for their labor with competition over resources while articulating their gendered projects of value. These acts by which women seek to represent themselves in order to negotiate with Fair Trade's hegemonic representations of them is an example of the kind of catachresis that Gayatri Spivak famously elaborated. Smallholder women tea farmers in Darjeeling are "reversing, displacing, and seizing" Fair Trade's "apparatus of value coding" (1993, 228). Women's skepticism around the meaning and material impact of Fair Trade directives is also an instance of catachresis, or creative abuse of the progressive ideals of consumer-based transnational justice initiatives to make such transnational regimes address the situated aspirations of subjects of justice.

At the time of this study, there were ninety-four smallholder women tea farmers in the Women's Wing involved in microcredit loans, as evident from the cooperative records. After the formation of the cooperative in 1997 to trade in milk, the Women's Wing was established so that collectively area women could access resources from government programs for maternal and reproductive health. Later with the arrival of microcredit loans, the Women's Wing provided the structure for the formation of self-help groups through which microcredit loans could be accessed. When I began my research in 2004, Women's Wing members were mostly involved in microcredit and assisting the cooperative. In the local power structure, the Women's Wing worked below the male governance body of the co-op that became a point of major economic and symbolic contestations as I detail throughout this chapter. The interviews used in this particular chapter are from my core sample of thirty Women's Wing members and also from women outside this core sample. I have followed the trajectory of these households since 2004 and the changes in women's collective organizing in the cooperative area are discussed in the conclusion.

To situate gendered contestations around Fair Trade, I first elucidate Fair Trade's gradual imbrication with local patriarchies and then demonstrate the ways women have contested this imbrication. I first briefly detail the political economy of smallholder tea production in Darjeeling, situating local tea production within broader changes in the tea industry, and I discuss how these changes have in turn affected gendered resource sharing in small tea farmers' cooperatives. I then provide ethnographic detail of women's mobilization at the time of Fair Trade certification inspections and describe women farmers' relationship with middlemen and how those relationships have affected their skepticism about and contestations of Fair Trade. Finally, I detail how smallholder women tea farmers have made critical connections between the multiple forms of disenfranchisement they face and how they remind themselves and interlocutors about their role in the economic and social reproduction of their families and communities by holding on to their gendered projects of value. This in turn has helped them develop a "vernacular calculus of the economic"—a gendered evaluation of Fair Trade from the vantage point of everyday struggles for resource and recognition (Ramamurthy 2011). They articulated their gendered projects of value from this vantage point.

Smallholder Tea Production and Fair Trade in Darjeeling

Before the advent of Fair Trade and the organic tea boom, local NGOs intervened to help these marginalized tea producers in many ways, encouraging them to form cooperatives and explore animal husbandry and other economic ventures for selling their produce. The cooperative that the women in this study belonged to was formed in 1997 but was not registered with the state until 2007. Seeing the economic potential of Fair Trade alliances for small tea producers, they formally registered the cooperative, with NGO help, so that they could better bargain with plantation managers. Because small-farmer cooperatives could not afford expensive tea-processing equipment, they had no option but to sell their tea as raw tea leaves. NGOs intervened to ensure that the cooperative received a competitive price for the raw tea that they sold to plantations. They also introduced safeguards so that the plantations could not sell smallholder grown tea under the plantation's own label, but would instead help with processing so that it could be marketed as cooperative-produced tea. Additional Fair Trade certification of the cooperative by Fair Trade Labeling Organization International (FLO)— a transnational governing body overseeing the trade and governance of Fair Trade operations across the world—ensured that good contracts with plantations were established and monitored. At present in Darjeeling, two formal tea cooperatives represent smallholder tea producers living outside plantations (Thapa 2012), one of which is studied here.

Although non-plantation tea cultivation is fairly common in Darjeeling's informal sector, it is rarely researched or written about because of the domination of plantations in production and visual representation. Only sixty thousand workers are employed in the eighty-seven plantations formally, but most of Darjeeling's rural poor subsist outside of these sites, and there is little data on how they survive by combining agriculture and trading.

In these areas, even though women overwhelmingly performed the actual work of tea production, it was male middlemen and male members of tea-farming households who sensed an important economic opportunity with the advent of Fair Trade, in part due to the lack of other economic opportunities in rural areas of Darjeeling. Men gained prominence in the process of formalizing the cooperatives, and local NGOs began to rely on these patriarchs. Smallholder women tea farmers, the "subjects" of Fair Trade, realized their worth in the organic tea production process but simultaneously felt a sense of loss as male

community members and local middlemen came to control tea profits by dominating the newly formed cooperative. Their realization of
self-worth led women to battle the male-dominated tea-farmers' cooperative over its failure to acknowledge their efforts to sustain organic
tea production, from which the cooperative itself was now benefiting.

As economic resources from Fair Trade agreements started pouring into the cooperative, smallholder women tea farmers realized these
resources were inaccessible to them because the money was being
invested in community development projects that did not involve
women. Women's contention that Fair Trade was not *swachcha vyāpār*
was a way to signal their disenfranchisement within their own cooperative. *Swachcha vyāpār* was also a critique of middlemen within their
own communities who now dominated cooperative affairs. Therefore,
swachcha vyāpār is a creative and powerful iteration of the Fair Trade
philosophy that incorporates a gendered awareness that male cooperative heads, male traders from their villages, and male Fair Trade
officials controlled the Fair Trade network.

Women continually debated what Fair Trade meant in everyday
talk since the current operations of the tea cooperative were inimical
to their aspirations of running their own businesses. For instance,
THulo yojanā was a pet plan of smallholder women tea farmers who
also belonged to self-help groups and accessed microcredit loans. The
Women's Wing devised *THulo yojanā* in order to begin an organized
business of their own that sold everything they produced besides tea,
whose trade was now monopolized by men. Women lamented that the
success of the Fair Trade cooperative did not directly help them or
their collective entrepreneurial ventures. Their repeated juxtaposition
of Fair Trade and *swachcha vyāpār* was a rhetorical strategy that smallholder women tea farmers used to make visible the precarious forms
of labor and entreprenurialisms that maintained their households and
sustained organic tea production (albeit by default). Furthermore, the
uncompensated labor of women was critical for running Fair Trade
awareness programs, internal control of organic standards, and organic
farming training classes that sustained the cooperative's Fair Trade
certification and hence its ticket to the financial resources of the global
Fair Trade movement.

Despite the marginality of Darjeeling's smallholder farmers within
the tea industry, their landownership and practice of agriculture, as
opposed to perceived lower-grade work like *coolie kaam* (menial or
plantation labor), shaped the identity of smallholder tea farmers' families, who considered themselves to have more freedom than plantation
workers. Smallholder women tea farmers in this study also highlighted

this distinction, since, as Piya Chatterjee (2001) has noted, plantation work was seen as demeaning and plantation women as wanton. Smallholder women tea farmers' self-identification as housewives working on their own farms and their receipt of microcredit loans shaped their subjectivities as housewife-entrepreneurs, the lens through which they assessed the significance of Fair Trade.

From Debating to Contesting Fair Trade

Beyond their discussions around the meaning of Fair Trade and the strategic juxtaposition of Fair Trade with *swachcha vyāpār* to interlocutors like me, Women's Wing members actively contested Fair Trade policies that affected their position within the cooperative without generating any real benefits in terms of advancing their economic entrepreneurial ventures. They voiced their displeasure by targeting specific aspects of Fair Trade's governing principles and their implementation in the tea cooperative.

Despite its aim of creating a better alternative to neoliberal trade and development, Fair Trade relies on technical interventions resembling the liberal methods of conventional development practice. For example, Fair Trade certification involves checklist-style, top-down, bureaucratic procedures for monitoring and inspecting farms and farming techniques, for examining on-farm labor relations, for tracking the use of Fair Trade premiums by farming communities, and for implementing empowerment directives from Fair Trade inspectors (Raynolds et al. 2007). I have argued elsewhere that these governance schemes make for an interesting biopolitics where people and process are measured against liberal notions of empowerment and development (Sen and Majumder 2011).

Smallholder women tea farmers encountered the technical rationality undergirding Fair Trade practices in the form of yearly inspection visits by a male Fair Trade inspector from Delhi. In order to continue to be certified, each community has to pass a Fair Trade inspection every year. International Fair Trade monitoring organizations such as the aforementioned FLO also send inspectors to check whether producer organizations are run democratically. Depending on how cooperative members fared in the inspection interviews, FLO inspectors decide whether a SPO (such as SKS) could continue to receive Fair Trade premium funds for economic development. Due to their significant consequences, inspections are tense times in the community.

In December 2006, I had the opportunity to witness one such inspection, as well as the dynamics in the cooperative as its members prepared for the inspection. In the days preceding the one-day inspection, male cooperative members were busy organizing documentation of tea sales and the cooperative budget. Women's Wing members were given the task of informing cooperative members' families about the meaning and benefits of Fair Trade certification, as well as cleaning and decorating the cooperative office and preparing meals for the inspector. Cooperative heads wanted to ensure that cooperative members would be able to answer basic questions about Fair Trade and organic production if the inspector decided to interview average members, which is why Women's Wing members were charged with the task of explaining the meaning of Fair Trade certification to each household. The inspector spent most of his time with the cooperative board. I interviewed him soon after the inspection and witnessed his interactions with male and female cooperative members. During the interview he made a notable comment about the women:

Figure 6.1. Woman Tea Farmer at an Internal Inspection with Her Organic Farm Diary. Photo by the author.

Figure 6.2. Women Tea Farmers Conducting Fair Trade Awareness Programs. Photo by the author.

> **Inspector:** Women in Darjeeling are much more forward than women in other parts of India, where society is more patriarchal.
>
> **Me:** Why do you think women are more forward here?
>
> **Inspector:** At least you see them sit in the meeting when you come for inspection, and they even answer my questions correctly. They are more free.

I was struck by the inspector's comments about women farmers' freedom, considering that he spent a total of two days in Darjeeling and six hours in the cooperative, talking mostly to the male board members. Moreover, the inspector was from Delhi and did not speak Nepali, the local language; most of his conversations with cooperative members were in Hindi, which the majority of cooperative members did not understand. Still, during his routine inspection, the inspector was impressed by the awareness and enthusiasm of smallholder women tea farmers within this male-dominated cooperative.

The aforementioned Women's Wing consisted of smallholder women tea farmers who were relatives of the male cooperative members. The Women's Wing operated at a level below the cooperative governors. The cooperative governing board made the major operational decisions and dealt with the management of tea within the cooperative community. Women's Wing members were involved in microcredit and assisted the cooperative by cooking for major events, running trainings, and the like. The inspector sensed this hierarchy. He wanted the smallholder women tea farmers to dissolve the Women's Wing and join the governing board in larger numbers. The inspector argued that women were ready for "more empowerment" and ought to be members of the main cooperative.

During our conversation, the inspector remarked that Darjeeling was not as patriarchal as the rest of India, which was borne out by the demographic fact that the female-to-male ratio in Darjeeling was higher than elsewhere in India—that is, there were proportionally more women in the population than in other regions. He had observed numerous woman-owned businesses in the marketplace. In addition, local women did not observe strict norms of *purdha* (veiling) that women did in the other parts of north India he had observed. Consequently, he assumed that smallholder women tea farmers would welcome his Fair Trade directives as guaranteeing them more political presence in the community and ensuring a more equitable distribution of Fair Trade resources, such as an annual Fair Trade premium to each certified community. Hence he used the word "forward" to imply that women were more advanced in Darjeeling. I could not rule out that the use of the word "forward" was an influence of the reigning negative stereotypes about women in Darjeeling.

Members of the Women's Wing, in contrast, did not endorse the Fair Trade directives. During my participant observation, I picked up terms women commonly associated with empowerment, such as *aggi barhnu* (to move forward/progress), *bato dikhaunu* (showing the way), *swachcha vyāpār garnu* (doing clear/transparent/fair business), *THulo yojanā banaunu* (making big business/big plan), and *balio hunu* (becoming strong). All these phrases invoke notions of empowerment and entrepreneurialism based on equality and imply particular kinds of economic action and accompanying household and community level interventions. Joining the governing body of the cooperative was never associated with these concepts or viewed as empowering. I wondered why the suggestion of joining the governing body did not sit well

with the Women's Wing. Why did they not want to make this potentially empowering move and give up their women's group? What were
women trying to achieve collectively by defying the inspector's directive, when they knew that such defiance could lead to the loss of
certification and subsequently Fair Trade funds for their community?

Through their persistence women wanted to publicly demonstrate their disillusionment with the governing board and the problematic operation of Fair Trade within their community. It was a way
to publicly express their doubt about Fair Trade's potential to break
the monopoly of middlemen in the cooperative and ensure transparent
business in their communities, as became evident from their constant
contrasting of Fair Trade and *swachcha vyāpār*. In the end, the cooperative's Fair Trade certification and funds were not revoked because
of the Women's Wing's defiance. The cooperative's certification was
put on probationary status with a warning to straighten out matters
within the cooperative, especially with the Women's Wing. The fact
that the cooperative received "probationary action," not a full-fledged
"pass," pleased Women's Wing members. It was a symbolic victory for
them, as I detail later.

The Women's Wing had asked the cooperative board for a share
of Fair Trade funds in 2005–6, before this inspection took place. Binu,
one of the active members of the Women's Wing, filled me in on this
background. The cooperative received Rs. 222,000 ($6,000) in Fair
Trade premium money. The Women's Wing members were happy
because the governing board told the villagers that the money would
be used for development. Leaders of the Women's Wing requested
Rs. 10,500 (less than 5 percent of the funds) as start-up capital for a
produce business, as an alternative to approaching a bank and bur-
dening themselves with a loan. Many smallholder women tea farmers
described this money as a reward for all their work on behalf of the
cooperative. The cooperative immediately refused the request, which
angered the women. As Binu explained,

> You know, it was all fine until we asked for our share of
> the FLO money; somehow we became everyone's enemy. We
> could not even imagine that the men would show their true
> colors, and there would be so much hostility. We have been
> taking individual loans from the bank for the last couple
> of years and always repay the money. After all, we get
> periodic suggestions and encouragement from the NGO and
> government officers running the SHGs [self-help groups] on
> how we should stand on our own feet and learn new skills.

When we are selling *raksi* [rice wine] and *biri* [cigarettes] it is fine, but when we want to found a big business, that is just not accepted. When we put pressure on the cooperative men to give us some money from FLO funds, they immediately asked us, "Who are you, what is your identity? Your group is nothing without the cooperative, why are you asking for a separate share of the money? If we invest the money into the community as a whole, you all will benefit, what makes you all special? Women also benefit from our rising tea sales, don't they?" I replied saying that women are the ones who provide the labor in the plucking season from which you get this money, and we are going to use this money to learn new skills. To tell you the truth, we absolutely have to make this business a success and show these men that we can do the things they can; otherwise, they are going to make fun of us again.

Binu further explained that if the Women's Wing dissolved and joined the main cooperative, then women would never get any money for this separate business. The middlemen in the cooperative would never allow the women a separate share of the money to start a business, arguing that funds spent on the entire community would benefit everyone. Women's Wing members like Binu were proud that they preserved their group and that the male governing board had to deal with probationary action because of their resolve. This was a key moment when the women felt they had received some redress for the cooperative's unwillingness to share any monetary resources with them. Binu elaborated,

We go for all sorts of training so that we can move forward. Then why not give us the money now, when we can gain some real training to better ourselves? It is okay if they want us to be on the cooperative governing board, but we really want to have our own organization. We women have *lāj* [modesty, shame] and we can support each other, even if it is just five of us. I know the men in the cooperative must have jumped at the inspector's suggestions because this was a way for them to wipe out our existence so that the cooperative would not have to share money with us again. By the time the secretary finally gave us the money, things had become bitter, but he told us then that this was the last time we were going to get our demands met.

Other women in the Women's Wing shared Binu's reading of the Fair Trade directives as collusion between male cooperative board members and the inspector. They interpreted the Fair Trade directives as the final step in wiping out the Women's Wing in retaliation for their request for Fair Trade premium money that the male-dominated cooperative governing board wished to monopolize. They saw the recommendation that they join the board as a way for middlemen to retain their voice in the cooperative, since a few women on the board could be easily silenced. The few women board members would hesitate to stand up for themselves based on local codes of honor and modesty that the women themselves invested in. Women in the cooperative community had a bigger battle in mind. They feared that dissolving the Women's Wing and joining the cooperative leadership might lead to middlemen coopting their business plan, destroying the collective space where they resisted male domination, and shaming them.

The Women's Wing, which on the surface seemed contrary to the goal of Fair Trade to empower women within the cooperative, in reality represented women's collective aspirations for economic justice at the community level. Smallholder women tea farmers understood that the success of the cooperative was important for getting a good price for their tea and for the general development of their community. But they also saw the Fair Trade–certified cooperative as standing in the way of their business ventures. Therefore they coded the Fair Trade cooperative as a men's domain that discriminated against them.

My participant observation and analyses of women's narratives revealed that the decision of Women's Wing members to reject the inspector's suggestion was a critique of the gendered spatial and ideological politics prevalent in their communities and reflected in the cooperative structure. This politics restricted the scope of their economic activities within the village, which made it difficult for them to succeed in their business ventures and repay their microcredit loans. In addition, as I detail in the next section, members of the Women's Wing faced ideological challenges because of their actions. The inspection and subsequent directives provided an opportunity for the women to publicly vent their anxieties about the challenges they faced in improving their families' economic situation. Refusing to accede to the inspector's suggestion was a way to question the appropriation of women's labor through gendered spatial politics and denial of Fair Trade resources.

I am not arguing that FLO's vision of empowerment is inherently depoliticizing, because the inspector did recognize the hierarchies within the community. However, his directive was based on the liberal modernist ideal of equal gender representation in numbers, without considering the context of empowerment. Hence his suggestion that it was important to have more physical presence of women on the cooperative governing body failed to recognize that the effectiveness of their presence was questionable. Examining how these women questioned the depoliticizing tendencies of Fair Trade as they charted out their own plan of empowerment and community participation revealed the significance of emerging forms of collective self-governance among women in rural India, within but against the market (Subramaniam 2006; Sharma 2008; Moodie 2008; Klenk 2004).

In recent years feminist scholars have used a transnational feminist framework to analyze aspects of the emerging global morality market and its specific manifestations (Chowdhury 2011). Feminist anthropologists and other social scientists have been preoccupied with issues around transnational justice regimes and the possibilities for local actors to connect their struggles to its promises (Adelman 2008; Merry 2006). Aihwa Ong draws our attention to the workings of modern justice regimes, the particular places that subjects of justice occupy in their own struggles, and the nuances of how these modern schemes of justice work. Commenting on the burgeoning justice initiatives in the transnational sphere, she writes:

> Increasingly, a diversity of multilateral systems—multinational companies, religious organizations, UN agencies, and other NGOs—intervene to deal with specific, situated, and practical problems of abused, naked, and flawed bodies. The non-state administration of excluded humanity is an emergent transnational phenomenon, despite its discontinuous, disjointed, and contingent nature. (2006, 24)

Ong characterizes these new justice regimes run by non-state agencies as "techno-ethical regimes" trying to bring justice to morally deserving yet excluded populations around the world. FLO's efforts resemble "techno-ethical regimes" in that they have devised technical directives for empowering marginalized producers. A Fair Trade label ostensibly implies quality, sustainable agricultural products, and well-governed people who understand and work within Fair Trade guidelines. Such a label reassures socially conscious consumers that marginalized producer communities are enjoying the material benefits of Fair Trade, such as social development premiums, and are operating in a democratic way. The process of certification thereby becomes a technical fix for existing inequalities in producer communities.

My encounter with the Fair Trade inspector demonstrates how the formula of justice emanating from the larger moral rubric of these liberal techno-ethical regimes was transformed in particular localities where subjects reinterpreted the rules to meet their own ends. Therefore, this book takes Ong's logic further by showing how women producers both reject and take advantage of elements of these techno-ethical regimes to gain prominence in their local communities, while all parties are working within Fair Trade certified institutions.

Ethnographic attention to the gendered cultural politics around certification also closes a major gap in the interdisciplinary literature on Fair Trade certification by providing a more nuanced understanding of how the broader goals of techno-ethical regimes do and do not translate at the local level and how such translations are gendered. In establishing the gendered nature of translations, I address what Tad Mutersbaugh and colleagues see as an exciting and important area that needs attention; that is, how producer communities are affected by these techno-ethical regimes and, more importantly, how people make use of these directives to substantiate and advance their own projects of justice (Mutersbaugh and Lyon 2010).

In this next section I discuss why the Women's Wing had a falling out with the middlemen and how this affected their skepticism about and contestations of so-called Fair Trade.

Middlemen, Gendered Spatial Politics, and the Government of Women's Work

Why is it that we get these stares when we walk down the village road? Are we different, now that we are trying to do big business?

This comment by Minu, one of the women tea farmers, alludes to the crisis of respectability that Women's Wing members experienced after they formally asked the cooperative for money to start a women-only business. Male middlemen called them names like *bāthi* (street smart)—a derogatory term when applied to women. What precipitated this slander was women's questioning of how middlemen used their clout and monopoly to control the women's entrepreneurial practices, even though these were critical sources of income for the middlemen themselves.

Before this cooperative was founded in 1997 and before the advent of Fair Trade institutions, local people depended on middlemen for credit and to sell their surplus produce and dry, "illegal" tea on the local market. These middlemen were not *sardars*—liaisons between the plantations and adjoining communities who recruited tea plantation labor. They were middle- to upper-caste, relatively wealthy Nepali men who negotiated between farming communities in rural Darjeeling and urban markets. Smallholder women tea farmers identified four important reasons for the role of the middleman: (1) middlemen had good contacts in town to sell products from the village, (2) they had money to hire people to transport merchandise from the villages to town, (3) they were necessary because women's family members resented them making frequent trips to town, and (4) the middlemen brought back supplies of food and other essential commodities to these remote villages. Smallholder women tea farmers often took loans from the middlemen and were obligated to sell their produce to the middlemen in return.

Although they were usually better off and better educated than the village farmers, some of the middlemen were distant kin of the smallholder women tea farmers. They were often larger landowners who had political contacts with the local party or low-level government jobs in town that supported their business activities. Some had become wealthy over time, and many also held important positions in the cooperative after it was formed.

With the formation of the Women's Wing, members started taking out lower-interest loans from a government bank through microcredit schemes, and subsequently the middlemen saw their income from moneylending to women decline. This history formed the backdrop of the hostility between Women's Wing members and middlemen, who spared no effort to impugn women's respectability, as Minu's comments in the epigraph attest. Smallholder women tea farmers welcomed the comparatively low-interest loans available from NGO microcredit schemes, and they reported that their family members did so as well. The advent of microcredit enabled women to free themselves from the high-interest loans from middlemen, but they still had to depend on the middlemen to sell their produce so that they could repay the loans.

The middlemen were not pleased with the NGO involvement and the microcredit schemes. Those who served on the cooperative board had tried to monopolize the sale of other local produce, such as turmeric, ginger, cardamom, milk, and vegetables. Most smallholder women tea farmers complained that the middlemen offered the villagers very low prices for their produce, but because of the lack of adequate transportation and contacts, the villagers had few alternatives. The formation of the cooperative had further entrenched the power of middlemen, as they could control who did or did not become members of the cooperative and learn how to get organic certification for their land. Most respondents also reported that they expected that in the future the cooperative would sell more goods besides tea. Thus, the local middlemen would become the virtual brokers of transnational market-based justice regimes in the villages.

After Fair Trade funds for development started pouring into the cooperative, Women's Wing members devised their plan of *THulo yojanā* (big plan/big business), to ensure that cooperative households would also get fair prices for their produce other than tea. From running Fair Trade trainings, they knew that Fair Trade supported women's income earning. Meanwhile, the middlemen were already upset with the smallholder women tea farmers because new sources of microcredit for the women had dried up previously guaranteed sources of income for the middlemen. Yet the middlemen still benefited from their dealings in selling other produce from the village. When the Women's Wing floated their business plan involving other produce, open animosity erupted between the middlemen and Women's Wing members. The middlemen defamed Women's Wing members, making use of existing gender ideologies to undermine the women's respectability (Hodgson and McCurdy 2001). They spread rumors that the smallholder women tea farmers were becoming like market vendors or women plantation workers, who were considered *bāthi* (street smart) and less than respectable.

One needs to understand the competing gender ideologies in Darjeeling to understand the power of these shaming practices for women's self-identification. Smallholder women tea farmers had a particular investment in distinguishing themselves from women plantation workers, who were considered inferior in social status due to their wage work and lack of control over their leisure activities. Smallholder women tea farmers and their families took pride in saying, "Our daughters, sisters, and wives do not go for *hajira* (wage work)." This gendered moral distinction had particular meaning imbued by past labor recruitment practices in the tea industry of Assam and North Bengal. As Jayeeta Sharma and Piya Chatterjee have both noted, sexualized and racial tropes accompanied plantation labor recruitment, which occurred mostly among tribal groups in east central India. In the postcolonial period, however, there has been a divergence in the identity politics of specific tea-producing communities in terms of how they situate themselves vis-à-vis these racialized and sexualized histories of plantation work. In Darjeeling, women plantation workers are also stigmatized as sexually immoral and alcoholic.

These specific stereotypes have shaped a gendered moral terrain of critical distinctions where women who do not work on plantations but live nearby, such as the smallholder women tea farmers discussed here, distinguish themselves from women plantation workers and their families, even though they likewise cultivate tea. Because among Nepali Hindu families the withdrawal of women from formal labor force participation marks upward mobility, these smallholder women tea farmers identified themselves as housewives and engaged in practices of social mobility. Smallholder women tea farmers also realized the limitations of this role identification. Despite their entrepreneurial ventures they were seen as housewives, not capable of organized business ventures and hence were denied Fair Trade resources. The spatial manifestation of these gender ideologies also put severe limitations on their ability to procure resources for their families, since middlemen used these ideological tropes to discipline women.

Smallholder women tea farmers performed as obedient housewives or good sisters who always asked for permission to go to town. Elder men and women in their households resented women's frequent visits to town, even if they relied financially on the women's petty trade. The smallholder women tea farmers tried to live up to these ideologies but also found them constricting because they left women dependent on middlemen who paid them very little to take their produce to town.

This form of spatial and ideological control hurt the poorest smallholder women tea farmers the most. Whereas comparatively wealthy households in the cooperative could afford to have the wives and sisters stay at home, poorer women were desperate to venture out of their homes to sell produce. For these women absolute confinement to home-based work was not economically feasible. Their families tolerated some amount of non-farm-related economic activities, such as loan taking and selling produce in the village. These women's non-farm activities were confined to the space of the village, preventing them from forming sustainable links with the market.

The persistence of gender ideologies not only confined women's economic activities to certain spaces; it gave some middlemen the moral resources to strategically question the actions of women who attempted to challenge the monopoly of middlemen in the village by going directly to the market. Practices of defaming were used to challenge the respectability of women who defied the dominance of middlemen in local business (see also Lynch 2007). Women believed that these shaming practices curtailed their earnings and thereby reduced their family income.

Thus, the smallholder women tea farmers determined to defend their Women's Wing articulated their gendered projects of value. They knew that joining the governing board of the cooperative would not end the existing double standard in their community pertaining to the appropriateness of women's business ventures. Fair Trade rules, as they unfolded, only strengthened men's control of smallholder women tea farmers' operations within the cooperative. This is why women read the Fair Trade inspector's directive about dissolving the Women's Wing as collusion among the men. They interpreted joining the governing board as giving in to the tactics of the middlemen, some of whom were important members of the cooperative. The change the Fair Trade inspector proposed in the interests of empowerment was perceived as giving in to the existing spatial politics in the community, which limited chances of women's economic success.

In the next section I show how women categorically engaged in practices of reminding community members and interlocutors such as myself that their labor was critical in sustaining their families and community. These reminders were responses to the shaming practices they were subjected to, and they became a key ingredient in developing Priti Ramamurthy's aforementioned "vernacular calculus of the economic." For Ramamurthy, the concept "vernacular calculus of the economic" helps explain the actions of subaltern actors that might not make rational economic sense. In explaining why poor Dalit Madiga farmers chose to cultivate hybrid cottonseed without the assurance of profitable returns, instead of laboring on other people's farms or migrating to cities for assured wages, Ramamurthy emphasizes how the practical consciousness to Madiga farmers in choosing this apparently irrational or nonprofitable act is shaped by a local "material and cultural grid." This grid consists of histories of economic and social humiliation associated with work and migration, which Dalit farmers have endured for generations. Similarly in Darjeeling, poor smallholder women tea farmers' decision to contest the Fair Trade bureaucracy despite its potential harm for the economic success of the cooperative was an instance of a "vernacular calculus of the economic" since it would not make rational economic sense to bring harm to the cooperative that helped legalize small-farmer-grown tea and ensured that small-farmer-grown tea in Darjeeling would fetch a good price from plantation owners. Smallholder women tea farmers were willing to settle for lesser economic rewards for their community based on their calculations of potential gains they would make in the local gendered political economy where their reputations were at stake (Kapadia 2002). In this case, "vernacular calculus of the economic" can be seen as smallholder women tea farmers' attempts to evaluate transnational justice regimes and their liberal rules from the vantage point of a localized gendered projects of value in order to gain access to resources and respect for their labor in a political field dominated by entrenched patriarchies.

"We Are the Police of Our Own Fields": Gendered Boundaries within Sānu Krishak Sansthā

Smallholder women tea farmers' rhetorical juxtaposition of *swachcha vyāpār* and Fair Trade in their daily conversations, their use of it to inform interlocutors of the distinction between the terms, and their subsequent actions within the cooperative were ways for the women to constantly connect the multiple forms of disenfranchisement affecting their everyday lives and also to remind themselves about their critical role in the economic and social reproduction of their communities. These reminders were necessary because women's own investment in seeing themselves as housewives at times prevented them from making these critical distinctions. These realizations and reminders also helped them cultivate a vernacular calculus of the economic through which they interpreted the value of the economic success of the certified tea cooperative and Fair Trade. These critical reminders were also attempts to insert themselves into global narratives of trade-based justice, which they sustained through creating virtualities about smallholder women tea farmers' lives. Hence Prema's comment in the opening section of the chapter: "You know, that smiling woman on that tea package is not us."

The reminders to themselves and to interlocutors took many forms. At the beginning of my ethnographic research I was just learning the routines of farm work, and from interacting with the male cooperative members, I got the impression from their descriptions that they were the farmers. When I began my detailed interviews with smallholder women tea farmers I always asked them to describe what farming duties male and female members of the household performed, in order to capture their perspective.

On one such occasion, I started my interview by asking Sumita *didi* (elder sister) when her husband was going to return from the field and what kinds of farming duties he performed. Sumita *didi* replied that her husband was in the army. Apparently, her sons were also preparing to join the army. Then, with a sarcastic smile, she said, "But, sister . . . we are the police of our fields." This short statement was an extremely powerful reminder: the "we" meant women.

The sarcasm was directed at me because on this visit, my first to Sumita *didi*'s house, having just conversed with the male cooperative heads, I assumed that her husband always assisted her in farming. Sumita *didi* alerted me to women's key contributions to farming and corrected my initial misunderstanding. This was a learning moment for me to understand how women were conscious of their household labor and were not ashamed to emphasize its significance, even to visitors. Both of us burst out laughing at the dry humor and sarcasm in the statement. It implied the de facto rights women had over their lands (even after the cooperative farmers received title to the land, most of the titles were in the name of the male family head) and also the importance of their labor and oversight for producing other cash crops in addition to tea. The extreme poverty in this community had forced many men to take up other occupations outside the village, particularly because the state considered farming tea outside of plantations illegal. Women at times were single-handedly responsible for the production and marketing of household agriculture. The statement was a very powerful reminder of how women interpreted their place within the community—the place from which they reinterpreted the meaning and value of Fair Trade.

Sumita *didi*'s statement also had dual meaning. Women in the tea cooperative not only had de facto rights over their land and produce, but they also needed to police the boundaries of their operation from the Fair Trade rules that enabled localized patriarchies to thrive. They needed to protect their dreams and desires of large-scale business within the community, even from well-meaning Fair Trade directives. Her comments were representative of how women perceived their contribution to their households and the challenges they faced within the cooperative at that time. Most visitors assumed that men were the farmers because they dominated the affairs of the cooperative. These misconceptions frustrated the women, and they felt compelled to remind people of their rightful place in the cooperative community.

Women in the cooperative community felt that they had sustained the production of organic tea even before the 1990s when there was no organic boom, no cooperative, and no NGO involvement. That is why Prema (as quoted at the beginning of this chapter) questioned the self-righteousness of Fair Trade institutions by asking, "Why now? Where were these people when we had no roads, when no one gave us loans, when we ate only stale rice?" Women performed the tedious jobs of plucking, hand-rolling, and drying the leaves, which they had hitherto sold to local tea shacks via middlemen because the tea board considered their tea illegal. This same tea had now gained the reputation of authentic, hand-rolled, traditional Darjeeling tea in NGO circles. As tea farmer Ashika commented, "It seems strange, some of us got arrested if the police checked our bags and found this loose tea. Now foreigners come and want to drink the same tea from us and praise it. They perhaps do not understand that our tea's fortune might have changed, but that did not change the fortune of smallholder women tea farmers." Ashika again subjected the celebratory narratives of Fair Trade—which they themselves recited to FLO officials during inspection visits—to the "vernacular calculus of the economic." She reminded me that Fair Trade bodies had made them visible in certain ways, but also concealed their everyday challenges.

Smallholder women tea farmers' everyday narratives were recollections and reminders of the dangers they had risked for their families. They had put at stake their reputation and physical life in pursuing invisible entrepreneurialism. The cooperative community did not have a proper road passable by car until 1996. Women, out of desperation to earn money, used *chor bāto* (hidden/thief's roads) to take the tea leaves to the town of Darjeeling, a distance of twenty kilometers. Before the road was built, people had to walk six or seven hours to get to the town to sell their produce. The women used to start at night to ensure that they reached the town early and that fellow villagers would not see them going to town. As tea farmer Gayatri told me, "Being arrested was a common feature; we slowly learned to pay bribes at police check posts and learned how to hide the tea under the vegetables. But these dangerous journeys were worth it, because they helped us put food on the table and send our children to school. Tea would still fetch us more cash than vegetables."

I heard similar narratives of risk taking from both older and middle-aged women. As Phulkumari, a woman in her eighties, reported,

We occupied plantation land and did not have *patta* [land title], the constant fear of getting ousted from the land was there. Like my husband, many men from the plantation villages then started looking for work in the town or outside Darjeeling: some went to Nepal, but the women had no choice. We lived on, tended the bushes which had grown wild and unruly because there was no one to maintain them. What you see now are the very remnants of those wild bushes. At times the bushes were as tall as me. But

we kept plucking and making *Hāthe chiā* (hand-rolled tea)
and made the long journeys to the town. Now that we have
the cooperative, it is so much easier, but still people fight.
I just don't understand why.

Phulkumari's comment that "still people fight" alluded to the conflicts
between the cooperative and the women that upset her. She, like many
other older women in the community, recollected and reminded me of
the specific contributions of women's farming practices and their role
in sustaining their households. She further mentioned that along with
some other women who used to go to town to sell tea, she had once
blockaded the local police office, without the knowledge of her family.
She stated that women had to take some action to stop the police from
regularly arresting them when they were found with "illegal" tea. She
said, "Women were good at this because if there were men protesting,
they would have been put behind bars immediately." Women used
their submissiveness and femininity strategically for economic gain.

The introduction of Fair Trade in the cooperative community provided smallholder women tea farmers, old and young, an opportunity
to reflect on, reevaluate, and remind themselves and people around
them of their indispensable role in keeping alive the production of
formerly illegal (now organic) tea and maintaining the economic well-
being of their households. It also helped them cultivate a vernacular
calculus that interpreted the value of Fair Trade. As tea farmer Lata
once told me, alluding to the use of women's labor for food preparation
during cooperative events, "We cook rice for our homes, we are not
going to do it for free for the cooperative." Lata and Binu later forced
the cooperative chairman to pay women for cooking for the inspection
event. Lata further mentioned, "How can we have *swachcha vyāpār* if
no one understands the value of rice we cook every day? We have to
make the Women's Wing survive to remind everyone about the value
of our work and sometimes get money for it." Lata's comments were
a reminder of the Women's Wing's efforts to make visible women's
contributions to their families, community, and cooperative through
creative cultural entreprenurialism. One of the ways they sought public
acknowledgment of their labor and time was through defending their
own organization, where women called the shots.

My interviews revealed to me women's very subjective interpretations of Fair Trade. Their goal of a *THulo yojanā* (big business)
was an attempt to retain the vantage point of the vernacular calculus
of the economic. They did not necessarily see Fair Trade practices
as enabling a fair distribution of resources within the cooperative

community and wanted to retain their collective space of critique—
the Women's Wing—to help remind everyone about their important
roles in the household and community. These subjective reflections
had raised deep doubts in their minds about Fair Trade's ability to
offer them *swachcha vyāpār*.

Conclusion: Empowerment Fix?

> While the language of enabling choice and "giving voice" to the
> marginalized sounds powerful in theory, in reality the terrain of
> empowerment is uneven and highly contested. This problem-
> atic emerges partly from a lack of shared political vision(s) or
> agenda(s) among those who advocate empowerment . . . and
> partly from the narrow frameworks within which development
> planners frequently attempt to "simplify and fix" long-term and
> deep rooted social inequities and injustices.
>
> —Nagar and Swarr 2005, 291

Political consumerism is often perceived as a panacea for redressing
some of the inadequacies of global free trade. Fair Trade, as opposed
to free trade, is seen as a new moral engagement that is better able
to articulate Western consumers' desire for justice promotion with
Southern farmers' empowerment needs. But does our well-meaning
daily caffeine fix provide a meaningful empowerment fix in places of
struggle? Or does it inadvertently support policies that try to contain
the multilayered struggles of women into static frames?

The ethnographic details of existing gendered resource struggles
in producer communities and events surrounding the implementation
of Fair Trade provide us with an opportunity not only to understand
the place-based gendered interpretations of Fair Trade in producer communities, but also to glimpse emerging modalities of women's collective self-governance in Darjeeling, which are in critical dialogue with
market-based "progressive" trade initiatives aimed at giving women
more voice. Women use available opportunities to insert themselves
into the global history of Fair Trade and expand its static frames of
empowerment. Their efforts to juxtapose Fair Trade and *swachcha
vyāpār* were thus a catachrestic effort to demonstrate the limitations
of the value frame of Fair Trade. This process reveals how subjects of
justice have to repoliticize the technical directives of the Fair Trade
movement to defend their own dreams of development and entrepreneurialism—their gendered projects of value.

The gendered resource battles around Fair Trade directives opened up a space for women to enact their gendered projects of value by refusing to give up their women's group. The Women's Wing was a public reminder to their community of women's refusal to fit themselves within the narrow frame of empowerment and of their long-standing efforts to sustain family and community—at times detrimental to their own safety. In the process, they also drew attention to the inadequacy of Fair Trade practices to address deeper gender-based structural inequalities in their community that maintained the hold of middlemen over people's lives. While removing intermediaries is one of the central aims of Fair Trade, in Darjeeling the inspector did not recognize the domination of the middleman because he was approaching the situation from a technical, results-oriented perspective.

What is perhaps more critical is that women used their knowledge from previous engagements with market-based development ventures, such as microcredit loans, to interpret the significance of Fair Trade as a market-based justice movement. Through microcredit, women learned the hardships of repaying loans. For them, Fair Trade offered an opportunity to avoid the burden of loans while planning a more sustainable collective business that would assist them to avoid being singled out through shaming practices of local patriarchs. Creative engagement with Fair Trade directives was a way for them to limit men's economic control of their lives and to reduce their dependence on microcredit loans.

An understanding of rural women's mobilization within the market has to acknowledge their complex desires around development, which they attempt to further by questioning the directives of transnational Fair Trade campaigns. While Western consumer-activists desire progressive social change in global trade, these reflexive desires are translated through technical inspections that leave larger procedural inequalities in Fair Trade–certified communities intact. Women did not believe that Fair Trade would enable *swachcha vyāpār* through a meaningless "empowerment fix" and therefore engaged in repoliticizing Fair Trade rules.

In analyzing the background and circumstances of this struggle and negotiations around certification, this chapter illuminates the ways in which women's collective agency can emerge within market-based production systems and how poor women farmers navigate inequities. Women in the cooperative did not perceive market-based trade as a problem; it was the gendered barriers within their community, unintentionally strengthened by Fair Trade initiatives that they regarded as the major impediment to their options for earning cash and supplementing their family income. Women's juxtaposition of Fair Trade and *swach-cha vyāpār* and their subsequent actions challenged the double standards within their community about the appropriateness and scope of women's economic activity. It was a way for smallholder women tea farmers to enact their new subjectivities as entrepreneur-housewives who defended their own dreams of empowerment. Their empowerment was made possible by their creative abuse—catachresis—of "neo"-liberal empowerment frameworks, which tended to use them as instruments for global justice.

Women's collective entrepreneurship ventures, as evidenced in Darjeeling's remote rural locations, reduce or calibrate the dependence on market and men. Such ventures produce values, tangible and intangible, i.e., enduring socialities and relationships based on cooperation and coordination that help women and their families in social reproduction independently of market and men. While Fair Trade and the discourse of entrepreneurship makes this possible, women use the significance and importance of the notion of fairness to collectively chart pathways slightly different from the ones originally imagined in individualizing narratives of Fair Trade. The next few chapters will also demonstrate how women's entrepreneurship moves to the sphere of the household and community to make visible multiple levels of complicity between culture, patriarchy, and capital which makes women's everyday unsustainable.

"Will My Daughter Find an Organic Husband?"

Domesticating Fair Trade through Cultural Entrepreneurship

Debating the value of emerging sustainability regimes, especially notions of fairness (*swachchata*) and organic cultivation (*jaivik kheti bāri*) were a regular topic of conversation in women's households both in plantations and the cooperative area. The everyday use of the word *swachcha* and the English *organic*[1] combined with the interpretation of emerging discourses of sustainability took an embodied form, where metaphors of organic and fair appeared in household conversations, Women constantly discussed their well-being in terms of the quality of their daily food intake, the medications they bought for daily ailments and extended the discussion on organics to reflect on the bleak future for their sons and daughters, but mostly sons. As stated in chapter 3, the massive male unemployment and substance abuse was a perpetual source of concern and therefore in plantations women's household dynamics was premised on the affective management of individual and collective crisis in Nepali masculinity (see also Elliston 2004; Freeman 2014). Therefore, local understandings of sustainable organic agriculture in Darjeeling must heed to reflection and analysis of these embodied manifestations of justice as they hold the key to women's self-understanding of their capabilities and resultant "gendered projects of value."

In this chapter I focus on the communicative and symbolic dimensions of women's labor within and outside their home to demonstrate how the cultural entrepreneurship of women at both sites effectively contained the disciplining through honor and shame. Noted feminist anthropologist Lamia Karim (2011) has rightfully designated women's honor and shame as the hidden collateral that results in an overwhelming rate of return on microcredit loans in Bangladesh. The dividends of honor and shame are very much related to appropriation of women's labor in plantations and in SPO/Cooperative villages, as is evident from previous chapters. I build on the works of Karim and other feminist anthropologists, like Diane Wolf, Carla Freeman, and Deborah Elliston, to argue that under certain circumstances honor and shame can also be creatively designated as a category of risk to unravel male hegemonic control over women's intimate material and affective lives by interpreting and establishing household work as risky business (Sen and Majumder 2015).

These everyday maneuvers help us problematize romantic understandings of the radical possibility of household politics as espoused by feminist philosopher Nancy Fraser (2013) and geographer Vinay Gidwani (2008). Instead the ethnographic attention to complexity of affective management of material and symbolic resources in households leads us to a more nuanced understanding of the possibilities engendered in the household sphere. Both Fraser and Gidwani identify that the "government of work" (Gidwani 2008) is an important aspect of understanding the dynamics of late capital and its articulation with varied modes of production. Theoretically both scholars have emphasized the radical potential of the uncommodified household sphere to provide a critique of capital as it penetrates every iota of our existence. Frazer, for example, suggests recognition of uncommodified activities of household work and care work to create possibilities of a postneoliberal society. Vinay Gidwani also shows how the flow of capital and its urge to maximize profit is interrupted in the spheres where withdrawal of labor from the commodity circuit of the wage labor is valorized. These spheres are not dialectically opposed to capital, such as the labor unions or political parties, but they inadvertently oppose capital because they champion affective priorities that do not seem to dovetail with the necessities of profit maximization. These frictions and interruptions hold the radical potential for a politics of value that contests values imposed by corporate-friendly neoliberal reforms. What is missing here is an analysis of contextual constraints.

Therefore, I propose that we attend to how the logic of regional politics and hegemonic notions of development provides the register for affective management of relationships. Women try to control the traffic in emotions and goods to simultaneously participate in hegemonic frames for social justice, but in opportune moments rupture this articulation of politics, development, and social reproduction, by advancing their own gendered projects of value and creative social entrepreneurialism in which bank loans and household chores are juxtaposed as detrimental. As Diana Wolf (2011, 137) suggests, instead of the "romantic assumptions about family and household unity" one should maintain "that there exist instead multiple voices, gendered interests and unequal distribution of resources." Unlike Wolf, missing from Gidwani and Fraser's conceptualization is an intersectional look at the minutia of household politics where radicalism may just be another face of appropriation, as demonstrated in chapter 4 and also in chapter 8.

Fair Trade–related activities produced a "new social landscape" (Schroeder 1999, 60) of community and household relations in the cooperative, which not only affected the "conjugal contract" but also relations between siblings and other household members. Women's reappropriation of Fair Trade ideas and their economic ventures in the cooperative area escalated household conflicts over the material and symbolic implications of women's work. In the plantation, household conflicts were independent of Fair Trade activities, although they also centered on implications of women's gainful employment and its symbolic dimensions.

The two most important distinctions between household relations in the plantation and the cooperative were the nature of intra-household conflicts and public exposure of household issues at the respective sites. The differences in household relations and community participation were influenced by the varying power structures that shaped everyday life in the plantation and the cooperative. Women's work in the plantation was surveilled and appropriated through restricted employment practices and male-dominated unions. In the cooperative women's work was appropriated by the cooperative through male policing of women's work within the village and through mobilization of gender ideologies about village women. Women in the cooperative were more adept at negotiating surveillance by publicly challenging the pressures put on them through household relations. Women plantation workers kept their household issues to themselves since plantation women were seen as "*chuchchi*" (with sharp tongue) and less respectable (as descried in chapters 6 and 7; see also Chatterjee 2001). Women plantation workers were deeply envied by their male family members who faced a gloomy economic future. Contrary to their stereotypical image of sharp-tongued *chuchchis*, women plantation workers rarely fought with managers, as they feared being shamed; they rarely "talked back."

The observation of household relations and close attention to the narratives of the women plantation workers and women tea farmers reveal that Fair Trade–related concerns had entered the micro-politics of household and community politics in the tea cooperative, unlike the plantation. Women tea farmers in the cooperative used Fair Trade trainings, certification processes, and public events to draw attention to the structural inequalities in their communities, which were sustained through household relations.

The home is a contested space. Partha Chatterjee (1989) shows that nationalist discourses made the domestic space—the home—a repository of tradition, a force of inertia against the ebb of colonial intervention. For smallholder tea farmers living in the villages of Darjeeling, confining the work of their women to the homestead was a way of maintaining their social distinction from plantation workers. Governance of women's work was used as a marker of difference and closely associated with discourses of social mobility. While the tea farmers in Darjeeling were only second-generation farmers and descendants of tea plantation workers, they liked to see themselves as essentially different from plantation workers. In their view they were the "farmers" and their wives didn't go to work, alluding to a difference in respectability and identity. Women plantation workers were accorded different class sexuality (Ong 1987; Stoler 1995) because of long hours they spent outside their homes. Male envy of their occupation also compounded negative portrayals of women plantation workers as evident from the casual use of the three Ws trope in chapter 2.

While on the one hand this spatial ethic of doing "home work" was prevalent at the discursive level, women tea farmers, as I discussed in chapter 6, have creatively worked to transcend the space of the home by engaging in monetary transactions and entrepreneurship under the garb of being dutiful housewives. Uma Chakravarti (1990) writes that Indian nationalists praised women for their support of anti-colonial nationalism activities of their men folk; at the same time deploring wage work. Ethnic Nepalis, while critical of mainstream Indian culture and nationalism (as demonstrated in chapters 1 and 2), share some common Hindu gender ideologies. Such commonalities are more pronounced among tea farmers who own their land—especially well-to-do villagers—who see themselves as economically better off than their counterparts in the plantations. Tea farmers see their women as distinct from market women, or plantation workers (see also Derne 2000).

A very different kind of visibility politics affected the household and social relations of women plantation workers. As I mentioned in chapter 4, women plantation workers occupied the lower-end jobs. However, because of the hyper-visibility of women plantation workers in gendered recruitment patterns, their male colleagues and household members envied them. The chronic unemployment of male youth escalated household tension. Women feared that if they took the issue of wages or new shoes for the monsoon to the unions, it would not be taken up by the union. Women were already seen to have a much more secure financial future in their families. In the plantations, women's relationships were tense with their male relatives, mostly with their brother's-in-law (husband's brothers) and sometimes even their husbands. Verbal abuse by male colleagues and harassment were never reported to the union, as male union members would rarely take up their case. Male plantation workers and male members of their family were disinterested in taking up these "women's issues."

In the rest of the chapter, I provide ethnographic details of household debates and dynamics in the plantation and the cooperative. By exploring women tea farmers' narratives around "risk," I show how women publicly discuss household politics. They implicate household members in their failure to reduce the dominance of middlemen in the economic lives of the villages. For women tea farmers, *swāchchā vyāpar* (clean or fair trade) could only happen when household members demonstrated honesty in acknowledging women's entrepreneurial skills and ambitions.

"She ate my work:"
Women's Work and Household Relations within the Plantation

Women plantation workers enjoyed a particular form of visibility in the tea industry. Most billboards in Darjeeling had an image of well-dressed smiling Nepali woman plantation worker engaged in effortless tea-plucking. Tourists who visited Darjeeling would find photo opportunities where local guides would ensure that women did not leave Darjeeling without a clichéd photo dressed like a tea-plucker with a *doko* (traditional basket) on her head. No male figures were present in the publicity material of the tea plantations.

Women plantation workers' visibility was not just representational, it was accompanied by stereotypes about women's work and their personalities. Plantation owners often fetishized women plantation workers as loyal and hardworking and men as idle and childish, denying the gendered labor recruitment pattern that resulted in making men unsuitable for plantation work, except in supervisory and managerial positions across the ranks. Such visibility was injurious; it complicated household relations when women workers' husbands or other male members of the family were unemployed. Male family and community members envied women's perceived financial freedom, and despite earnings women were constricted in money allocation and spending, i.e., maintaining a separate purse (see also Dolan 2001).

Women plantation workers' social relations and their subjectivities were deeply impacted by both positive and negative connotations of the gendered meanings of their work. The politics of shaming also influenced their entrepreneurialism, both economic and cultural. Many women commented that their work was both an advantage and a disadvantage for them. The result of these gender ideologies and the effects of such subjective reflections were best revealed in household debates and interactions. It strained their conjugal relations and relationship with the extended family. The plantation pay, despite a major increase in 2011, was very little, and women reared chickens, and pigs if they had the space, or made *raksi* (local Nepali rice liquor) for sale to village men. They played *ghumāuri* to meet their household financial needs. *Ghumāuri* money was crucial for buying clothing, furniture, school supplies, and medicines in case of a major illness in the family, or during the festival season to buy gifts. Many women said that they saved money so that they could make everyone in their homes happy.

Out of the forty women plantation workers I interviewed regularly in the two plantations, twenty-nine women had husbands without regular work, five had husbands who had migrated to work elsewhere and sent remittances, and six women plantation workers' husbands had work in the plantation. Regular employment put women at a disadvantage in household relations. I used to frequent Bimla's house often in the evenings when she would come back from work. She was in her early forties and had started work in the plantation fifteen years ago when she eloped from an adjoining village and married Khim Bahadur. Khim Bahadur's mother was a plantation employee and was retired; his father had already died. It was common practice in plantations to give employment to one member of a family in which there was a retired plantation worker. This was also a way for workers to retain the right of living in the plantation quarters. Khim Bahadur and Dāl Bahadur were two brothers, and their sister was already married and lived in another plantation.

Everyone in the family was happy when Khim Bahadur married Bimla, a girl from a neighboring plantation. Bimla became instrumental for the family to retain a regular source of income. Khim Bahadur worked as a cook in Goa (Western India) for six months in a year and spent the rest of the months at home. The family had meager earnings and Khim Bahadur's mother took care of household work for her daughter-in-law, who worked outside the house in the plantation. Khim Bahadur and Dāl Bahadur's relationship had declined tremendously after the former's marriage. Dāl Bahadur was expecting to get a job in the plantation as his mother's replacement, but there was low demand for men's work. It was much easier for women to find work, even if it was of temporary nature, as an apprentice tea-plucker.

Like most unemployed youth, Dāl Bahadur was always playing Indian Carrom Board with his friends, but we used to chat a lot. We discussed films, TV shows, and life in the United States. Dāl Bahadur frequently asked me whether I knew about the migration of Nepali drivers to the U.S. The local village men at times also shared their frustrations. Dāl Bahadur and I were stuck in Kurseong at a bus stop one monsoon day. He asked me whether I liked Bimla, then asked me whether he could share a secret. I showed interest. He started talking about Khim Bahadur, portraying him as a simple man who did not understand Bimla's tricks. "Bimla *Bhauju* (sister-in-law) thinks she is doing a lot for the family; she does not realize that she ate my work. *Ama* (mother) and Khim *Dāju* (elder brother) are always engaged in making her happy; no one cares about me. I am sure if I marry I will be economically dependent on *Dāju* and *Bhauju*; I cannot marry the girl I love. I am trying so hard to find work. Bimla *Bhauju* has no conscience. She should have tried to get me a job too, but she is very selfish."

Dāl Bahadur was a very pleasant person, but fights in their household were common in the months when Khim Bahadur was back in Kurseong, having finished his six months in Goa. Fights took place during lunch time when Bimla was at work and Dāl Bahadur returned home for a meal and shower. Their mother tried in vain to stop them; she told me once, "I am so glad that Khim Bahadur's dad was the only son, and all his sisters married outside this plantation, so there was no problem for me to work in the plantation."

Gendered labor recruitment in the plantation created these tense situations in households. Women's work outside the home was not a problem per se; but it had these negative consequences. Dāl Bahadur saw Bimla as opportunistic and street smart since he did not get the replacement job, implied by his comment in Kurseong, "she ate my work." Whenever Dāl Bahadur was asked to feed the chickens or pigs he would not bother to do it; he would tell his mother that if Bimla gave all her money to the household they would no longer need to raise chickens. Bimla wanted to alleviate this feeling of animosity; Bimla always gave Dāl Bahadur clothes. She once told me, "I wish Dāl Bahadur could understand why I was recruited." Plantation workers' reputations were thus spoiled by their own family members. Gendered labor recruitment in plantations on the one hand gave women economic security, but at the same time created these household tensions.

The above example is not the only instance of where women faced adversities at home because of plantation recruitment patterns. In my time at the plantation, I spent a lot of time talking to male and female household members of the plantation workers. Pooja's mother worked in the plantation tea-packing department and her father had died. Like many of her friends, Pooja had studied until middle school. She quit school after she failed the school's 10th standard board exam. This was a common feature in the plantation; many women studied until they got to the board exams. Pooja's brothers also had the same educational level. Her elder brother had worked at a pharmacy in Kurseong town but had lost his job after the pharmacy started hiring better educated men. Pooja's younger brother Rakesh was twenty, just a year younger than she. Rakesh was unemployed, and was very uncertain about what he should do next. He had also recently failed the Indian army's recruitment test.

Pooja's daily routine was to cook, clean, and run errands for their household. She used to knit well and took orders from neighbors, making sweaters and socks for the winter to earn cash. One afternoon she had made plans with her friends to go to the town and asked her younger brother Rakesh to cook the evening meal. Rakesh's routine in the afternoon was to play carom with Dāl Bahadur and some other local boys. When we were eating lunch, Pooja made this request to Rakesh, at which he immediately replied, "I am not going to cook rice in this house till you are married or you get work in the plantation." Pooja replied, saying, "Maybe that day will never come and I will spend my life making rice for you and your wife." These sorts of exchanges were common in homes between siblings. Along with the metaphor of the organic husband to designate the complexity of household politics, plantation women often worried about good marriage prospects, as reflected in Pooja's comment "that day will never come."

Many elderly plantation workers sometimes saved money to send to their sons who had migrated to Delhi or Mumbai to work in restaurants. Dayamani used her *ghumāuri* savings to send money to her son. Her son complained that his salary from working as a cook in a private home did not leave enough money to buy him winter clothes. Dayamani's daughter, on the other hand, wanted to take a beautician's course, for which her mother never gave her money. Dayamani told me that if her son left that job in Delhi and came back to the plantation her household worries were going to increase, or he would just waste time with his peers. It was best to keep him away. She hoped that her daughter would find a good match or that she would get the replacement work when she retired.

The stereotypes that were associated with women plantation workers affected the way they could/could not negotiate with their employers. Sita was a nurse at the hospital dispensary; her pay in 2007 (Rs. 1,800) was higher than an average worker (a plucker). Her mother-in-law and father-in-law were both ex-employees of Phulbāri plantation. Her husband worked for a government concern in Siliguri. She was the only one in her family who worked in the plantation. Sita was chosen to receive nurses' training because her father-in-law worked in an important position at the plantation office. Sita was envied by other plantation workers because she enjoyed the benefits of being the daughter-in-law of an influential man. Her father-in-law was close to the present plantation owner, and hence, she got the job. Sita was also in the Joint Body and she did many hours of work apart from her nursing duty. This family was better off than Dāl Bahadur's, they had a bigger house and Sita's husband had no brothers. But Sita's son was a cause of great anxiety in the household. Unlike Sita's daughter, her son was not interested in studies. He watched television all day. There was a tendency among many families to be protective of their sons, as they were anxious.

Sita told me that she was scared; her son Kumud would not find employment either at the plantation or elsewhere. Her anxiety was more about the quality of job that her son would get, since her family was better off than the other plantation workers' families. She told me one day:

> I worry that Kumud will stand nowhere when we are old. Lipika (the daughter) will be fine; she will get a job as a teacher or get married. If Kumud does not study he will be given a field job, which he will dislike. I cannot fight like other women; I cannot create a scene for Kumud. The owner likes me because I always respect him and because I am not *chuchchi*; it worries me so much.

Plantation work and recruitment patterns had created many complications for women plantation workers, whether they worked as low-paid pluckers or as nurses in the plantation health center. On the one hand, they enjoy the fruits of assured employment, but on the other, their actions were underwritten by the motive to defy common stereotypes about them. Sita had a comparatively better job, but one that put her at a disadvantage, especially because she was seen as docile by the plantation owner and she saw herself as not being *chuchchi*; different from an average plantation worker who is *chuchchi*. Gendered cultural stereotypes were often kept alive by women plantation workers themselves. If her son had been good in studies he would have had a chance at gainful employment, but now he was dependent on Sita's bargaining power, which she was hesitant to exercise because of the unwritten terms of her own employment. The plantation owner had once told me that Sita was a very presentable woman, she had a pleasant personality, she was also very judicious, and was not a troublemaker. The way she gained visibility in front of the employer decreased her bargaining power and created tension within her household. Women plantation workers like Sita were always careful not to upset their young boys because as she told me, "If there is no peace in the home they will start using drugs."

Plantation surveillance and employment tactics put great pressure on women's household politics. Households that had a women member already working in the plantation had a difficult time finding work for other members. The pay, which was approximately a little more than a dollar a day, was highly insufficient for putting children through school. Most plantation workers' children had a primary- and middle-school education. High school and college were expensive and were unaffordable for most families. For women, seasonal plucking work in a plantation was always available, but for male youth, the pressure to find work was immense. Male youth were extremely envious of management officials, who were mostly Bihari, Bengali, or Punjabi[2] college graduates from elsewhere or upper-class and upper-caste Nepali men with good connections to the local political party.

During my stay in Phulbāri, a group of male youth assaulted the senior manager. The manager suffered head injuries and was admitted to the hospital. These kinds of sporadic incidents of violence were common and mostly performed by young male youth belonging to the plantation. The father of one of the Nepali managers whom I interviewed was murdered by another unemployed plantation male youth. The paucity of employment for men and lack of proper educational opportunities put great strain on plantation households and women plantation workers, which resulted in these occasional outbursts. In addition, during my stay, there was often gossip about violence between spouses and alcohol-related abuse.

There was also great anxiety around sharing/pooling of existing resources within the family. Women often reared chickens, made rice wine, and knitted during the weekends to make money. They usually sold these in the plantation villages. Lachmi *didi* usually woke up at 5 a.m. and lit the oven in her kitchen to make the morning tea. She also boiled water to make rice for lunch, which she and her husband took with them. Her daughter Mala would leave for work (she worked as a cook in the assistant manager's house). The two sons would still be sleeping. The elder one had just returned from Delhi with his wife who was expecting. After washing, Lachmi entered the living room where the younger son was sleeping. She told him, "Ramesh wake up and at least do things around the house, feed the chickens and make sure they don't flee or the neighbors' dogs will eat them." She then turned to me and told me:

> At least the girls find work in the plantation, if not full time, part time work plucking tea in the neighboring plantations. But my sons worry me. My elder son went to Lucknow to work as a cook. There he discovered that other *madeshi*[3] cooks threatened them to leave so that their own people could join. Even if our sons travel outside, they cannot find safe employment. There are no opportunities for them, and if they sit idle for too long, they take to drugs. There are so many managers and office workers hired from outside the plantation; why can't our sons be trained to work in the plantation? This kind of system would at least motivate them to study. Our sons have no future.

Ramesh hung out with some union guys and Lachmi hoped that the party leaders in the union would help him find a job. Lachmi's feelings were representative of the anxiety within households in the plantation.

Male youth that I had befriended in the two plantation often asked me this standard question, "*Didi, hāmi driver ko kām pāondina? America mā, teta to dherai car cha?* (Elder sister, will we not get a driver's job in America where there are so many cars?"). Widespread nepotism in the plantations, along with fewer opportunities for men's work, resulted in mounting tensions within households about men's economic future. Most household conflicts were centered upon supplementing household income and securing the economic future of their families. In Sonākheti, Phulbāri, and other plantations the gendered labor recruitment resulted in disillusionment of male youth.

The plantation owner's constant emphasis on the "strong women of Sonākheti," and his public exposure of negative feelings about the capability of Nepali men only furthered plantation workers' tension about the future of their children and complicated their household relations. The owner was very conscious of his support for the "ethnic" needs of his workers, though he frequently used ethnic stereotypes of "childishness" and "immaturity" to discriminate against Nepali men, when hiring male workers for office or supervisory positions. He built temples for workers but did not recruit local youth in the plantation, except to do weeding work.[4]

Male family members of plantation workers tended to see their wives/daughters/sisters as more privileged. In many families women had regular income and men did occasional wage work in town or they would be unemployed. Jang Bahadur and Gita had frequent fights over their son's future. Jang Bahadur had no employment; he sometimes did part-time work in the plantation. His wife Gita, although sympathetic toward his unemployed status, sometimes could not control her frustrations about her husband's status. One evening when I was staying with them, I returned from a day's work in the field. Jang Bahadur was drunk, and Gita was giving him a piece of her mind. I did not enter their home and stood outside to talk to their neighbor, Thule, who incidentally was also unemployed. Gita shouted to Jang Bahadur, "Why can't you sell some of the *raksi* (rice wine), why do you drink it all with your friends, do you know that my *thikā* (wage) is insufficient?" Alchoholism among men and women was common. Yet making alcohol also was a way to stretch the family income, selling it to neighbors and friends.

In many households, men helped in making alcohol to be sold in the plantation. Bindu was an average plucker, but her family was better off because her husband was a retired army man. Her husband received a pension. Bindu's husband used his pension money to improve their home and marry off her two daughters. In his spare time, he made *raksi* (local rice wine) and reared pigs. If husbands had regular jobs they were much more supportive of women and helped out at home. When I lived in their house, Bindu's husband would make meals.

Household Relations in the Cooperative
(Sānu Krishak Sansthā)

As evident from my ethnographic examination of household relations in the plantation, Fair Trade activities were far removed from worker's everyday lives. Household conflicts centered on the dim employment prospects of male family members. In the cooperative, household relations were affected by the increased visibility of Women's Wing members and their business plan, which went against their dominant image as housewives. Tension was particularly strong in the homes of women tea farmers who were active Women's Wing members and were going to town to sell produce for the Women's Wing's business.

In the cooperative, women's image as housewives had naturalized "home" as the sphere of work for women. Women tea farmers faced problems because of their active participation in the Fair Trade activities of the cooperative. While family members did not object to women taking out loans, they complained if women went to too many meetings. The differential politics of class related to women's visibility in the public sphere affected gendered work struggles within and outside the household.

Another notable difference in household relations in the cooperative was the effect of socioeconomic inequality among cooperative members and the way it affected women's position within households. Gendered mobility politics worked through household politics. Women in the cooperative area had different backgrounds depending on their socioeconomic position. While caste was an important marker of identity in Darjeeling, socioeconomic standing (class) played an important factor in shaping people's identity. The cooperative neighborhoods had a majority of Rai, Tamang, and Chettri (Nepali ethnic groups). Economic inequities were based on education, family wealth, access to political power, government employment (whether in the army or local government offices), and size of land and affording hired labor.

Active Women's Wing members who regularly came to meetings were comparatively less wealthy compared to women who were interested in loans but never came to the meetings. I also observed that husbands of women who were active in the Women's Wing mostly worked as wage laborers in town or farmed at home. Women whose husbands had gainful employment, large holdings of land, or successful business ventures apart from selling tea in the cooperative were more apprehensive of participating in the meetings. The latter were also not ashamed when they defaulted on microcredit loan repayments.

For instance, Ashika, the wife of a shopkeeper and middleman in the cooperative area, was no longer a Women's Wing member. I knew from my interactions with other senior Women's Wing members that she had been a very active member in the initial years and also took out loans. After a while her husband's shop started doing really well and she left Women's Wing. When I asked Ashika to describe her experience in the Women's Wing she made the following comments:

> When the Women's Wing started out we were encouraged
> to do *social* [emphasis mine] things. We campaigned in the

villages against alcoholism, encouraged pregnant women to
go to the hospitals, campaigned for polio awareness among
new mothers and did ICDS child development work.[5] We
did a lot of good work. But today the Women's Wing is
only interested in loans; women have become very money
minded and that is why their household members object
to their activities.

It was ironic that Ashika ran her husband's shop when he was not in
the village. The shop was in their house. She would switch on her TV
and sit in the shop the entire day. She nevertheless blamed Women's
Wing members' household conflicts on their "money minded" attitude.
She repeated what many older men and middlemen said when asked
about their thoughts on the Women's Wing. One of the male cooperative members told me that business was not a woman's thing; that is
why it is bound to fail.

The active members of the Women's Wing mostly came from
households with smaller land-holdings, or households that did not
have enough tea bushes and felt the need to generate income from
other sources. These women were interested in taking loans and usually returned them to ensure that they could take more loans each
year. Women from neighborhoods which were not near the service-
able road that ran through the cooperative area became most active in
the matters of the Women's Wing because they we more exploited by
middlemen. At times there were exceptions—women from supportive
wealthy homes who could spare some time from agricultural or other
household chores were also active. As occurs in any organization,
some women were more articulate than others, and this was not necessarily tied to education or wealth.

When I asked members why they joined the Women's Wing, most
women frankly admitted that they wanted to access loans by joining
the Women's Wing. When I asked why they stayed on in the Women's
Wing, women explained that they now felt a sense of camaraderie,
while also admitting the possibility of taking part in future income-
generation schemes of the Women's Wing. The most common response
was, "We love the fact that at least once a month we can forget about
our homes; now we know people on both sides of the hill. We learn
so many new things, get training." During interviews, many women
mentioned that they became members so that their daughters could
learn new business skills and get service *kaam* (work). One often
repeated explanation was, "Times are changing, and women need to
learn new skills to keep up. I hope my daughter will also join when

she is older so that she can go for different training camps organized by the NGO." Non-members or ex-members usually said they liked the Women's Wing but did not have time, very similar to responses of women who had left the Women's Wing. Another important observation was that single women who got married to better (well-to-do) homes left the Women's Wing, even if they were active before marriage. Age was important, but economic inequities outweighed age in determining spontaneity of women's involvement in the Women's Wing.

These differences between women also affected household relationships. During my fieldwork I stayed in a combination of households to see how socioeconomic differences influenced household relations. Economic difference affected the way men and women were socially evaluated in their communities, which in turn affected their household relations. For instance, in one wealthy household the daughters-in-law, Poonam and Rajni, were never allowed by their mother-in-law to become members of the Women's Wing. In my conversations with the mother-in-law, who was never a member of Women's Wing herself, she told me that her daughters-in-law did not require loans, and they would rather spend that time doing household chores. "Our family's daughters-in-law do not need loans. There is much to do at home."

After some time, the youngest daughter-in-law, Poonam, decided to become a member of the Women's Wing. She was the more outspoken of the two daughters-in-law. Her husband did not have regular employment, and she decided that she needed to make some savings for the future. Poonam's decision was not welcomed in the household; her husband was also indifferent. There were arguments over her impudence. Poonam's father-in-law frequently cracked jokes at dinner time about the failure of the Women's Wing's milk business and ineffectiveness to dissuade Poonam from joining the Women's Wing. Poonam's father-in-law had five acres of land, almost three times the average holding size in the area. He was also a loyal supplier of one of the middlemen from this region.

Poonam's father-in-law, like many other wealthy families, had a material interest in defaming the Women's Wing because he wanted his individual milk business to survive. Jokes about Women's Wing's business ventures were common in wealthy families. Sometimes, even women who had benefited from Women's Wing microcredit schemes earlier and now had more stable income sources denigrated women Women's Wing members as "*bāthi*," implying that active Women's Wing members had transgressed the boundaries of existing social norms in the *basti* (non-plantation village area). These rumors of failure were damaging for the confidence of Women's Wing members and their family members who were already doubtful about their daughters' or wives' new ventures.

Poonam's family was not the only one with this problem. Women from families with sufficient income were always reluctant to allow their women outside the homes. In contrast, women who felt the need to increase their income would be most active in the Women's Wing so that they could take more loans. They would be regular at meetings and would pay their dues on time.

Household Conflicts in Sānu Krishak Sansthā

I was awakened from my sleep on January 12, 2006, by a loud altercation between Manju and her brothers. Manju was the most active Women's Wing member of her neighborhood. She was in charge of helping the milk business along with Dipika. The night before, she had come to know that Kabita, another Women's Wing member who took the milk collected in the village (by Manju and Dipika) to Darjeeling town, had threatened the Women's Wing to start her own business. Kabita was upset when she was requested by Women's Wing members to give another economically struggling woman a chance to go to town and learn the skills of selling milk and vegetables.

Manju was extremely upset because she thought Kabita was betraying the Women's Wing's objective of a rotating collective business. Kabita, it seemed, was very upset that she would lose her turn to take the milk to town eight months after she took charge of the Women's Wing's business.[6] Kabita believed that not everyone should get a turn since her economic condition was not good. The rotation system was institutionalized by the Women's Wing so that every economically struggling woman in the Women's Wing would get a chance to learn business skills. So when Kabita was requested by other Women's Wing members to give up her position, she took it personally. Manju's anger at this incident was compounded by her brother's comments. When I lay awake in my bed, I heard her elder brother Dipesh sarcastically saying:

> You should not feel frustrated now; I had warned you before that Kabita will take advantage of you. It was the Women's Wing's aim to make sure that women stand on their own feet; well at least one of them has. You should be satisfied and Women's Wing should also stop this business since it is not working out. If you cannot digest this reality you all

are not fit to do business. That is why the cooperative is
not giving Women's Wing Fair Trade money this year.

Manju's brothers and their friends in the locality were otherwise very
supportive of the Women's Wing's business and helped them with
accounts. I had seen them defending their sisters when people made
fun of their business plan. Manju's brother also used the money Manju
borrowed from the microcredit loans. They nevertheless made fun of
Manju because she was spending a lot of time outside the house going
to meetings, going to the town, and visiting people's homes campaign-
ing them to give their milk to the Women's Wing business. Manju and
Dipika would hold meetings in the village to make sure that villagers
gave their milk to Women's Wing and not the middlemen who mixed
it with water after buying milk from villagers and sold it in town at
double the price. Manju snapped back:

> Don't talk to me like that. The next time you are upset
> because the middleman cheated you with your goats, I will
> remind you about your failures. It is common for beginners
> to make mistakes in business, but we want to do *swachcha
> vyāpār* (*clean/fair trade*). You must understand that Women's
> Wing does not want to be like middlemen; we want profit
> but not by exploiting others. So try to understand what the
> Women's Wing is trying to do. Do you stop taking your goats
> to town during *Dashāi* (annual festival) because you were
> cheated by one middleman last year? Why do you want us
> to stop? I think you are paying too much attention to village
> rumors. Try to apply your brain and see what the Women's
> Wing is trying to do. And where would you get money to
> buy the goats if I was not a Women's Wing member.

The exchange between Manju and her brother typified interactions
between active Women's Wing members and their families. Among my
thirty key women informants in the cooperative community consisting
of members of the Women's Wing, most commented that they do not go
to town regularly and face opposition in their homes if they spend a
long time outside their homes. I asked all of the women I interviewed
whether they needed to get permission if they were going to go to
meetings; most of them said yes. Women's work inside the home was
considered materially and symbolically important to maintain inter-
household distinctions within the village.

Socioeconomic issues underlined Manju's altercation with her brother. Manju's family was sufficiently well-to-do. She lived with her aged father and two elder brothers. She had a sister who was married. They had a large land holding, but tea was not the main produce of the family. Manju took out loans and gave it to her brothers for buying young goats for their animal husbandry business. She also ran a small shop from her house selling cigarettes, soap, and biscuits. She told me that she paid back her loans from the earnings of this small shop but her brothers also gave back a large share from the sale of their goats and ginger during season. Because Manju's family was comparatively wealthy her brothers frequently asked her to give up her Women's Wing work. The standard discourse was, "You don't need to." Socio-economic differences were manifest by restricting women's visibility to the household. Upwardly mobile families were especially conscious of the movement of their women outside the household.

Men were also very self-conscious if their wives or sisters were working outside the home. While I was staying at Kabita's house, her husband, Harka Bahadur, often asked me, especially if he had had too much *raksi* (rice wine) to drink, what I thought about their household situation. In the beginning I did not understand what he meant by "household situation." Gradually, I mastered village gossip; I understood his self-consciousness and concern about the reputation of his household. I continued pretending not to understand, and finally he elaborated, "You know Kabita goes out in the morning to the market and I stay at home. Do you think that is okay? How do you feel about that?" I told him that to me it was normal. He should not feel bad about it because Kabita was earning for him and their two sons. My participant observation in the *jungās* (village vehicles) while traveling back and forth from the town also helped me to triangulate these frustrations among men whose wives were active Women's Wing members.

Kabita and Harka Bahadur were looked down upon because apparently they had violent fights. According to male cooperative members, Harka Bahadur apparently drank too much. Kabita was seen as cunning because she went to town often and was not afraid to argue with male members of the community. Even her closest neighbors looked down upon her. She also had a smaller agricultural plot and her household output of tea was little, so she had much less income compared to households with large holdings of tea.

Harka Bahadur knew that people talked badly about his wife. But there was nothing he could do. Kabita was smart, she could sell things in town, and the two did not have enough tea bushes to just rely on tea. Harka Bahadur also helped his wife, collecting vegetables from the village and packing them in a bag in the wee hours of the morning, cooking for his sons, and taking care of their small plot of land. Harka Bahadur had failed to secure regular wage work in town. When I stayed with Harka Bahadur and Kabita, he used to call his female cousin to make lunch for me in Kabita's absence because women serving food to a guest was the norm. I always requested him to let me cook my own food, which he appreciated. This saved him from being ashamed about his wife not serving his guests.

Household conflicts could not be seen just as an interaction between spouses; conversations within the household were often influenced by rumors in the cooperative community and actions of the cooperative board. Harka Bahadur was sidelined in the cooperative because he drank too much, had little education, and also because his wife had a bad reputation as being cunning. On the other hand, Hiren, the secretary of the cooperative, was also very cunning, but he was not ostracized like Harka Bahadur. His wife had no reputation and was not a member of Women's Wing. He was educated. He probably did not drink as much as Harka Bahadur. He also had a job at a government school. Because of his class position people did not speak badly of him. However, he was criticized heavily by Women's Wing members because he played an active part in the cooperative's decision to not share the FLO premium with the Women's Wing.

People did not speak well about Punita, another active Women's Wing member. She was also nearing thirty and was not married, which was a major cause for gossip. Punita was very independent minded and had a very sharp tongue, but people talked about her also because she was an active member of the Women's Wing. Punita's family had little land. Her parents farmed and her brother was trying to get into the Indian army each year. Even her brother was uncomfortable that she was still not married and reminded her occasionally that he would not get a wife if she did not marry. Punita had told me numerous times that these comments in her household did not bother her anymore. She would not marry because she loved watching TV in the afternoons and was concerned that her future husband might not let her. Women's Wing members who were single were very apprehensive of marrying men from the neighborhood for the fear of being subject to the norms of being a "housewife."

These kinds of wealth and gender inequalities were regular in the cooperative area. Well-to-do men and their wives always maintained composure, but community members constantly scrutinized economically struggling families. Gender ideologies survived through these gendered discourses about men, women, and their households.

Women's reputations affected their husband's participation in the cooperative and their own household relations. These gendered politics were challenged by women tea farmers in the cooperative. Women plantation workers on the other hand are not able to challenge the domination of the management (and male co-workers) even in spite of greater freedom to meet outside the house.

Household Politics and Public Discourses of "Risk"

It was because of this gendered class politics that active Women's Wing members felt vulnerable. They blamed this not only on their husbands and family members but also on the cooperative and community who held on to gender ideologies about women's work. A recurring theme in women's narratives was a discussion of risk. Women used the English word risk but when pronouncing it, it sounded more like "*riks.*" The theme of "*riks*" was a way for women to talk about the gendered struggles they continued to face in their community and households. Through a discussion about risk, women found a way to connect their past sacrifices (before the cooperative was formed) with the present ones to justify their entrepreneurialism and activism within the cooperative.

At the time of my research, women thought that their biggest risk came from male middlemen who dominated the trade of produce and milk from the cooperative villages and were related to their families. Since their families had depended on middlemen for many years, women were having a hard time convincing their family members about their business venture. This risk was compounded when their family members did not realize or object to the extent of middlemen's exploitation of villagers (like Manju's brothers). Women told me that they had always been forced to take more risk for their families and communities without much support. By "*riks,*" women not only implied greater workload but also the increased possibility of losing their reputations, especially if they were poor and became active in the Women's Wing. Some of the important members of the cooperative were middlemen who collected vegetables and produce from the neighborhoods at very low prices and sold them in town for profit as detailed in chapter 5.

After the Women's Wing fought with the cooperative over the FLO money for their business plan, powerful men in the village spread rumors that the Women's Wing business was bound to fail because women were inexperienced. Poonam's father-in-law is one such man.

Like Poonam's father-in-law, other *Goālās* also found out that the milk depot in town to which the Women's Wing was selling their milk. The *Goālās* told the depot owner that women were disorganized and were unethical. Women tea farmers now constantly felt they were at risk because their reputations were at stake. Their own family members at times felt the pressure of being loyal to some middlemen questioning women's skills. This created household anxiety. However, if women tea farmers succumbed to these rumors and stopped their business, they would risk losing their chance to convince villagers that they could conduct their successful business. Their failure would ensure that the cooperative never gave them FLO money for their projects.

In the December 2006 Women's Wing meeting, the driver of the car that carried the Women's Wing procured milk to town was called to a meeting to settle accounts. He never arrived with his car at the designated time to take the Women's Wing produce and milk to town. This was a major issue because of the perishability of milk and vegetables. Though he was very helpful to the Women's Wing's business, his immediate public response was to hide his delay. The car owner quickly added: "You women are blaming me for your business not doing well but you all do not even know how to talk to the milk depot owner in town. If you knew that then your business would have been running smoothly." The comment implied that village women were inexperienced about how to conduct business. At this Manju quickly responded,

> Thanks so much for taking time out to come here and for helping us to realize our mistakes. However, it is also my duty to remind all you people from this neighborhood that no milkman was offering you Rs. 8 per liter of milk before we started this business. We don't have a pliable road, so please remember the days when you had to throw away your extra milk in frustration for not getting a good price from the middlemen in other villages. None of you encouraged your *household members to start a business* [emphasis mine]. Now that we are doing well, you tell our brothers and fathers that Women's Wing members have become *bāthi*. We took a great risk by starting this business so that you all did not have to waste your milk and we women could also learn how to do organized business. We shell out our own money when the customers in the town delay their payments, just to make sure that our business is fair, and that you are getting your money on time. Please have some

appreciation for the risk that we are taking here. We are
here to learn, so let us have some productive discussion
about how we can sell your milk more efficiently, instead
of trying to create problems in our homes.

Reminders of risk-taking for the community were regular in meetings and in my personal conversations with women. Manju frequently
reminded her brother (as in the last example) about the efforts of the
Women's Wing to do *swachcha vyāpār* (clean/fair trade). Women told
me that the cooperative was a microcosm of society where women's
work outside their family farms was criticized. The conflicts they faced
in the household were compounded by the attitude of comparatively
wealthy board members and their wives.

On March 16, 2007, there was a general strike in Darjeeling called
by the GNLF. On the day of the strike women risked going to town
to sell the milk. I met them in town and waited with them beside
the train station. I quietly listened to their conversation, which again
centered on the topic of risk. In spite of a strike women tea farmers
risked coming to town because they wanted to capture the market
there. Women did not want potential customers to feel that they were
not serious about the business. There were no cars running in Darjeeling that day. All schools were shut and all shops were closed.
During such strikes, the government allowed only emergency service
vehicles to use the road, which included emergency food supplies like
milk. So the women made their own "emergency milk duty" poster
and convinced the driver to take them to town. Apparently, all the
other male milk vendors from hamlets within the cooperative and the
driver were hesitant to travel to town. The men were not sure about
the circumstances in town. They feared they would get caught by the
police and would have to pay bribes to the cops. The Women's Wing
members said that because they agreed to pay up for any monetary
loss the driver agreed to come to town.

Binu told me later, "There are lots of men who come regularly
to town and know what a strike entails, but none would come for the
fear of being caught. It was because the women took the monetary risk
that the men could all sell their milk. Women are always asked for
more sacrifices in the home and community; yet there is no faith in
their capacity to do big business." She felt pride and frustration at the
same time. She was proud because they were able to sell their milk
and frustrated because whenever the women's group decided to start a
new business venture their business integrity and capacity to take new
ventures was questioned. Men mobilized existing gender ideologies in

the community to express doubt about whether simple village women would be able to conduct big business like men. Poonam's father-in-law kept telling her that joining the Women's Wing was a waste of time because their business was a failure. Manju's brothers made fun of her when she spent time at the Women's Wing. Binu told me that men, who perceive women as potential competitors, use these statements to show concern. In reality such comments are meant to create a lack of confidence about the Women's Wing's business. Once the women got their share of the FLO money, such concern had quickly turned into hostility. Active Women's Wing women were now defamed with negative representations like "*bāthi* and *chuchchi*,"[7] which made their household relations tense.

Women farmers never interfered with the business of the middlemen who were friends of their male family members or their kin. Wealthy middlemen were active in the cooperative too. They had more land and kept very good relations with families who were well off. Class relations in the village worked through these inter-household ties. Women felt frustrated when these men defamed Women's Wing members. Women's Wing members who were engaged in small entrepreneurial activities felt that they had taken all kinds of risk in their community starting from selling illegal tea, to taking out microcredit loans to support their families and now in this business, which the male middlemen were out to destroy. They were willing to take risks for the men, such as on a day of the strike. Such compassion could not be expected from the men. Women told me that they took risks but never let their temper overtake their diplomacy. They knew the motive of all men but never got into any kind of altercation with them because it went against notions of honor. Whenever they felt cornered, they found friendly ways to get their point across. In such a circumstance women felt that they could not let their group dissolve. It was through this group that women could critique male dominance and the use of their labor. The hope was that the group's continuation and success would convince their household members that they were on to something important. It would convince family members that their wives, daughters, and sisters were trying to accomplish something important for their household and community by trying to raise household earnings by cutting out the middlemen.

When women took loans, they felt that they took a risk due to various reasons. Their husbands and other family members used this money for their own use, but the responsibility of returning the money fell on the women. Since the Women's Wing women had been taking out loans for the last seven years, they felt that they were being exposed to the risk of running their homes all alone. Manju had once told me, "Men just go out, earn a little bit of money and think that they are the ones running the household for which their wives should be grateful to them. The truth is that wives run the household, they stretch that little amount of money and make things look okay. It is because of the effort of the women that their husbands can feel a sense of pride which is highly misplaced!" Sunita *didi*, another committed Women's Wing member, once told me, "The work inside the home is rarely seen, that is the nature of our work!" After my extended interview I realized that by "work inside the home" Sunita *didi* not only meant physical household labor, but also the difficult process of negotiating identity and acceptance within the household. Women whose families owned cattle had a common joke, "We get the grass, he takes the milk," to describe the inequality of resource sharing within cooperative households. Women spent a lot of time cutting grass for their cattle and most of them hated this work. This comment implied how men enjoyed the fruits of women's labor.

Women tea farmers also used Fair Trade trainings and public events to address household issues. During the Fair Trade *Janajāgaran Kāryakram* (People's Awareness Campaign detailed in the next chapter), Women's Wing members made speeches about the significance of Fair Trade and urged people to remember why they were getting development money from Fair Trade. Somewhere in these speeches Women's Wing members always mentioned that they were also trying to practice Fair Trade (*swachcha vyāpār*). Sabita mentioned, "When all of you trust and respect the Women's Wing and value it as much as the cooperative then our community will see true Fair Trade happen. Every household member should send all their women to the Women's Wing so that they can all learn business skills so vital in today's world. Don't make fun of your wives if they spend time in meetings; don't make their lives difficult." I had recorded many public speeches that women made in the cooperative in which they made these moral appeals to the cooperative community to pay attention to how women were treated in their homes. In this particular speech Sabita related women's household relations and Fair Trade.

Gendered resource politics was thus compounded by economic hierarchies making economically struggling families and their women more vulnerable to the effects of inequality. Sunita, Kabita, Binu, Punita, and Shanta had various economic disadvantages. Manju faced great opposition in her family because her brothers thought she did not need to take loans. When Manju's family did not need loans, she took a loan in her name and gave that to other women in the village who had not become Women's Wing members. Shanta and Sunita complained that their husbands were giving them a hard time in the community after the Women's Wing floated their business plan. Comparatively wealthy women also deplored Women's Wing members, saying that they were money-minded. As I detailed earlier, the wife of a wealthy shopkeeper in one community who was previously involved with the Women's Wing told me, "These days women are just interested in loans, in our days we were doing social things. We were not business minded." When the Women's Wing started they were not involved in microcredit but did health campaigns, campaigns against alcoholism, which were common programs, run by the Indian government (see Sharma 2008). When microcredit started everyone welcomed loans and the only way to get one was by making their daughters, wives, or mothers members of the Women's Wing. Some women dropped out a couple of years later, mostly because they had defaulted or their families now made enough money from selling tea. By this time, the local *panchāyats* also started lending money to people in the locality. These wealthy ex-Women's Wing members were the most critical of the present Women's Wing members, implying that it was not appropriate for women to be interested in business. These women spoiled the reputation of the Women's Wing's present members through village gossip.

In their monthly meetings women often spoke of solving the "household problem." In the January meeting, Punita raised her hand when the Women's Wing president was deciding on the meeting agenda. She said that women now had to take greater risks, and the fault lay with the Women's Wing members. She requested women not to be dumb/*lāti*. She urged them to go home and convince their household members that business was not a bad thing. It was all for the community. Premlila, another Women's Wing member, mentioned "Many of our community's problems were because of household issues. People do not understand that household work (*sakaune kaam*) is also like running a business."

Some women farmers identified that *riks* was systemic due to the barriers to women's economic freedom, as Nita explains:

> You know how these NGO brothers talk about *riks* to us, they tell us we should pay up on time and not being able to do so will harm our future loan-taking ability. I say we are the ones who really understand *riks*, we have to return the money, it is us women; we have always taken *riks* for our community.

Women used the word *riks* creatively to draw attention to the inequities, some of which have escalated along with new economic opportunities. In their daily discourse, loan-taking women identified several aspects to the notion of *riks*. Sheila reminded me that: "we frequently have to take risks; now the task of household procurement (*sakaune kaam*) has become risky." Instances like this were noted in regular conversation where women invoked the notion of *riks*.

Through their various acts of cultural entrepreneurialism women tea farmers tried to show how male power worked through the linkages between community and household relations. By publicly talking about the "household problem" during Fair Trade trainings women exposed their household anxieties as will be demonstrated in the next chapter.

Consequences of Differential Visibilities of Women's Work

Deborah Elliston writes that household relations emerge "as sites central in decision-making about laboring projects and as the moral and affective centers structuring the ascription of meaning to labor activities" (Elliston 2004, 610). These micro-contexts of everyday life become the testing ground for judging the effectiveness of ethical regimes for addressing structural gendered and socioeconomic inequalities in certified communities and promoting everyday sustainability.

In recent years the household studies literature has emphasized the study of intra-household relations to understand the consequences of women's bargaining power within the household (Jha 2004). Kabeer stresses that the "visibility and extent of women's gainful work" within households remains important to arrive at conclusions about women's bargaining power within households (1994, 110–11). In her more recent work, Kabeer emphasizes that women's agency (read in her study as the ability to join public sphere) is not only influenced by particular household relations but to a large extent influenced by the social milieu in which households are immersed. Both Kabeer (2000) and Fernandes (1997) call attention to looking at gender identities in households in conjunction with class, caste, or immigrant identity politics of the community in question. In this chapter, I have looked at household politics simultaneously with socioeconomic inequities in the community to understand the significance of women tea farmers' political action in the public sphere and their household politics. Women plantation workers and women tea farmers both live lives negotiating their respective social reputations with trying to cope with the growing economic concerns of their families—balancing economic and cultural entrepreneurialism. While Fair Trade–related economic activities affected women's household relations more directly in the cooperative, in the plantation, women's household relations were not affected in any way to Fair Trade. While in the cooperative women tea farmers used Fair Trade–related public events to draw attention to structural issues within the household that devalues women's labor, entrepreneurialism in the community, and in the plantation, household matters were kept secret. My findings in this chapter finds resonance in the work of feminists economists (Iversen 2003) advancing the idea that to develop a more robust understanding of women's capabilities one must address women's power to bargain within households.

"Tadpoles in Water" versus "Police of Our Fields"

Competing Subjectivities, Women's Political Agency and Fair Trade

Having described the everyday activities of the women tea farmers and plantation workers, in this chapter I attend to their respective political agency. In my analysis of political agency among women plantation workers and women tea farmers, I give equal weight to their practices and narratives around practice, in order to analyze how women tea farmers and plantation workers read institutional power structures and think about their own capabilities to navigate them. To conceptualize political agency, it is important to see their situated practices and their own subjective interpretation of these practices.

Women use their "practical consciousness" (Williams 1977) to shape their political action and to also reflect on what kind of actors they become as a result of their actions. I also show that women tea farmers' direct participation in Fair Trade–related awareness workshops have increased their confidence about the purpose of their economic and political activities. While both groups of women take action to deal with the inadequacies of their lives, tea plantation workers' narratives reveal a sense of decreasing possibility for action, while women tea farmers find new thresholds of action opening up for them, due to the advent of Fair Trade. Even if they do not make concrete gains all the time, the altercations over Fair Trade's benefits have enabled women tea farmers to create a space for publicizing their role in community development.

It is not my intention to see taking action as the ultimate form of political agency, but I start from the narratives of the women. It is in their narratives that I locate a preoccupation with "doing," "changing," and "not being able to do/change/speak" that forms the basis of my argument about political agency. It is their narratives about capacity for action and change that I analyze in this chapter. Women's political agency is best deciphered by looking at what women subjectively construct as possibility or impossibility. I see women's political subjectivity as situated understandings of their own gendered projects of value at this given historical moment.

Women's self-knowledge or subjectivity (Foucault 1994), was shaped by the institutional structures which governed their lives. Their specific self-knowledge affected the way they interpreted their own actions. I have argued throughout this book that women plantation workers found a situation more adverse to large-scale collective organizing, limiting their capacity to mobilize federally granted labor rights. Even individual actions challenging systemic nepotism or workplace hazards—everyday resistance—are rare, as I will show later in this chapter. Women tea farmers, on the other hand, were engaged in activities that challenged male domination in the cooperative. They were refashioning themselves as entrepreneurs, challenging existing cultural productions, trying to undo the exploitation of middlemen and seek respect for their activities in front of household and community members (as seen in the last chapter).

In this chapter, I locate how the difference in the subjectivities of women at two sites impacts the way women plan to use their specific collective organizing efforts. In the cooperative, women's collective organizing was aimed at gaining a public voice; in the plantation women's collective, organizing was aimed at surviving a system by not ruffling too many feathers. The distinct goals of their collective organizing influenced how women tea farmers and women plantation workers saw themselves as actors. The institutional structures also influenced the type of resource that each group could mobilize. In the cooperative, women's husbands owned the legal titles to their land and women felt that they had some ownership of what was produced on that land, as detailed in chapter 3. Since individual tea farmers came together to form the cooperative in 1997 and in every matter each co-op household had an equal vote, women tea farmers had a different understanding of their organization (the cooperative) and its relation to the Women's Wing. Women plantation workers were much more insecure about the status of their employment and there were limited ways in which they could use the plantation land. Although plantation workers had lived on plantation lands for generations, they feared being ousted due to perceived wrongdoings. They could not use their living quarters the way they wanted and always had to ask for permission. These kinds of differences influenced the way women interpreted their capacities as a group and as individual actors. The social milieu, institutional structures, and types of resource access all combined to produce different kinds of "practical consciousness," which became part of their political agency—their ability to understand and navigate power through specific action.

Women tea farmers also found themselves in the midst of a less hierarchical organization than the plantation. In the plantation, the strict bureaucratic hierarchy, top-down obedience structure, and corrupt labor union practices limit the ability of the women workers to know and bargain for Fair Trade benefits from the plantation administration. Thus, women in the two plantations neither had a say in the ways in which the Fair Trade premium (that the plantation receives each year) should be used, nor did they have any clear idea of what Fair Trade entailed (its history and benefits). Most women from the plantation described it as *zamindāri* or feudal domain, and asserted that their grievances mostly remained unheard. Plantations that were certified Fair Trade usually had a Joint Body that decided how the Fair Trade premium money would be spent in various labor welfare and development projects. In my participant observation and interviews, I found the effectiveness of this group to be limited in fulfilling this goal. While more than 50 percent of the members of the Joint Body (ten out of sixteen) at the plantation were women, they hardly ever participated actively in these meetings. While the plantation website and publicity material advertised that women made all Joint Body decisions, the reality was very different. Such an oppressive milieu had given rise to covert practices of economic reciprocity (*ghumāuri*) among women plantation workers as described in chapter 2.

In the small tea farmers' communities, the nature of women's participation was very different from that of women workers on the plantation. Male and female representatives of the cooperative and the Women's Wing, respectively, were elected through unit-wide public meetings. Cooperative elections were held every year and candidates, whether male or female, had to stand up to the test of leadership skills. Joint Body members in the plantation, on the other hand, were handpicked by the plantation owner as amply demonstrated in chapters 4 and 5.

The more non-hierarchical, democratic structure of the cooperative provided more space for discussion and dissent among its male and female members in the co-op decision-making process. Cooperative meetings were therefore important places where women tea farmers through open debates questioned gender hierarchies. While men outnumbered women in the governing body of the cooperative, some members of the women's group were always present at meetings. The Women's Wing had a separate meeting on the eighth day of every month. Women cooperative members felt that the Women's Wing should receive a separate share of the Fair Trade premium money and were not afraid to claim it, as they knew they could not be ousted from their land. These differences affected how women conceptualized their own capacities in the plantation and the cooperative. In their daily conversation, plantation workers frequently mentioned that they had "lost the power to speak." Women tea farmers, in recounting the evolution of the Women's Wing, emphasized that they were now "ready to beat the table," implying that they were not going to be taken for a ride. Women tea farmers frequently sought out avenues to reduce their dependence on the tea cooperative.

In the rest of this chapter, I analyze how women tea farmers' and plantation workers' subjectivities were influenced by the institutional structures where women worked and lived. The latter also affected the scope their collective organizing, through *ghumāuri*/Women's Wing. The limits and nature of collective organizing, in turn, reinforced the subjective feelings women had about their own selves and future, affecting the tactics and intensity of women's negotiations with structural power.

Being "Tadpoles in Water" vs. "Police of our Fields"

In this section, I analyze through narratives, how the different institutional structures have influenced women's subjectivities at respective sites. I analyze the "patterns of talk" women use to describe their own condition.

In early March 2007, I was in Darjeeling town doing research at the NGO office which has been working with the tea cooperative for many years. As I interviewed one of the male NGO members on his perceptions about the activities of the Women's Wing, he made a comparison between them and the women workers from Sonākheti. He had seen both groups of women in action at a state-sponsored women's development workshop in Siliguri. Women from both plantations and non-plantation areas were invited. The male NGO employee,[1] who had accompanied Women's Wing members to Siliguri, was very proud of the confidence and public speaking skills of the Women's Wing members. He said that the women from Sonākheti kept smiling when asked about women's development and its effects on their communities. He further added, "Our Women's Wing members on the other hand were prompt with responses. The workshop leaders were impressed. When asked about women's activities, Binu immediately sketched a brief history of the community's engagement with FLO and what the Women's Wing was doing. I could not believe how clear their understanding of Fair Trade–organic was." I suspected that this comparison was a publicity stunt, until the NGO worker's observations were corroborated by women plantation workers themselves.

Months after I had heard this comparison from the NGO employee, I was at a *ghumāuri* meeting in Sonākheti. The meeting was taking place after a Joint Body meeting, where I was also present. In the *ghumāuri* discussion, Sita asked me about my work with the women tea farmers. The plantation workers always spoke of *basti*[2] people (women tea farmers) with envy. Shinu, another plantation worker, teased me, saying that every time I returned from the *basti* I looked fresh because the *basti* people grew their own organic vegetables, which made me look good. Plantation workers had to depend on the bad quality vegetables of Kurseong town, the bad ration rice and *dāl* (lentils); they did not have their own land. I used to get the plantation workers' vegetables from the cooperative area as gifts, which they otherwise had to buy at high prices in the market shops. Whenever I ate a meal with women plantation workers, they would ask me what I ate when I was in the cooperative area.

Sita (the nurse) had arrived to the meeting late because she had to make a couple of house visits to distribute medicine. Sita joined the conversation by declaring that women in the *basti* were more aware about FLO. She soon started talking about a workshop at Siliguri that she had attended where there were women from the *basti*. I confirmed the dates with her and knew immediately that she was talking about the same workshop discussed by the NGO worker. She said,

> I have never been so ashamed of myself. In our Joint Body meetings, we never discuss the history of FLO, we don't know why the white people are paying more for our tea, and what we are supposed to do with FLO. We only discuss useless (*fāltu*) things. The sisters from the *basti* knew it all. They were so smart (*chānkho*). Not only are the *basti* girls eating more nutritious food, they know how to speak, they know more about FLO. *Bahini* (younger sister) you must tell us more about this FLO business; we must learn more before you leave. Please tell us about FLO, we do not want to be *lāti* (ignorant/stupid) any more.

I was now convinced that the NGO employee was not being partial to the Women's Wing's members' performance at the Siliguri meeting. Sita then asked me the names of the Women's Wing members. I told them. Sita became very excited when she learnt that I had lived with the two Women's Wing members she had met at Siliguri. She told me "please take out your camera and show other women present here that you know the *bahinis* from the basti." I brought out my camera, and the entire group was excited about seeing the two Women's Wing members from the co-op. Soon other comparisons ensued between *basti* and *kamān* women followed by quizzing me on FLO. I gave them information on FLO and they thought it was very complex. I told them what kinds of activities Women's Wing members were planning to do with FLO premium in the cooperative. They were very impressed. They regretted that they never had Fair Trade trainings. The management did all the talking at meetings and inspections. In fact, the women told me, they did not understand when the inspections had taken place, although outside officers interviewed them at times. Women plantation workers agreed that the meetings were a big waste of time. Pushpa said, "We attend so many meetings, yet we are still stupid, we have lost our ability to speak effectively. This is why I tell you sister, when you leave, take all of us with you so that we can all escape this dreadful life."

The above example is one among many narrative instances that revealed women plantation workers' perceptions about themselves and their capabilities to change the plantation system for their own benefit. They frequently used the word *"lāti"* (stupid, ignorant) to describe themselves. In their statements, there was emphasis on becoming stupid, almost implying that plantation work produces this negative effect on workers. Another phrase that recurred in their conversation was *"hami bolnu birsechu*/we have forgotten how to speak." The latter expressed their fear of arguing with the managers.

These negative reflections were aggravated by the poverty of their daily lives. They blamed the plantation for all their misery and complained incessantly about the lack of proper pay and effective unions. Phulrani, now fifty-two years old, told me, "Of course our condition is a bit better than when I started. Then we were threatened that we will be stripped naked if we did not pluck and clean well. The managers and *Chaprāsis* were abusive. Even now they are very harsh, but at least we get our salaries." She then said, "The last good thing that the union did for us was in 1984 (pre-GNLF), when they fought for making most workers permanent,[3] and soon after, the retirement benefits started. That was 20 years ago, our wages are little compared to what the times demand, but we have been doing the same work for ages."[4]

The references to being "stupid" and "losing the power to speak" were always connected with the lack of options in women plantation workers' conversations. When I was at a different *ghumāuri* meeting a month later, Lachchmi made this revealing comment reflecting on the condition of plantation workers. She said,

> I try to motivate the women in my group. My group's record of plucking tea leaves in the factory is very good. These women plantation workers have no new ideas, no new ventures to take. How will they; nothing can happen without the owner's permission, even if they spent their own money. We follow this dreadful routine every day and are mostly interested in feeding our children and giving them some education, in the hope that they can escape the *thikā* (wage). If they want anything extra, anything good they have to depend on loans from the money lender. Women who are strong and fit can make some extra income during the plucking season.[5] For the average workers, they are tied to the dictate of the *thikā* (wage).

This notion of being tied to the dictate of the *thikā*/wage was another recurring theme in many interviews. The phrase implied the discipline imposed by the insufficient wage that made workers' options limited. The small wage limited the scope of better education for their children. It made them dependent on informal money-saving ventures, like *ghumāuri*, to stretch their buying power. I also interpreted the use of the phrase, "being tied to the wage," as a way for plantation workers to express how other systems of patriarchal control worked through the wage. Women workers could never ask for more wages because the management was tied by the state-permitted minimum wage which was uniform through the Darjeeling area. However, the dictate of the *thikā* was made ever more binding with the male union leaders devoting their attention to party activities (as outlined in chapter 5). Women complained that the shoes, umbrellas, and socks that the plantation was supposed to supply for safety were never replaced in a timely fashion. Women used their own money to keep themselves safe. In many ways the *thikā* was insufficient.

Thikā was also used to denote the strict disciplining of their work life, the verbal abuses from the male managers and male supervisors which guided how they lived in the plantation premises. Women plantation workers secretly kept their savings through *ghumāuri*. The long work hours meant that they could not engage in other money-making ventures, such as knitting or rearing animals, as much as they would have liked to. Women plantation workers also used the word *thikā* as work. I frequently noted them saying, "*Hāmilai thikāmā jānu parcha*"/ "We have to go to work." They implied that they were bound by the wage which limited their freedom of movement. The *thikā* became more binding as it could not be changed easily. A further layer of insecurity was added because *thikā* (or work) led to household conflicts. While male members of their homes were envious of their work and wage (as demonstrated in chapter 4), women knew that this wage was not enough to meet all household needs. The dictate of the wage was felt at many levels reflected in these sets of comments.

Lachmi concluded her reflections with this statement, "Women workers here are like tadpoles in water; they do not dare to come out of the known waters for the fear of being engulfed." The tadpole analogy again drew attention to their lack of freedom and work options. Plantation work was the bread and butter; if they left one plantation, it was also very hard to get work in another plantation, especially as a permanent employee. Plantations rarely recruited new workers, since the new workers (whether temporary or permanent) were always recruited from the family of a retired plantation worker. Working in the plantation was also a way of holding on to the house. In spite of the drudgery of plantation work, women rarely left their jobs.

The example of the *thikā*, when read together with constant references to being stupid or losing the power to speak, points to women plantation workers' subjective states. As I moved back and forth between the plantation and the cooperative, stark differences emerged as to how these two groups of women thought about their lives, their futures, and the collectives they had formed. Women's self-reflection about their capability at both sites was important for how they understood their political futures, the role of their collectives (*ghumāuri* and Women's Wing), and the power of their collective gendered projects of value.

During my time at the cooperative, life was routinized as well. The 1 p.m. lunch siren from neighboring plantations meant that women tea farmers, working in the mountain slopes, had to now return from work and make lunch as referenced in the introduction. I was surprised that the plantations' routine had such a hold on the lives of women tea farmers, at least temporally. Tea farmers (whether men or women) always made it a point to remind me that their work lives were very different from plantation people. I asked them why they followed the plantation siren. Premila told me that it helped them organize their day better. If they were away in the field, the siren reminded them that it was now time to go back and eat. After answering my question she paused for a moment and then said, "I know why you asked that question. You want to know what makes us different from your friends in the plantation." By this time Premila had a good idea of my research objectives; she always complained about my frequent stays in the plantation.

Women tea farmers, however, rarely envied anything about life in the plantation. They knew that being a plantation worker was difficult and was associated with negative gender ideologies in the region. One of the biggest complaints that plantation workers had was about their inability to possess land. In fact, male members of the tea cooperative always had the option of agricultural work. Possession of land provided a disguise to the male unemployment which plagued people in both plantations and the cooperative.

While the siren gave women direction in their lives at both sites, in the plantation the 1 p.m. siren meant that workers had to start their afternoon shift. The women tea farmers had a choice to go back to the field after 1 p.m. or to stay indoors and take a nap. This sense of freedom from a fixed schedule was something that the tea farmers relished and was a defining feature of their identity. They were not bound by the discipline of the *thikā*. The potential for choosing when and how much to work was critical to the women tea farmers' sense of freedom, which they shared with men. As the cooperative president explained to me, "Here any day could be a Sunday." This flexibility meant that tea farmers had more control over their time. Women tea farmers from wealthy households would spend the afternoon watching TV if they had the resources to employ other people from the village to work in their agricultural fields.

People in the two sites spoke about each other as if they came from two very different worlds; hence they were different kinds of people. While outsiders could not distinguish between the lives of the women who pluck tea and appear on the label of tea packets, there is a sharp difference between *kamān ko mānche ra basti ko mānche* (people of the plantations vs. people of the *basti*). These were different people, not because they belonged to different ethnic groups, they were all Nepali, but because their daily lives were structured differently. I took it upon myself to analyze these different claims about work and freedom, which brought me to explore the different effect that Fair Trade had on their respective lives. Throughout this book, I have shown that women tea farmers have been able to utilize Fair Trade to their benefit, albeit despite notable failures. For women plantation workers, Fair Trade was something that the management does. In this chapter, I show how the ability to claim some Fair Trade benefits has increased the existing confidence of women tea farmers, unlike women plantation workers.

It can be argued that women tea farmers needed to take aggressive steps because of their economic insecurity and their vulnerability in the tea industry. However, it is important to note that women tea farmers could take aggressive steps, in spite of being shamed, because they could not be fired, and they cultivated their own lands. The cooperative relied on their labor in producing tea and during important cooperative activities. Women tea farmers had de facto ownership of their land and what they produced, as was evident from the comment in the earlier chapter about women being the police of their own fields. Too often, economic well-being becomes a lens to gauge empowerment (Kabeer 1999). Women in the plantation of course had a regular source of income, but women tea farmers' household income was not terribly different from that of plantation workers. The average income of households at both sites ranged from Rs. 1,800 to 2,000 per month (based on income-related reflections during interviews at respective sites). This economic explanation of political activism is therefore too simplistic as it forecloses the possibility to explore the complexity of how people understand themselves at the two sites and conceive of their capabilities.

Both groups of women played important economic roles in their families and community and had done so for years, yet women tea farmers retaliated against male domination and women plantation workers did not. Women tea farmers directly negotiated practices of defaming and the double standards that existed against women in their community. The difference lay in the way the two groups of women understood themselves, their self-knowledge vis-à-vis existing moral standards to which they were subjected and which impacted their actions. Women plantation workers constantly felt that they had lost their power to speak because of the dictate of the *thikā*, expressing their alienation from the fruits of their labor. Women tea farmers on the other hand felt that they had rights to everything that they produced. They used Fair Trade to make moral claims on their land and justify their economic ambitions. The two groups of women thought about themselves as different kinds of actors.

The question of institutional structure and resource access was also very important for the way women perceive possibilities and how they imagine their future. Hence, plantation workers see their state-accorded rights to ask for a decent wage, benefits, and health provisions decrease over time because of the changes in the union priorities. Women tea farmers take the opportunity of Fair Trade stipulations to put a price on their labor and efforts to secure the economic future of their families and community.

Ghumāuri vs. Women's Wing Meetings

At both sites, women were highly aware of the systematic workings of structural power, yet there was a difference in the way women at both sites strategized to negotiate hegemonic practices. Their subjective states influenced the nature of their collective gendered projects of value. *Ghumāuri* meetings were a safe space to vent anxieties and make exploitation more habitable—a therapeutic space. Women's Wing meetings provide a place for careful planning to negotiate structural inequality. As I will soon show, Women's Wing meetings were used to plan how women could benefit from Fair Trade. They were more than places for venting, they provided time and opportunity for careful planning to change attitudes toward Women's Wing's ventures and publicly shame the male cooperative members for their double standards and their use of women for raising Fair Trade awareness.

Let me return to my previous example of the Siliguri workshop with which I began the previous section. In explaining the circumstances, Sita mentioned that the Joint Body meetings were useless, and they were not aware of inspections; they were never told about inspections. Fair Trade as a topic was also not part of their *ghumāuri* meetings, although it was a space where they discussed plantation politics. As I mentioned in an earlier chapter, the *ghumāuri* groups were very much under cover, having no formal presence. The meetings were held on holidays, every one or two months. Women plantation workers often discussed issues of loyalty and productivity in the *ghumāuri* meetings. Even when they discussed problems at work they tried to come up with help and solutions within the group. They strategized about ways of placing their concerns with the owner individually, not any organized plan of action to involve union members to take up the issue. There was no paper trail of anything that they proposed. *Ghumāuri*, as a collective space, had little potential to systematically address the structural constraints placed on women workers through low wages, unsafe work conditions, nepotism, and strict disciplining. In spite of this safe space, women felt that their futures were not going to improve any time soon; hence they are "tadpoles in water."

In *ghumāuri* meetings women often discussed the mistrust that the management displayed toward women workers in daily affairs. While otherwise extolling the skill and sincerity of women workers in front of visitors, plantation authorities would often accuse women workers of insincerity when they personally met women at work. One day, in the peak plucking month of June, I was with a group of women workers. The owner was doing his rounds. He came up to two women and made this comment, "*timihāru lakshmi chineko chainau*." When translated literally from Nepali, the statement means "You don't know your Lakshmi." In Hindu custom, Lakshmi is the goddess of wealth and prosperity. The plantation owner implied that women workers were not loyal to their work, and they did not pluck enough leaves; this was read as disrespect for work. The statement was ironical because in the peak season, women were paid extra rupees, three per kilo of plucked tea, in addition to their eight kilos of daily plucking requirement. Women looked forward to the monsoon months in spite of all the dangers (like landslides, leeches, and slippery terrain), because they could earn a little more. These kinds of comments from the owner really made women angry.

In the next *ghumāuri* meeting the two women, Nita and Kala, started talking about this comment. They complained that the productivity of tea was much lower than when they started. There was a constant pest problem after pesticide use was stopped in the plantation. One of the retired male supervisors had also told me during an interview that the discontinuation of pesticide use was not beneficial for pluckers because there was loss of productivity, i.e., fewer leaves to pluck in the high season, hence, less extra income. Nita regretted that she could not talk back to the owner. She told the group that the owner thinks that only he knows how to care about tea. Then she said, "It is because we worship tea that he makes so much money. That is why for *sāhib* the plantation is like Lakshmi. For us, tea is like our second mother, we have to be loyal and careful. We offer the season's first leaves to god, but he does not understand. We take pride in our work, and that is why we come back to worship our Lakshmi every day. So what if we don't have a temple in the factory." She made fun of the daily praying rituals in the factory temple that the owner performed.

The analogy of tea as mother was important. Most of the plantation workers were born and brought up in plantations. This was their social world and their lives had an indelible link with tea plants. The ties between the plantation and women workers were like those between a mother and her daughters—a strong bond. One could never sever ties from one's mother nor from the plantation because it was one's source of nourishment. Then Kasturi pointed out the key difference between a real mother and the tea mother. She said, "When a small child is upset, tired or sick, the child can rest on their mother's lap. They cry and mother soothes their pain, but the second mother (tea) is not that caring. We come to her, rain or shine. We sooth her pain, but she is loyal to her sons." Kasturi implied that tea as mother was more generous toward her son—the owner—who enjoyed the fruits of women's labor.

This comment can also be read as the constant neglect of women's needs within the plantation, which was perpetuated by women's own cultural production of being obedient, formed against the sexualized tropes through which they were represented.

After this comment, Nita brought out a small container and opened it in front of me. She told me "Younger sister, now I will show you the real thieves of the plantation, we catch them often." Then as soon as she opened the small container, I could see small mosquito-like insects, some half dead and some alive. These were the pests which drove down the productivity of the plantation. They could not be controlled by organic methods. She continued, "The owner does not have any idea how we protect our mother. She is only Lakshmi (wealth) for him, but she is our mother. We care for her; he is only interested in selling her." She kept saying that she would continue her work because if they stop then they will die hungry, the plantation will close. We *pahādis* (hill people) have no other option but to toil in this land. We have to be a good worker; that's the only way we can survive." Kala told me, "You have to be sincere, and then you will have no guilt." Through these kinds of *ghumāuri* sessions women plantation workers constructed meaning from their toil. The constant reiteration of sincerity was how women formed a parallel moral universe opposed to what people actually thought of them, as promiscuous, insincere and *bāthi* (street smart). In chapter 1 I demonstrated gendered, sexualized tropes about plantation women in daily life.

Attending *ghumāuri* meetings in both plantations provided me the space to understand how women made exploitation habitable. It is in their reasoning that I saw how they were treated in the plantation and how that affected their self-knowledge. Women saw their labor as indispensable for the prosperity of the plantation in its organic avatar. While they protected their second mother—tea—from harm and blemish, they themselves had to live a scarred existence, always suspected, underpaid. *Ghumāuri* meetings were like group therapy—women narrated their stories while other women listened. Sometimes the meetings would be charged. Some women would break down, but by the time they left for home, they had new ideas about where to buy the cheapest books for their children on their next visit to Kurseong town.

Women's Wing meetings were very different. They were more regular (monthly) and provided critical space for planning. Although women tea farmers were subject to norms of obedience and respectability, they also found ways to subvert these norms creatively by participating and using Fair Trade events. The Women's Wing meetings were not merely safe spaces to vent; they were more. Women tea farmers met on the eighth day of every month at 1 p. m. at the cooperative office. When they started in 1999, they were taught by the NGO to keep detailed minutes of the meetings; they continued this practice. They also had elections every two years when they changed their president, secretary, and treasurer. The Women's Wing secretary kept written records[6] of their requests to the cooperative board and their specific interactions with cooperative members. The cooperative households were spread across steep slopes and women from different villages used the meetings as a way to keep tabs on gossip about the Women's Wing's activities. There used to be small votes on issues such as who would be selected to go to training, who would go to the cooperative board meetings, who would collect savings. Women often discussed the adversities they faced in their homes.

Women's Wing meetings were also critical for consciousness-raising about Fair Trade and how the Women's Wing could benefit from Fair Trade. Active women would frequently quiz new members or the shy ones to get them to speak up in the meetings. On special occasions, like the International Women's Day, the Women's Wing president would urge all the women to reflect on why they had joined the Women's Wing. Shanta, the new president, was a really timid woman when I first met her. In the beginning of my work she was voted to be the new president so that everyone could share the leadership. In the beginning Shanta used to stammer and kept her speeches very short, but as the months elapsed her speeches grew longer and she stopped asking the other active members, "What shall I say?" Sima told me at the end of one such meeting that she could not believe how far Women's Wing members had come compared to their state in 1999. She said, "We used to sit at the back of the room during main cooperative meetings; we used to be scared talking to the men from the NGOs and our community. Now, we can also beat the table and argue when we want to."

If a woman tea farmer repeatedly failed to come for meetings, leaders of the Women's Wing would make a big deal. If someone missed a meeting and justified her absence saying that her family members got upset if she came to meetings, then the leaders would ask them, "What did you tell them in response? Much of the problem lies with the fact that you all go home and don't tell your family members what the Women's Wing is doing. If you explain they will understand. You must tell your daughters and sons about the importance of our work. We are not here to chat; we make plans here. You have to explain what our *THulo yojanā* (big business) means for the community." While making these kinds of allegations, women also knew that the problems with the Women's Wing's declining membership and the recent smear campaign by the middlemen and rich housewives had its roots in the cooperative. Women's Wing members were concerned about the exist- ing social and economic differences within the cooperative and how it impacted the future of the Women's Wing. Meetings were crucial for strategizing on confronting the president of the cooperative.

In March 2007, the governing board of the cooperative learned that the Fair Trade premium they were to get that year was consider- ably more than the previous year (a 40 percent increase). The sale of their tea had gone up in the Fair Trade–organic market, but there was also a note of caution from FLO. FLO had requested that the coopera- tive file legal registration with the West Bengal Government Societies Registration Act.[7] The letter also mentioned that many people in the cooperative were not clear about the history and specificities of Fair Trade. Among other warnings the letter also mentioned that women would have to be made part of the main cooperative board. If inspectors found these issues unresolved by the next inspection date in December 2007, the cooperative's premium would be stopped by FLO in 2008.

The letter had caused great alarm for cooperative board members who immediately came up with a *FLO Janajāgaran Kāryakram* (FLO People's-awareness campaign). They decided to use some of the 2007 premium money for these events, which would be held in all the neighborhoods within the cooperative. Soon the cooperative sent let- ters to the Women's Wing members for a general meeting with them to discuss their formal inclusion in the cooperative board. Women's Wing members already knew about this warning from FLO; they wanted to discuss the possibility of their participation in the *FLO Janajāgaran Karyakram* after careful negotiation with the cooperative president. News spread in these villages very fast. Women's Wing members knew that the president would soon request their labor for the *FLO Janajāgaran Kāryakram*. It was common for the cooperative president to request Women's Wing members to help out with the cooperative's activities. This was another way the cooperative appropriated wom- en's time and labor in official matters. Officers of the Women's Wing decided to call a meeting with the co-op board to straighten out the relationship between the Women's Wing and the cooperative and clear out the air between them. If women were going to give time and labor outside their homes for the awareness campaign, they needed some explanations from the president about his previous actions vis-à-vis the Women's Wing.

On May 8, 2007, thirty-five women tea farmers gathered at the cooperative office. The president, secretary, and treasurer of the Women's Wing were all present. It was decided in the April 8th Women's Wing meeting[8] that the agenda of the May meeting would comprise a discussion with the president of the cooperative about the specificities of the relationship between the cooperative and the Women's Wing, and would include taking stock of the activities of the women's group. In light of recent decline in the membership of the Women's Wing, women were concerned and decided that they would use the *FLO Janajāgaran Karyakram* to further their own goals of recruiting more women into the Women's Wing. Active members of the Women's Wing thought that the cooperative's male members had a role in this declining membership. Some Women's Wing members rationalized that the opposition women tea farmers faced at home about spending time in the activities of the Women's Wing, especially after the big business plan was publicized, could not be blamed on individual household members. Women tea farmers were aware of the gender and wealth differences in their community. The cooperative president's denial of sharing FLO money in 2006 (chapter 6) and then again in 2007 propelled Women's Wing members to censure the wealth and gender politics within their communities that created impediments for the women's group who were out to start a new venture. These inequalities also affected household politics (as I show in the last chapter).

At noon on May 8, 2007, Shanta *didi*, the current president of the Women's Wing, started her inaugural speech for the Women's Wing's monthly meeting. Shanta *didi* said that the Women's Wing will be successful when every household in the cooperative sends their mothers and daughters to the monthly meeting of the Women's Wing. Then she decided to answer why that was not happening. According to Shanta *didi*, the Women's Wing members could not effectively explain what went on in the women's group meetings to their family members. At the height of her speech, Shanta *didi* mentioned that women have to learn to better explain "What we do in these meetings." There was a need to justify the labor/time spent outside the house in a way which made sense to family members. "We have to tell our husbands and elders that we discuss important matters of the community in our meetings which do not just concern women, but concern the well-being of all the villages within the tea cooperative area. It is not just about chatting and taking loans, we are making plans here which will be beneficial for every household."

At around 1 p.m., the president of the tea cooperative arrived. Women's Wing members greeted him and requested him to put forth his agenda. The president started explaining that with the new Fair Trade regulations the cooperative would have to include more women. The president of the Women's Wing would now become the ex-officio member of the cooperative. The Women's Wing would now have to make a new constitution and bylaws so that their bylaws would not negatively affect the cooperative or its members. In his speech, the president continuously emphasized how the rules of the Women's Wing will only be effective once the cooperative governing board approves of it. These new Women's Wing bylaws, which would include a list of Women's Wing's future business activities, would have to be approved by the governing body of the cooperative. He also requested that Women's Wing members should help the cooperative in their *FLO Janajāgaran Kāryakram* as anticipated by Women's Wing members even before the president arrived.

At this point Shanta *didi* interrupted the cooperative president's speech and informed him that the Women's Wing wanted to use this *Janajāgaran Kāryakram* to raise awareness about the Women's Wing's activities because the Women's Wing needed new energy. She emphasized that people needed to know more about the new activities of the Women's Wing and the economic problems women faced. The president of the cooperative sarcastically replied saying that the Women's Wing was not doing "*rāmro kām*" (important work), did not have a proper agenda, and hence people thought it was a waste of time. He started complaining about the difficulties of running an organization; a skill which women were just beginning to learn.

The meeting quickly turned into a heated session between the president and the Women's Wing members. I was present, but did not speak a word. I was recording the meeting. It was too emotional a moment. I knew from previous Women's Wing meetings that women were planning such a discussion for the last six months to express their collective anxiety about the cooperative board's attitude toward women's business ventures, which they related to the legitimacy crisis women faced in their households and neighborhoods.

Shanta *didi* continued her questioning of the president and then finally asked the controversial question regarding the president's household matters. At this point other Women's Wing members joined in and cornered the president. The Women's Wing members questioned the president about his and the cooperative's role in defaming the Women's Wing's business and reputation. Here I quote a section of my recordings from this significant meeting to demonstrate how Women's Wing members related household politics and the cooperative president's actions. The cooperative president's constant disavowal of his and the cooperative boards role in neglecting the Women's Wing was clear from his utterances. Women's constant repetition of references to the politics in the president's own home was an indication of their collective desire to shame the president for his actions. This kind of a meeting was in the books for the Women's Wing ever since October 2006.

> ***Shanta didi:*** But you are aware of Women's Wing's activities and you just now told us that Women's Wing was a part of the cooperative registration. Women's Wing's president will be an ex-officio member of the cooperative board, and you support the Women's Wing. Yet your wife, who is the member of our Women's Wing and has been part of our microcredit ventures, never comes to our meetings; your house is next-door to the office. What do we make of this?

The photograph below captures the mood of the meeting.

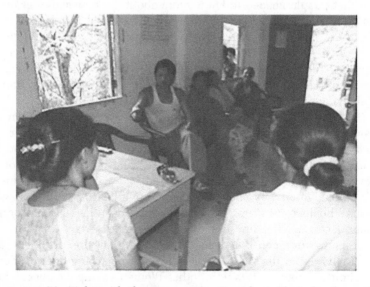

Figure 8.1. Big Fight with the Cooperative President. Photo by the author.

The president was angry and grew extremely uncomfortable and some women started smiling (as is evident in this photograph). Local village youth peeped inside from the office windows as they heard loud exchanges in the office. The president pointed a finger at the active Women's Wing members accusing them of asking personal questions, which he was not required to answer. The president kept insisting that women did not know how to keep organization and household matters separate. At this point Manju replied, "What happens in our homes is important for Women's Wing's future."

President: who is going to take charge of farming and household work? If she does not take care of my home, then how am I going to give my time for the organization? How is the cooperative going to run?

Binu: *Dāju* (elder brother), you must understand that your actions have far-reaching consequences for the survival and legitimacy of the women's group. We need to know what happens in your household. If your wife does not come to our meetings, maybe you don't let her come, maybe she does not like us. We need to know. Maybe other women are thinking the same way as she. You are like our elder brother, a respectable member of our community. Because of your experience and contribution, our cooperative will prosper, but let me reiterate something which you seem to misunderstand. Please do not interrupt me. We need to know where we as a community are making mistakes.

President: You all are blowing my family matters out of proportion. You should not let these feelings of animosity creep into your organization. This is a mistake.

Punita: These are not your personal matters anymore especially if you are the board.[9] We want you to know the reason why we need a Women's Wing. You keep telling us that we are only interested in microcredit money, but your wife also used to take loans by being a member of our group. Now your contracting business is going well, and she does not come. However, your family matters have far-reaching consequences. What happens in our families is important. You all keep saying in public meetings that women should have the same respect as men; they should move forward, be confident. In our homes women should be respected

and they should take important decisions in the household.
If all these things were happening we would not need a
Women's Wing. Men have some responsibility to support
Women's Wing.

President: My goodness . . . you are all too emotional . . .
how can you run an organization if you bring up personal
matters all the time?

Manju: For once don't speak to us as the president of the
cooperative. Don't hide behind the cooperative banner. Talk
to us as an average man who is the head of the family,
who wants women in his family to succeed. Do you ever
honestly tell your wife to go to the meetings?

President: She is a human being, not a sheep. Can I force her
to come? It is her judgment. If women want to exercise their
rights they have to do it themselves . . . no one will give it
to them in a platter . . . men cannot force them . . . every
individual should take their own decisions . . . if other
people base their decisions on joining Women's Wing looking at my household, then they are like sheep.

Punita: If it's all an individual's own decision, then why
have *FLO Janjagaran Karyakram* about Fair Trade. People
will find out for themselves before the next FLO inspection . . . they do not need awakening, because they all
have minds . . . they are not sheep! Why do you need the
Women's Wing to spread Fair Trade awareness; people can
just learn about these things on their own.

President: I am not sure why my wife does not come.

Manju: People need to understand that women's work is
important both inside and outside the home . . . this should
also be one of the messages about your upcoming *Janjagaran*
(awareness) program. You have a duty towards Women's
Wing. When you give your speeches please tell other people
not to emulate your wife, because Women's Wing is doing
important work . . . tell every women in your village it is
time to awaken.

President: Do you think if I order women in my village they will listen?

Binu: Why do you think they won't? When you gather women in your village and put them to work on your farm or on your road-work business, they listen don't they? They all listen because they know they will get money; everyone understands the significance of money . . . if we tell everyone that Women's Wing is doing something profitable just like the cooperative, I am confident, they will understand.

Manju: Please go and start a *Janajāgaran* (Awareness Campaign) about the Women's Wing in your own village before you ask us to participate in the cooperative's business.

The Women's Wing meetings were extremely important for women to address economic and social inequalities in their communities which persist to the present. The president constantly tried to put forth that the weakening of the Women's Wing and its present impediments were in no way related to the activities of the main cooperative. He emphasized that women have to become powerful by themselves; they could not ask for help. In the meeting, women's constant emphasis on the president's household matters and its relation to the defaming and weakening of the Women's Wing was a critical connection to expose the attitudes of upwardly mobile wealthy families toward the Women's Wing.

The Women's Wing members constantly made the president feel conscious about his double standards and opportunism. He sent his wife to Women's Wing as long as they needed loans. I had interviewed the cooperative president's wife, Hema, in 2004, which the president had forgotten. In 2004 Hema's husband was not the president of the cooperative. I had met her at the Women's Wing's monthly meeting. She was introduced to me as an active Women's Wing member. She had told me in that interview that women had to do more work in the home and there was constant need for money and she was taking loans. When I returned in 2006 for my formal fieldwork, Hema was a different woman. She would never come to meetings. She watched TV in the afternoon when the Women's Wing had meetings. Hema's house had more expensive furniture, her husband was thinking of buying a Jeep (secondhand car). She told me one day in 2006 that she did not have time for any organization work because she had to entertain her husband's clients in his new constructing business by making lunch and tea, and she could not come to meetings because they were held at lunchtime. Hema's comments about her preoccupation with helping her husband's business reflected discourses and practices of upward mobility in Nepali Hindu households in rural Darjeeling. Wives of rich villagers withdrew from manual labor in their own house and community.

Ghumāuri and Women's Wing were different kinds of spaces. They were shaped by the larger institutional structures in which they were embedded. *Ghumāuri* was largely underground, whereas Women's Wing saw itself as a parallel organization to that of the cooperative. This positioning gave women tea farmers a different kind of motivation, which affected the way they dealt with structural inequalities. Women's Wing directly participated in Fair Trade activities, they questioned it, whereas *ghumāuri* members had very little to do with Fair Trade. Women's Wing members identified the socioeconomic inequalities manifested itself in the sexism of cooperative board members. *Ghumāuri* members collectively narrated the indispensability of their labor for the plantation's wealth and found new hope and motivation.

The Politics of Clean Hands vs. the Politics of Clean Trade

Both women plantation workers and women tea farmers aspired to be economically better off, but their battles were pitched at different levels. As I mentioned before, instances of "everyday resistance" were sporadic among women plantation workers, but they found novel ways of protecting their bodies and souls. The focus of activism for women tea farmers was not merely protection, but also seeking economic justice and respect within their community and families for their labor and efforts. While both groups were highly conscious of the limits of their action, I contend that women tea farmers could take their struggle to a level higher than the women plantation workers. Women tea farmers used more confrontational tactics than women plantation workers to question their exploitation.

As I spent time with plantation workers for days on end, I gradually started noticing what tea plantation workers did and said to make their harsh work environments more bearable. These acts were often reflections on the plantation surveillance structure and became evident after the first couple of months of fieldwork. I would start my days waking up with them in their homes, going to work, sharing lunch, returning from work, washing, cooking, watching TV, going to worship, and chatting. I was close enough to also see how they kept themselves motivated and went about their daily work routines, which they frequently described to me as drudgery.

One such day I set out to the tea fields with Lachmi *didi's* group. After lunch we all sat in the shade till the 1 p.m. siren blew. During lunch hour (between noon and 1 p.m.) the conversation centered on what these women did to protect themselves, particularly their bodies, from plantation work. Working in the plantation meant long hours away from home; the so-called "nimble fingers" were frequently scratched and there were dark red marks on their fingers from tealeaf stains. Women often wore plastic boots, supplied by the plantation, and layers of socks to protect themselves from leeches, which were a daily threat to their health. Women had to carry umbrellas to protect themselves from the sun and rain. They also carried local medicinal herbs with them in case of a slight stomach pain or fever in the field.

During the time I spent in the plantation health centers[10] the most common complaint from workers were fever, headache, and body ache. A medical report in the plantation dispensary also noted that "women were thought to report more illness than men." Being sick was a way for them to get a day off. Their work involved heavy climbing through the steep hillslopes leading to fatigue. Women consumed a lot of painkillers. When I told one of them that painkillers were not good, I was told, "If we had enough time to rest our feet and hands we might not have consumed these medicines." If women lived too far from the health center, they would just drink a glass of warm homemade rice wine to ease their pain.

Women were very interested in cleanliness. At 7 a.m., they would be immaculately dressed, with their *sindoor* (vermillion used by married women), *bindi*, powder, and lipstick, and most importantly they would keep long polished nails. Plantations forbade the latter. Organic certification rules forbade any use of knife, blade, or plucking with nails. The correct way to pluck was with one's fingertips. Women's obsession with clean manicured hands was a way of concealing their drudgery. When I used to travel to town with the plantation workers, they would never fail to buy a nail color. Bindu told me that keeping clean hands was very important, especially when they went to town. They did not want people to know that they were plantation workers. "Our hands give out our occupation. When we go to town, we want to momentarily forget our lives of misery and hardship. We want to be clean for some time."

Women plantation workers often wore gloves while plucking leaves. If they were caught in the act of using gloves while plucking, they could be suspended. They stitched these gloves at home from old umbrella cloth, because the material for the gloves had to be waterproof. They never bought gloves in town because word might spread that gloves are being used in the plantation. The obsession with a clean appearance was more pronounced among the young women workers, who were between the ages of eighteen and forty-five. Older women rarely wore nail polish. Lachmi *didi*, their group leader, explained why these little ways of protecting their bodies were important. She further explained that the *thikā*/wage allowed women to take these small steps to keep them happy; there is no one to care for them. The Darjeeling tea logo, which distinguishes it from other Indian teas, displays the

Figure 8.2. Woman Plantation Worker with Gloves On. Courtesy of Sue and Jon Hacking.

hands of the plantation workers as perfect, not showing bruises or stains, making this representation different from the actual physical appearance of the workers. Official advertisements of Darjeeling tea on billboards also depict well-dressed women plantation workers concealing their painful toil.

Women plantation workers' perseverance and toil was written on their hands. They were proud of their work, but for them their hands embodied their struggle and their limited options. They never asked me to photograph them with their gloves on. In spite of these ways of protecting themselves, women plantation workers came back to work day after day, without fail. While the plantation owner used essentialisms to explain women's motivation, women put forward very different reasons for their motivation. Women who worked in the sorting department were exposed to different kinds of hazards; there was so much tea dust that they could develop breathing problems. There were about a dozen women in the sorting department. They would make fun of me and ask whether they would all fit in my *kameez* (Indian shirt) pocket so that they could escape.

Pluckers envied sorting department women. Plantation workers in the sorting department, who were slightly better paid than plain pluckers, had their own anxieties. Gangā *didi*, the leader in the sorting department, in her mid-fifties, was a motherly figure. I was more helpful for the sorting department women when I was around. Sorting involved less skill for a novice like me. Gangā told me that I should demand my *hazirā* (pay) since I spent entire workdays with them. Then she asked me whether I had a breathing ailment. She told me "You think our work is easier than the pluckers', but the dangers here are silent, don't you see that many of us wear glasses; we have to sort all the bad leaves out; it's hard work. Come winter you will not even recognize your Gangā *didi*. When sickling begins, we spend days in the winter sun, we become black and our skin is burnt." Gangā *didi* almost implied that in winter they step down in the plantation hierarchy to join the ranks of ordinary pluckers. A sense of everyday erasure.

The politics of clean hands signified a struggle that women wanted to forget in their everyday lives. They were extremely aware of their misery and the limited options for organized resistance. A lot of thought went into keeping one's hands clean. The plantation workers would frequently tell me, "The least we could do is keep our hands clean. What else can you do in this life of *thikā* (wage); maybe my next life will be better?" In the absence of large-scale collective organizing, women plantation workers performed these acts as a form of escaping the governance of the *thikā*. The subjective understanding of their possibility for action resulted in these small acts, accompanied by their constant lament about losing their ability to speak.

Women plantation workers and tea farmers were engaged in different kinds of visibility politics. Unlike women plantation workers, who were always trying to hide their toil, women tea farmers were engaged in making visible the value of their labor in the prosperity of their community. Male members of the cooperative would frequently talk about the cooperative as a movement of small farmers, reinforced by the rhetoric that they got from the NGO and the plantation to which they sold their tea.

In March 2007, the cooperative had an annual general meeting. During this time festivities were planned to greet the plantation owner and honor him for his support of small farmers. This was a way to ensure the durability of the plantation–co-op contract. The plantation owner was the chief guest and in his public speech he extolled the efforts of the women. He said that women possessed the natural quality of *māyā* (love/care/compassion), which they infuse in the tea leaves throughout the year. Without the *māyā* of women, the cooperative movement would not have been successful. He proclaimed that the plantation was their partner in fighting for the rights of small farmers, but it was the women who gave Darjeeling tea its quality through their *māyā*.

While the plantation owner made his speech, I was with the Women's Wing members, taking pictures. They wanted a picture of their activities at the ceremony. As soon as the plantation owner spoke of *māyā*, the women tea farmers laughed out aloud. Then Sushila laughed and said, "We don't believe in doing things for *māyā* anymore, those days are gone." Women's Wing members had agreed to prepare the feast for the day for a small fee for Rs. 500 ($11). Previously the Women's Wing would provide such services for free. In a recent confrontation, Binu had told the president of the cooperative, "We are not here to cook your rice and pluck leaves." The dispute was settled with an agreement through which the cooperative board agreed to pay money for the Women's Wing's services.

In the picture on the next page we can see male cooperative members sitting in on the celebrations, while a board member makes his speech. On the speaker's left there are huge rocks behind which Women's Wing members were cooking the meal. The smoke coming out from the fire is also seen around the rocks. This time the Women's Wing members demanded money for their labor, which was previously mostly hidden. Through this act, women made visible their silent work which

Figure 8.3. Scene at the SKS Annual General Meeting. Photo by the author.

was important for the cooperative's success. As Karuna later told me, it is because we have *māyā* that the men can count on us, but too much *māyā* will result in the obliteration of our group. It is also because of *māyā* that women can do *swāchchā vyāpar* (clean/fair trade). The comments of the plantation owner and the Women's Wing members were laden with gender essentialisms. Gender essentialisms became a way to communicate the battle over labor and resources in the cooperative. The desire for clean trade drew on a gendered moral economy through which labor was mobilized in the plantations and the cooperative. Women tea farmers, however, were able to cash in on this essentialism by putting a price on cooking for this important occasion.

Conclusion

The institutions in which women worked and lived and resources they could access affected women tea plantation workers' and smallholder tea farmers' subjectivities and aspirations. Plantation workers'

subjectivities were affected by an understanding of the limited possibility within the plantation system. Their sense of limited possibility was reinforced because the *ghumāuri* activities only helped them
cope with the discipline of the *thikā* (wage). Women tea farmers, on
the other hand, directly negotiated with the cooperative to fulfill their
desires. The possibilities available to them within the cooperative
structure gave them relatively more confidence. Women tea farmers'
narratives about their economic and political action revealed a sense
of confidence. Women tea farmers frequently mentioned that they had
come a long way and were no longer afraid "to beat the table."

Women plantation workers and women tea farmers were engaged
in different kinds of battles—they mobilized at different scales with
their gendered projects of value. Also important to note here is the
mobilization of Fair Trade ideas by women tea farmers in interpreting
themselves and their struggles, through the invocation of *swāchchā
vyāpar*. The greater exposure to Fair Trade training in the cooperative
made women aware of what they could do (or not) with Fair Trade.
Fair Trade gave them a new language to publicly enact their subjective
desires. While both groups exercised agency, their battles took different
shapes depending on how they navigated multiple intersecting inequities through their everyday cultural and economic entrepreneurialism
and networks of talk.

Conclusion

Everyday Sustainability

Over the last eleven years, every time I saw a neon lit billboard at a
U.S. airport with smiling faces of women refugees posing with their
pretty Fair Trade–certified handicrafts, or Fair Trade publicity material celebrating the survival stories of women beneficiaries across the
globe, the voices of women from Darjeeling's out-of-the-way places
have reverberated in me. Their rebuke of development, their anger,
their excitement about new business plans, and the sharp humor with
which they joke about all *yojanas* (development projects including
Fair Trade) have filled me with cynicism and hope at the same time.

Cynicism comes from witnessing the hubris of social justice, as
it plays out in the global stage of activism, with distinct local manifestations and material effects, oblivious to women's situated histories, entrepreneurialisms, and everyday realities. Hope, because this
decade-long feminist ethnography has convinced me that no development policy is able to sap poor women of their creative potential: their
everyday innovations that keep them grounded in an everyday street
feminism deeply wary of agents of the aid or the academic world.

In the middle of 2015 I learned that some of the women in
SKS have formed a new self-help group called *Makhmali* which was
completely independent of SKS or any NGO. Women pooled together
money and made small items for consumption like knitwear, pickles,
snacks, and also *Hāthe chiā* (homemade raw tea) in nearby villages.
The business was running well for these twelve women and they were
now planning to access local bank or *panchāyat* loans based on their
savings. I asked Binu why the name *Makhmali*? She quickly grabbed
my hand and took me outside her house pointing at the bushes of
purple flowers called *Makhmali* in Darjeeling. *Makhmali* flowers look

fragile but endure the harshness of Darjeeling winter bringing color and charm to the garden before spring arrived. The emphasis in Binu's explanation was on beauty, endurance, and survival. "We could not find a more befitting name," she said; "its like our ambitions and work which survive the dictates of the cooperatives' men." Thus, gendered projects of value took many turns in the tea farming villages in the last decade, sometimes trying to engage with Fair Trade, sometimes avoiding it by establishing *Makhmali*, but never losing sight of what was possible for them—their everyday sustainability.

Their understanding of what is sustainable is not without blind spots, just like our engagements in social justice that are grounded in our lifestyles and political choices. I want to refrain from all possible essentialisms in proposing something akin to "all solutions are at the grassroots" and Vandana Shiva-like deeply problematic celebrations about women's intrinsic understanding of sustainability and so on. Yet it is at the grassroots that one witnesses the drama of gender and sustainable development unfold in its excesses. That is where one witnesses the catachrestic (Spivak 1993, see also chapter 6) dissection of the "good" in commodified global justice, aka, Fair Trade.

In this book I have upheld the catachrestic possibilities created through enacting "gendered projects of value" at the margins of conscious capitalism. These gendered projects of value weave economic and social entrepreneurialism bringing about women's situated justice imaginaries. I reiterate that long-term ethnographic analysis of gendered projects of value can contribute to current understandings of gender and sustainability, scholarship on transnational justice regimes, and feminist debates over empowerment under neoliberal systems of development and governance as well as contemporary research on Fair Trade.

The creative way women sustain their everyday loves—albeit with its imperfections—the way they organize their lives and exercise their power at opportune moments stands in such sharp contrast to the pop-feminist notions of individualized gender justice, where an individual loan is prioritized as solution from poverty as opposed to bolstering existing collective bargaining mechanisms and making states and state agents like plantation owners more accountable. The global call for privatized gender justice now stands at an all-time high. Publicity materials for nonprofits and Corporate Social Responsibility[1] campaigns frequently bombard the public with giant neon images of poor women of color from the global South accompanied by captions like "I Am Powerful." An excerpt from Oxfam's recent campaign for legal support of women farmers' land rights states, "I plough. I till. I sow. I water. I harvest. I feed. I am the farmer. I want my land."[2] While well-meaning and promoting private property rights for farmer women, the campaign paints women's rural work lives in monochrome. If the reality of women-headed households in India were factored in I think the representation of the farmer, in addition to carrying a plough, would have to include instances of her engaging in petty trade in non-agricultural products for starters (see also Lahiri Dutta 2014).

This agentive celebration of women's individual power without attention to any structural impediments is the key ingredient of books in the moral marketing shelves at leading bookstores and upscale grocery stores like Whole Foods, adorned with Nick Kristoff's *Half the Sky*. These books advocate for care and compassion to rescue otherwise resourceful women from the clutches of patriarchy in their own communities. Liberal justice czars like Kristoff and his ilk (in the global South) mirror the activities of the well-meaning gender specialists advocating for global solidarities to empower women. However, the ideas of powerful women they advance are "enframed" (Brooks 2006) in static notions of who these individual women are. Marina Lazreg (2002, 133) aptly describes these problematic global feminist interventions in discourse and practice as "containment through inclusion" where the radical critique of market-based development is drowned out with the hysteria of doing good. Hence, subaltern women may speak but only a selection of their statements will be heard and disseminated—those phrases or words are then quickly coded in the register of benevolence as another success story.

My book's contention is that in this impetus to save women there is a categorical disavowal of the impending political economies of marginalization as the chapters in this book have amply documented. Good intention is not enough; one needs patience, less sympathy, more critical empathy, and extended time to unravel successive betrayals of economic development as seen from the grassroots. Self-appointed advocates also have to understand that Fair Trade is just a drop in the ocean in the face of continuing inequities related to consumption and production, where 75 percent of the world's energy, and 80 percent of its other resources, are consumed by the mere 20 percent of the population found in the OECD members (Sexsmith 2012, 43).

Interestingly Fair Trade enthusiasts from the United States are shocked to find poor people watching WWE wrestling and sporting Bob Marley T-shirts, but they have not reconciled their own privilege of driving SUVs and drinking Fair Trade–certified lattes and English

Breakfast tea every morning. In the drive to "do something" for poor women in the global south, I wonder if they think about women in the U.S. inner cities whom they could help with less carbon foot printing—would that not be more sustainable? The answers to these questions require that we engage in a healthy dose of reflexivity and know our place in the justice machine. The women in this book are also India's daughters[3] with much less privilege to tell their stories, since they do not have the networks in place like Leslie Udwin and they do not have the necessary feathers and bobbles to get them a noticeable place in the global "Oppression Olympics" for a sensational documentary (see also Tania Li 2000, 2001; Chowdhury 2011).

In this age of sound bites and app-based donation possibilities (like kiva.org micro-loans, see Moodie 2013), the sky is the limit for making the world a better place, but we must also address the mixed messages of our willful engagement to save women (Abu Lughod 2011). I recently saw a publicity image in Fair Trade USA's Facebook site celebrating the activism of César Chávez, the noted Latino labor activist. For me it was another instance of mixed messages, since in Darjeeling Fair Trade is assisting with union busting in very sophisticated ways (see chapter 5) that César Chávez would probably not approve for celebrating plantations and certifying them Fair Trade.

Uma Narayan probably has the best assessment of the current justice-scape epitomized in Kristoff's book. She writes:

> The book offers little sustained analysis of what it would mean to recognize poor women in impoverished countries as rights-bearers, though it pervasively represents them as victims. They appear to be most victimized by local patriarchs, who subject them to rape, to pregnancies that result in maternal mortality and to sexual trafficking and who insist on spending sparse household cash on alcohol, tobacco and sugar. While I have no objections to underscoring the brutalities inflicted by local patriarchy, I do have serious objections to what is left out of the causal picture. One is given very little sense of the vast global economic and political forces that impoverish these women's lives and cause them to attempt to survive in the middle of armed conflicts and economic chaos. The huge disparities of wealth between rich and poor nations and between the global affluent and the global poor appear to simply exist, without cause or explanation. The authors' stress on the

charitable activities of affluent well-intentioned Westerners
as a central mode of securing the empowerment of poor
Third World women is, arguably, at odds with their status
as rights-bearers. (Narayan 2010, 5)

Fair Trade is another chapter in this "enframed" global-justice
drive, where people are not just donating a tiny part of their disposable income for the needy; they get to consume their stories of
survival and the wonders of Western intervention when using their
disposable income to pay a tad bit extra for their morning cup of
English Breakfast (albeit produced in SKS) Fair Trade Organic Certified Small Farmers' organization that is actually illegal in the Indian
tea industry. Trade-not-aid may be the mantra of Fair Trade advocates,
but for women in Darjeeling Fair Trade is like "missionary impulse"
(Fernandes 2013) where mostly rich brown and white people come to
their communities and tell them what's best for them and ask them
to subscribe to another *yojana* (scheme, policy). As they often asked
me "money must have overflowed in the west, right? Or why will
they pay more for our tea?"

The comment about cash-overflow drives home that we need to
understand how the poor create their own literacies (Massey 1991),
sometimes their own fetishes to engage this vastly unequal world.
Such counter-fetishes about the novelty of Western development are
produced to navigate the commodified essentialisms about their pre-
political lives circulating in justice-scapes (as seen in chapter 4). They
have to translate what Fair Trade means for them even when the NGO
officials have left. They learn through practice and through meta-con-
versations about their everyday realities reflected in what I have conceptualized as "gendered projects of value." We do not need a big data
set to get the smoking-gun proof that the poor may have ways to reap
benefits of Fair Trade—they have learned to make hay when the sun
shines since the time of the *kuire sahibs* (white men). One needs to
understand how women are finding solutions to economic and political exigencies facing their communities in non-essentialist ways.

The solutions women come up with are not because they are
closer to nature in some kind of essentialist ecofeminist way. They
are not telling us to abandon all plans for development; how can they,
since their self-images are very much tied to what we all desire—prosperity, security, and the availability of disposable income. Something
that policy feminists, as soon as they read my book, will interpret as an
indication of full-fledged endorsement of market-based development.

Figure. C.1. Little Girl Going to Office. Photo by the author.

In this image a little girl in a tea-farming household is seen engaged in the "play" of going to office. Note the sharp contrast of this little girl's outfit from her *nini* (grandmom). Her *nini* explained to me that dressing up, taking that bag, and wearing her shoes was her favorite thing to do when she is not at elementary school. In a way this little girl's play reflects women's engagement with Fair Trade since many women farmers wanted their daughters to have *"service kaam* (work)*"* in a school or bank and they hoped that their entrepreneurial ventures would support such dreams. Everyday cultural productions in household and community life reflect a desire for mobility and economic stability not associated with agricultural life.

These depictions of village life will also upset armchair leftists (with their upper-caste and class privilege intact). They would read the celebration of "cash overflow" or these cultural productions (like in image C.1) as the deafening of the indigenous alternatives and hegemonic conquest of indigenous ways by NGO-ization. Leftist feminists in India are not far behind on such quick conclusions about what the poor need; everyone has a sound-bite solution ready, but not the time to engage in the everyday. The reality in rural Darjeeling is of course much more complex; it takes time to understand where the rubber meets the road, costly time which cannot be made up in fly-by-night activism including instagramming about odd service-learning projects in a village (Kascak and Dasgupta 2014), while simultaneously shopping your hearts out at your local co-op. It requires that we address everyday gendered realities of social reproduction and cultural production in the West and the rest, which has reached the point of ecological crisis due to over-consumption (although some would even deny that we are indeed on that path).

Amidst promises and proclamations of gender justice via populist marketing and commercial feminist projects, I always ponder the questions women tea plantation workers and smallholder tea farmers, two distinct producer groups in Darjeeling's certified Fair Trade–Organic tea industry, repeatedly asked me during my ethnographic research over the last nine years: "Why now, sister; where were these people when we needed them most? What can Fair Trade do to change our plight? Our smiling faces are famous all over the world, but does anyone care about us in Darjeeling? No." This book, I hope, has driven home the point that sustainable development is only possible when the everyday is in focus in a grounded way by reckoning with "gendered projects of value." It is precisely because of this lack of respect for the everyday that women in Darjeeling feel the need to disassemble and reassemble the tenets of the Fair Trade movement to write, converse, and make visible their own justice imaginaries and practices. Northern propaganda around Fair Trade and its impact is replete with smiling faces and upbeat stories—survival narratives—from women in producer communities—hyper-representations that conceal situated gendered activisms around Fair Trade.

I find hope in the writings of fellow feminist scholars who are thinking about sustainability in the context of gendered processes of social reproduction. Kathleen Sexsmith (2012, 42–43) in analyzing the failed negotiations of the "Ten Year Framework of Programs (10YFP) for Sustainable Consumption and Production (SCP)" of the UN Commission on Sustainable Development's (UNCSD)'s 19th session writes that

> . . . by taking Western consumption trends for granted and refocusing energies on the environmental impacts of production processes the debate has obscured the need to address inequalities ascribed in social relations. Gender-based inequities have been marginalized in the SCP debate, in particular. By proposing technical fixes and tweaking around the environmental margins of the global chains of labor and products that structure the world economy, this discourse has rendered invisible the feminized spheres of reproductive work that support activities at every node of the production chains. The new solutions therefore falsely presume the gender neutrality of consumption and production relations, and, in doing so, preclude development alternatives that would situate environmental improvements in relation to the gendered contexts of productive, consumptive, and reproductive work.

My insistence on the importance of a gendered power-inflected discussion of social sustainability is very much in line with what Sexsmith has outlined above.

Proponents of decentralized sustainability practice need to move beyond the discussion of economic and ecological (of the triple bottom-line approach) efficiency if they really want to understand how women interpret emerging sustainability regimes.

The concept of social and cultural sustainability also enables a more nuanced understanding of two important concepts relevant to gender and sustainable development: vulnerability and livelihood diversification. I believe that women's situated conceptualizations of vulnerability vis-à-vis their resource environment are mediated by their self-perceptions of their social vulnerability, which in turn drive the individual and collective search to diversify their livelihoods. Women plantation workers often emphasized to me the bondage of *thikā*. *Thikā* in practical terms meant much more than wage-work; it was a metaphorical representation of the intense patriarchal disciplining of women at the workplace and at home. The gender ideologies pertaining to women plantation workers helped in controlling their actions; specifically, managers strictly monitored the women's non-plantation economic activities and awarded bonus payments accordingly. Even though the women workers took concrete actions in their own informal collectives—*ghumāuri* groups—they recognized their structural vulnerability by describing themselves as "tadpoles in water." Women are well positioned to understand the possibilities and limitations of sustainability policies in their particular political and cultural situations.

Smallholder women tea farmers were also under patriarchal scrutiny, some of it self-imposed, because they perceived themselves as housewife-entrepreneurs who had higher social status than plantation women. In the absence of a regular wage, they were always planning new ventures to sell various produce and diversify their livelihoods. In such a scenario, single-commodity Fair Trade certification imposed "unfair" structures that limited their attempts at diversification. They chose to negotiate with local patriarchs in the cooperative as part of a larger strategy to gain recognition for their invisible labor. Further, their somewhat successful encounter with development programs and access to land had greatly heightened their self-esteem despite their struggle against patriarchal constraints. These concrete, gendered self-perceptions led them to bargain very differently with their families, cooperative members, and Fair Trade bureaucrats, as evident from many ethnographic instances in this book. They often referred to themselves as the "police of their fields." Consequently, women plantation workers limited their engagement with Fair Trade, whereas women tea farmers actively engaged with Fair Trade ideas and practices. The institutional structures of which these women were a part—namely, the plantation and the cooperative—were both patriarchal and exploitative of women's vulnerability, but they did alter women's self-perceptions. Such self-perceptions of vulnerability or strength within distinct political fields need to be factored into any assessment of the success of sustainable development.

Thus, women tea farmers and plantation workers engage in different kinds meaning-making around sustainability projects based on self-perceptions of their social location and associated gendered projects of value. Their self-making projects tempered by gender ideologies of respectability at the two sites (plantation and cooperative), result in different kinds of "gendered projects of value." In Darjeeling sustainable development, in the garb of Fair Trade policies and practices, is frequently subjected to these social expectations (Ferguson 1990) driven by women's situated assessments of how Fair Trade can (or cannot) enable them to advance their gendered projects of value.

This book focuses on "gendered projects of value" and will enable scholars and practitioners to recognize how development ventures acquire gendered meaning at the "Bottom of the Pyramid." Such mean-ing-making, evident in their narratives, help us understand women's chronicling of their own empowerment pathways while exploring new collective possibilities for community-level change. Gendered projects of value direct our attention to processes (political, cultural, economic) that have shaped the threshold of their contemporary maneuvers at the individual and collective level. It also facilitates our understanding of where contemporary sustainability initiatives figure in these efforts.

I propose that a bottom-up method of dealing with notions of sustainability since a return to indigenous or communal practices might not get us very far when thinking about the alternative collec-tive desires nurtured by poor women. This is why on a theoretical, methodological, and political level we need to engage hybridity (see also chapter 1) We also need to think about what kind of "location" we communicate in thinking about these alternatives and representing the everyday lives of poor women as feminists. Do women who are critical of Fair Trade not use it in any way? If they do use Fair Trade poli-cies, does that mean they are in some way subordinated? What kind of "Global Literacies" (Chatterjee 2009) do we produce about women's engagement with market-based sustainable development? Here I heed Amanda Swarr and Richa Nagar's (2011) caution to scholars engaged in representing the local and the global in feminist collaborative trans-national praxis where the local becomes the unquestioned place for engendered pure resistance or counter-hegemony.

Swarr and Nagar raise an important issue when thinking about "oppositional consciousness" to neoliberal hegemony. In this book I have dealt with this question further by exploring whether women in Darjeeling's tea sector display what could be called a global under-standing of their specific location as they chronicle their own pathways to empowerment. During my fieldwork I often heard statements such as "everything in the United States must be Fair Trade, or else why were people prosperous there" or "there must have been an overflow of cash since we are getting money in Darjeeling" or "why would they care about Fair Trade in Darjeeling." Women imagine their well-being, capabilities, and everyday economic and cultural entrepreneurialism in comparative monetary terms. Whether working inside or outside of the plantations, they constantly devise ways to better their financial situations. Therefore, they often contemplate affluence in the West, of which Fair Trade is clearly a product, and why it does not attend to their financial inadequacies. They are also deeply aware of the appro-priation of their images and stories to increase the value of Fair Trade. *Ghumāuri* is a shield against that. This desire for monetary stability is not necessarily evidence of adopting neoliberal entrepreneurialism. Women's ambition for respect and success are much more complicated, as many chapters in this book have upheld.

The women smallholder tea farmers I write about have had many years of exposure to microcredit policies. It was through their encounters with microcredit that women reimagined their labor of social reproduction (*sakaunu*) as a form of *business* (see also Sen and Majumder 2015). Women cultivated an entrepreneurial subject position in which they avoided loans and turned to mutual lending. Their entrepreneurialism was geared toward eliminating intermediaries and reducing dependency in their small businesses. Everyday entrepreneurialism was celebrated but not the burden of loans. Such decisions and reinterpretations illustrate the difficult cultural terrain women have to navigate in engaging in various forms of entrepreneurialism.

The creative appropriation of this global discourse of entrepreneurialism then became a "register" (Foucault 1987) through which women interpreted the effects of Fair Trade. The juxtaposition of *sakaunu* with the modern, small-business directives of NGOs enabled them to secure local resources on their own terms. To be just and "fair," Fair Trade had to become more accountable to their everyday needs. Their appropriation also exposed the interdependence of global regulations with local patriarchies and with their desire to preserve their reputations and respect for their labor without giving up the idea of a "business." When we look in detail at how women apply their newfound entrepreneurial subjectivities to make Fair Trade policies more suitable to their gendered political field, we realize they play off one kind of global ethics of empowerment against another, challenging the assumption that their agency lies in only reviving the indigenous, local, and communal (such as *ghumāuri* activities of women plantation workers). Even when they fall back on homegrown cultural resources like *ghumāuri*, one needs to understand that as a "traditional" practice *ghumāuri* has always been about sustaining the everyday needs of eating, living, and aspiring in a very different historical period.

Ever since I began this project eleven years ago, my colleagues and students have asked me "So does Fair Trade work for the women you research with in Darjeeling?" My default response has always been "It is complicated." This response has been received with mixed feelings by my graduate and undergraduate students who still hope to do something good somewhere in the world. So many times they have asked me to take them with me to Darjeeling to help with Fair Trade. They have brought me boxes of Fair Trade tea from big grocery chains since these students are not members of co-ops, they are mostly working-class folks who are strapped with debt. Some of them know that I have a perspective on Tom's shoes and I have discussed their guilt of privilege many times. But every time they ask me when they can come along with me to do "Fair Trade" work, I have hesitated and asked myself whether the structures are in place to translate their passion and potential hard work into something meaningful. Are they prepared to navigate the fault lines of the emerging global morality market with their commodified affect (see also Brondo 2013; West 2012; Freeman 2014)?

In 2013 my undergraduate students in "Anthropology of Gender" read an article that I wrote about women's struggles with Sānu Krishak Sansthā. At the end of the class discussion one of them asked me why there is no Fair Trade store in her rural southern town. I really had no answer, I asked her to think about why. What kind of Fair Trade would her small-farmer family in Georgia want to see? While women in Darjeeling's rural areas ask me whether in the USA everything is Fair Trade, in the United States some rural college students in Georgia do not understand why they cannot buy Fair Trade products in small towns so that they can help. The structural challenges of sustainable development are interconnected. Yet current transnational sustainability and social justice initiatives isolate products and people to be Fair Trade–certified in niches leading to partial solutions. Unless systemic questions about gender, work, consumption, profit, and everyday sustainability are raised by everyone to understand collective complicities and mutual responsibility in non-patronizing, non-essentialist ways, we shall only see Fair Trade, not *Swachcha Vyāpār*.

Notes

Introduction

1. According to Fair Trade Labeling Organization International, organizations like SKS are called Small Producer Organizations or SPOs.

2. I detail the nuances of what Fair Trade and organic stipulations are in chapter 3. Generally when a food or beverage product is Fair Trade certified it indicates that it was produced under the international standards of organic farming as stipulated by the certifying institution. Fair Trade certification is an ethical stamp of assurance, which tells consumers that their food or beverage was produced under sound labor and humanitarian conditions. Certified products are premium priced, where the premium is routed back to producer communities for capacity building projects of which women's empowerment is a key emphasis area. In Darjeeling's certified tea plantations Fair Trade and Organic certification went hand in hand.

3. Plantation workers commonly referred to non-wage plantation monetary resources as "fund."

4. Informal revolving support and money saving groups found among women in Darjeeling's plantations. I detail them in chapter 5, 6, and 7.

Chapter 1

1. Another term for Nepalis popularized by the British Colonizers. Also spelled as Gorkha.

2. Both plantation and cooperative names, as well as participants of research participants are pseudonyms unless they are public figures.

Chapter 2

1. A spacious car made by the Indian multinational TATA popular in Darjeeling as privately run shared-rides vans.

2. Lepchas are popularly known as the original inhabitants of Darjeeling before the Nepalis migrated to work in plantations.

3. The intention of this book is not to provide a comprehensive his-torical account of Darjeeling and Indian tea production. Other scholars such as Sharit Bhowmick (1981) and K. Ravi Raman (2010) have written in detail about the political economy of tea production in North Bengal and South India, respectively. Piya Chatterjee's feminist historical and ethnographic work in North Bengal lays the groundwork for understanding these gendered political economies and I build on her contributions to demonstrate the specificity of Darjeeling's gendered landscape of tea production within and outside planta-tions (Chatterjee 1995, 2001).

4. Early scholarship on the "politics of recognition" concentrated on the efforts of marginalized groups or citizens within a nation to gain public recognition and prominence (Taylor 1992, 34). The formulation was used to highlight the limitations of liberal justice systems, under which people belong-ing to specific cultural groups were not respected or represented in public insti-tutions. Fraser (1997), through a discussion of the "recognition-redistribution" dilemma, challenged the contours of the liberal democratic models of justice. For her "politics of recognition" was expressed in the "New Social Move-ments," which made identity politics the centerpiece of struggles.

5. By "subnationalism" I refer to the political and cultural struggles of Nepalis in India who face cultural marginalization within the Indian nation. Nepali workers migrated to Darjeeling and adjoining areas in the early 1800s to work in the tea plantations of the East India Company and they have lived there ever since. They have been fighting since the 1980s to demand their homeland—Gorkhaland—a separate state for them within India. The movement was spearheaded by the Gorkha National Liberation Front (GNLF), a local political party, devoted to the ethnic cause of Nepalis in India. This struggle has taken various forms, but recently it has centered on the preoccupation among Nepali leaders with creating a unified Nepali identity, which I refer to in this book as the "cultural politics of subnationalism" and frame it as a form of "politics of recognition" using Nancy Fraser's (1997) terminology. The first Gorkhaland movement began in the 1980s culminating in the formation of Darjeeling Gorkha Hill Council, a semi-autonomous administrative unit within the state of West Bengal. This was also a time when many subgroups within Nepalis sought scheduled tribe status and also found ways for Dajreeling to be under the sixth schedule. Since 2007 a new movement began to revive the cause for statehood for Indian Nepalis living in Darjeeling, India, which led to the formation of Gorkhaland Territorial Adminstration (GTA) under the new party Gorkha Janamukti Morcha (GJM). These successive subnational move-ments have also resulted in the formation of political outfits such as the Demo-cratic Front and the Darjeeling wing of the TMC and the BJP are also gaining hold along with the formation of "development boards" for "tribals" like the Lepcha Development Board and many others trying to gain in the oppression olympics as demonstrated in Darjeeling's regional context.

6. I use the word cooperative to talk about the institutions representing non-plantation smallholder tea producers in Darjeeling. Fair Trade organiza-tions refer to these as Small Producer Organizations (SPO). My use of the word

cooperative also reflects the struggle of Sānu Krishak Sansthā (SKS) to become a formally recognized cooperative. They later settled for "Society Registration" and replaced the word cooperative with the word *sanstha*, which in Nepali means an organization.

7. The Nepali word *pāhāDi* means people belonging to the hill areas. It denotes a particular kind of place-based identity distinguishing Nepalis from people in the plains.

8. Henchmen of the plantation owner, supposedly his favorite Nepali male supervisors.

9. *Partybazi* implies working for the local political party. At the time of this interview the Gorkha National Liberation Front (GNLF) was fighting for greater cultural and political recognition for Nepalis of Indian descent living in Darjeeling and other places in India.

10. It is another name for the plantation owner. It is also spelled as *Sāhib*, but in Darjeeling it is pronounced differently and hence I use "*sahib*."

11. It means people of the hills. People in Darjeeling tend to think that they are not as cunning and opportunistic as plains people.

12. Nepali migrants came to Darjeeling almost 180 years ago, and through their stay have acquired citizenship rights. Barring new migrants, most Nepalis in Darjeeling now have voting rights and ration cards. Ration cards entitle them to subsidized the purchase of food items from government-run grocery stores. In India, ration cards are used as proof of Indian citizenship.

13. This talent contest is very similar to "American Idol."

14. *Momo* is a Nepali style dumpling very popular in India, and primarily considered as a Nepali delicacy. *Momo* is originally a Tibetan delicacy.

15. GNLF stands for Gorkha National Liberation Front the dominant political party based in Darjeeling. The reason why the word "Gorkha" is used to designate Nepali people in India has a very complicated history. For this chapter, I use Gorkha and Nepali as synonymous. When I was doing my book fieldwork this was the dominant political party in the Darjeeling Gorkha Hill Council (DGHC) and also in the plantation labor unions. Before GNLF was formed, in the pre-Gorkhaland Agitation days, CPIM (Communist Part of India, Marxist) and ABGL (affiliated to the Congress party) were the dominant political parties influencing the labor unions. After the Agitation, this party lost all its political teeth in Darjeeling. The Communists in India are parliamentary communists, more like social democrats.

16. The majority of the population of India's North Eastern States, Nagaland, Manipur, Tripura, Meghalaya, Mizoram, Arunachal Pradesh, and parts of Assam have different physical features. In common parlance they are said to have "mongoloid" features. They have much lighter skin, straight hair, and smaller eyes. Dietary practices also differ. These differences are used as markers of racial difference, which then are used to culturally marginalize people from India's North East. In my own experience of having many close friends from Nagaland and Manipur, they would jokingly call me Indian. They would complain to me that other girls from "India" think that women from India's North East were sexually promiscuous. States in India's North East are also

under-developed, perpetuating existing feelings of marginality among people from the North East, including Darjeeling.

17. A recent newspaper article discusses the deliberate strategy of the 2nd Gorkhaland Movement and its solidarity with women from all walks of life, which was not the case in 1986. In fact, the first martyr of the new movement was a woman who died in a recent police shooting. The 2nd Gorkhaland Movement started in October 2007.

Chapter 3

1. When I began this research the tea farmers in this study were struggling to get cooperative registration. Over the years they decided that cooperative registration was not the most fruitful bureaucratic means to formalize their existence within the Darjeeling tea trade as it would jeopardize their access to Fair Trade resources (as detailed later in this chapter and the book). Instead they went for society's registration and replaced the word Cooperative with Sanstha. I have used a pseudonym of their original name retaining the word Sanstha to reflect this transformation. However in common conversation people in the area still call it a cooperative.

2. From my interviews with Darjeeling Tea Association officers, I understand that there are no official statistics about the exact number of organic gardens, but I was given a rough estimate that thirty plantations were certified organic and the number was growing.

3. When I returned for fourteen months of fieldwork in 2006, the DPA was renamed as Darjeeling Tea Association (DTA).

4. Hand-rolled tea made by the farmers and their families.

5. Like the plantation, I have not used the name of the cooperative; I just refer to it as a tea cooperative or by its pseudonym, Sānu Krishak Sansthā. Translated from Nepali it means Small Farmer's Organization.

6. I have found out from my life history interviews with older plantation workers that the British planters did not use any pesticides. They used cow dung. Chemical-intensive methods of tea cultivation were introduced in the 1960s when India adopted the green revolution.

7. The italicized words indicate the various Nepali caste groups present in the co-op area.

8. The plantation where I did my fieldwork was not buying tea from this particular cooperative.

9. It is not my purpose in this book to write the history of Fair Trade. There have been numerous interventions by scholars to chart its history (see Raynolds et al. 2007 for a very detailed history, also Jaffee 2007).

Chapter 4

1. One the voluntourists in this ethnography Kate Curnow made a documentary called "My Life With Fair Trade" which was recently available on

YouTube and is now removed. I possess the full version of it because Kate shared it with me when we met in the U.S.

2. When we met in the U.S. many years after the original encounter in Darjeeling in 2007 she gave me a copy of the uncut footage with my interview in it. I appreciated that, but the fact remained that the public (who chose to watch her five-minute video) only got to see her celebration of the "cooperation" which according to the documentary was due to Fair Trade. This student was one of the most conscientious I met and yet her documentary was full of essentialisms.

3. To protect the identity of my informants I have abstained from citing the websites where they wrote their accounts or using their real names. If my informant's comments or activities are made available by them to the general public I have used their real names instead of pseudonyms to document their acts of "witnessing Fair Trade"—a central theoretical and empirical claim of this chapter.

Chapter 5

1. Leela Fernandes (1997) and Amrita Basu (1992) also write in detail about the union and political party nexus in India. In Darjeeling the alliance has a specific history with consequences for labor politics.

2. This treaty allowed Nepalis and Indians to settle, work, and trade in each country without the right to vote, as I have described in chapter 2.

3. From October 2007, Darjeeling is under the sway of the second Gorkhaland Agitation, this time lead by Gorkha Janamukti Morcha (GJM), a breakaway party from the GNLF.

4. Chhāyā's views about the coercive politics of GNLF are shared by many informants (both male and female), some of whom are not as articulate as Chhāyā and do not share her leadership qualities. Women who were not explicitly critical of GNLF also complained about nepotism and the uselessness of unions in raising wages and upholding their concerns.

5. Criticizing the leaders of the 2nd Gorkhaland Movement, an opposition party leader in Darjeeling expressed concern over the anti-democratic means of this movement for social justice in an English newspaper. The GJM (Gorkha Janamukti Morcha) is being accused of diverting attention away from many other problems in Darjeeling by promoting this single issue movement.

6. Phone interview with Chintamani Rai in December, 2007.

7. The Joint Body is a recent phenomenon in many Fair Trade–certified plantations in Darjeeling. It is supposed to be a group of workers representative of different interests within the plantation community. The group was supposed to be drawing up plans on how to spend money coming from Fair Trade product sales in the West.

8. Ghumāuri is the informal saving group popular among women plantation workers. I detail it later.

9. When I was in Darjeeling in 2005, and then again for a year in 2006–7, the second Gorkhaland Agitation had not started. The members of the

Darjeeling Gorkha Hill Council were preoccupied with their efforts to get the 6th schedule for Darjeeling district. The latter was thought to be a panacea for the under-development of the region. It would prevent people outside Darjeeling from buying land and also have special job reservations for "backward" people in Darjeeling in government jobs all over India. Ghising spearheaded this drive of the Hill Council. Ghising invented new tribal traditions and people objected to them. He banned the worship of certain Hindu gods, which upset a large section of the "Nepali Community" who were staunch Hindus and did not identify as tribal. Local youth were used as vigilantes to ensure that no Nepali person observed the favorite Hindu festivals, so that the community could prove that it was tribal and should have their own land. While this was just a proxy for an actual state, it gave GNLF party workers a new preoccupation. Like many people, Devilal was frustrated with their efforts to "tribalize" Nepalis and the invention of new religious traditions. Hence he said that people were more into religion.

10. In the early 1980s the GNLF was born out of the collective desire of Nepali people in India to have their own state within India, which would be called "Gorkhaland." Whenever I refer to Agitation, it means Gorkhaland Agitation of 1986–88. Darjeeling was under the grips of a 2nd Gorkhaland Agitation because the first Gorkhaland Agitation ended without a separate state being formed. In 1988 the DGHC or Darjeeling Gorkha Hill Council was formed, which just led to more decentralized administrative power for the DGHC whose chairman was Subhash Ghising. Ghising was seen as a dictator by many locals, and twenty-two years after his rule his closest allies ousted him from power by forming a new party, Gorkha Janamukti Morcha (GJM). The new party, GJM, has similar viewpoints to those of the GNLF lead by Ghising, but the new movement promises to be less violent, more Gandhian in its approach and tactics. It still wants a separate Gorkha state. From my content analysis of newspapers and personal interviews with people, I gather that this new party, GJM, and its tactics were being questioned by minority political groups in Darjeeling as being non-democratic and coercive, just like the first Gorkhaland Agitation.

11. The question of community is not only significant for anthropologists but has been important for scholars of South Asia to understand the consciousness and practices of people in this region. Scholars studying the region have debated the significance of community in explaining dominance, hegemony, and cross-cutting loyalties of subjects. The question of community gained significance in studies of working-class consciousness. Particularly notable is Dipesh Chakrabarty's (1989) discussion of the importance of community in determining how the working class experience domination and resist powerful forces. More recent work has focused on the production of class and community (Fernandes 1997) with special emphasis on gendered exclusions. Scholars studying environmental conservation have also focused on the contested nature of communities in South Asia and its significance for resource managements (Agrawal 1999; Agrawal and Sivaramakrishnan 2000).

12. *Ghumāuri* originates from the Nepali verb *Ghumaono* (to move something in circles). Workers explained that they move money in a circle "like a ring." It is named so because money, food, stories, and emotions are circulated between groups of workers by their own volition.

13. Although I was asked by some women to not reveal the existence of *ghumāuri* groups on the plantation, I have since conferred with some members, and they qualified their request. They agreed that it was alright for me to talk about the groups, since the plantation management did indeed know about their existence. But they asked me to try to protect their identities, since management does not know which individuals are involved. I have therefore done everything I can to protect their identities, including the use of pseudonyms, masking/changing of details, and delinking critical quotations from individuals.

14. "Bonus" is a payment made to workers during the Nepali Hindu festival of "*Dashai.*" The money for the bonus comes from a section of a worker's salary and the management also puts in a proportion depending on the harvest year.

15. Plantation workers, both men and women, sometimes refer to themselves sarcastically as *coolies*, a Hindi word for day laborers who made their living by carrying heavy loads. It is a derogatory term for unskilled laborers.

16. Information used from http://www.mercycorps.org/countries/india/2108, accessed on December 12, 2008.

17. For further evidence of the influence of party politics on national and local-level labor organizing, see Leela Fernandes (1997) and Piya Chatterjee (2001).

Chapter 7

1. Since the organic and Fair Trade inspectors rarely used the Nepali translation of organic, *jaivik*, in training programs, men and women used the English—organic. I would also like to note that I have witnessed an increase in the use of the words organic and Fair Trade over the last eleven years. With the declaration that the neighboring state of Sikkim (which also has a sizeable population of Nepalis) would be an organic-certified state the intensity and envy has affected the use of organic as metaphor in Darjeeling.

2. Bihari, Bengali, and Punjabi are other regional groups within India.

3. *Madeshi* is another Nepali term for designating people from the plains.

4. This work involves cleaning the weeds between the tea bushes.

5. One of the earliest gender and development programs that women in Sānu Krishak Sansthā took part in was the Government of India's Integrated Child Development Program (ICDS), also called *ānganwādi* in other places in India.

6. The Women's Wing had decided that the person who took the milk to town would get a share of the profits from the milk sales as her daily salary.

The same person would not take the milk to town for more than three months in a row to ensure that everyone, depending on their need, would be able to earn from the Women's Wing's collective business.

7. Nepali derogatory terms for implying that women were street smart and had sharp tongues.

Chapter 8

1. The majority of NGOs in Darjeeling were run by Nepali educated middle- and upper-class men and women. This NGO worker was a Nepali upper-caste male.

2. *Basti* when literally translated from Nepali means an area of human settlement. *Kaman* is another local word for plantations. In Darjeeling, people talked about localities through the *basti/kaman* dichotomy.

3. Plantations in Darjeeling are very secretive about the percentage of workers whom they hire as temporary workers during the high season—the plucking season. Newspaper reports and conversation with NGO members reveal that at times plantations can keep the majority of the workforce as seasonal labor. In the plantation where I did most of my ethnography I was unable to find out the exact number of seasonal labor employed from the plantation management.

4. Personal interview with author May 15, 2007.

5. While plantation workers get a daily wage, they can earn some extra money between the months of March and October when tea leaves grow in abundance. In the plantation where I did this research, they were paid Rs. 3 for every extra kilo of tea they plucked beyond their minimum daily plucking requirement of eight kilos a day.

6. If the Women's Wing secretary was illiterate, then literate members helped in keeping meeting minutes.

7. The tea cooperative where I did my fieldwork was not registered with the state government until 2006. The reason for it being unregistered is outlined in chapter 3.

8. The Women's Wing had monthly meetings on the 8th day of every month. The 8th day of the month was originally selected in 1999 by the NGO working with women tea farmers to spread awareness about International Women's Day and women's issues and every year on March 8. The Women's Wing celebrates women's day in their own style.

9. Equating him as the "board," meaning Cooperative Board, was a way for women to show respect and at the same time make the president aware of the severe implications of his smallest actions.

10. The dispensary provided basic services and medicines, with no provision for surgery, for which plantation workers had to be taken to town. Often plantation workers would not have money to afford town doctors. It was largely the owner's discretion to whom he would pay for the doctor's expenses in town. You had to be in his good books for this service.

Conclusion

1. In India state-level CSR intervention is enshrined in the recent legislation which states that all Joint Stock Companies have to invest 2 percent of their share of profit toward CSR projects. According to the UK daily, *The Guardian*, India is the first nation to stipulate such a law (http://www.theguardian.com/sustainable-business/india-csr-law-debate-business-ngo).

2. http://theladiesfinger.com/why-do-we-tend-to-think-farmer-man/.

3. I am referring to the sensational documentary "India's Daughter" (directed by a white British woman, Leslie Udwin) whose reception in India brought out a deep divide among Indian feminists. In my opinion the documentary uses every trope of representing the poor as violent and India's educated lower-class women as voiceless. My critique of this documentary also reflects Nepali women's reaction to the massive protests against rape in New Delhi as I have indicated in a previous chapter.

References

Abu-Lughod, L. (2011). *Do Muslim women need saving?* Cambridge, MA: Harvard University Press.

Adelman, M. (2008). The "culture" of the global anti-gender violence social movement. *American Anthropologist* 110 (4), 511–14.

Agarwal, B. (1994). *A field of one's own: Gender and land rights in South Asia.* Cambridge, UK: Cambridge University Press.

Agarwal, B. (2010). *Gender and Green Governance: The political economy of women's presence within and beyond community forestry.* Oxford: Oxford University Press.

Agrawal, A. (2005). *Environmentality: Technologies of government and the making of subjects.* Durham, NC: Duke University Press.

Ahearn, L. M. (2001). *Invitations to love: Literacy, love letters and social change in Nepal.* Ann Arbor: University of Michigan Press.

Alexander, J. M., and Mohanty, C. (Eds.). (2013). *Feminist genealogies, colonial legacies and democratic futures.* London: Routledge.

Alexander-Floyd, N. G. (2006). *Race, gender and nationalism in contemporary Black politics.* New York: Palgrave McMillian.

Anderson, B. (1991). *Imagined communities: Reflections on the origin and spread of nationalism.* London: Verso.

Babb, F. E. (2005). Autonomy in the age of globalization: The vision of June Nash. *Critique of Anthropology* 25 (3), 211–16.

Bacon, C. (2005). Confronting the coffee crisis: Can Fair Trade, organic, and specialty coffees reduce small scale farmer vulnerability in northern Nicaragua? *World Development* 33 (3), 497–511.

Baldez, L. (2002). *Why women protest: Women's movements in Chile.* Cambridge, UK: Cambridge University Press.

Batliwala, S. (2002). Grassroots movements and transnational actors: Implications for global civil society. *Voluntas: International Journal of Voluntary and Nonprofit Organizations* 13 (4), 393–409.

Batliwala, S. (2007). When rights go wrong: Distorting the rights based approach to development. *Seminar,* January 2007. http://www.justassociates.org/sites/justassociates.org/files/whenrightsgowrong.pdf.

Barrientos, S., and Smith, S. (2007). Mainstreaming fair trade in the global food production networks: Own brand food and chocolate in UK supermarkets." In L. T. Raynolds, D. T. Murray, and J. Wilkinson (Eds.). *Fair Trade: The Challenges of Transforming Globalization.* (pp, 103–23). New York: Routledge.

Basu, A. (1992). *Two faces of protest: Contrasting modes of women's activism in India.* Berkeley: University of California Press.

Becker, E., and Jahn, T. (1999). *Sustainability and the social sciences: A cross disciplinary approach to integrating environmental considerations.* London: Zed Books.

Beneria, L., and Roldán, M. (1987). *The crossroads of class and gender: Industrial homework, subcontracting and household dynamics in Mexico City.* Chicago: University of Chicago Press.

Berger, M. T. (2006). *Workable sisterhood: The political journey of stigmatized women with HIV-AIDS.* Princeton, NJ: Princeton University Press.

Bernard, H. Russell. (2002). *Research Methods in Anthropology.* New York: Altamira.

Besky, S. (2014). *The Darjeeling distinction: Labor and justice on fair-trade tea plantations in India.* Berkeley: University of California Press.

Bhowmik, S. K. (1981). *Class formation in the plantation system.* New Delhi: People's Publications.

Bhowmik, S. K. (2003). Productivity and labor standards in tea plantation sectors in India. In *Tea Plantations of West Bengal in Crisis.* New Delhi: Centre for Education and Communication.

Bisen, J. S., and A. K. Singh. (2012). Impact of inorganic to organic cultivation practices on yield of tea in Darjeeling Hills: A case study. *Indian Journal of Horticulture* 69 (2), 288–91.

Blowfield, M., and Dolan, C. (2008). Stewards of virtue: The ethical dilemma of CSR in African agriculture. *Development and Change* 39 (1), 1–23.

Bourdieu, P. (1977). *Outline of a theory of practice.* New York: Cambridge University Press.

Breman, J. (1996). *Footloose labor: Working in India's informal economy.* New York: Cambridge University Press.

Breman, J. (2003). *The laboring poor in India: Patterns of exploitation, subordination and exclusion.* Delhi: Oxford University Press.

Briggs, C. L. (1986). *Learning how to ask: A sociolinguistic appraisal of the role of interview in social science research.* New York: Cambridge University Press.

Brondo, K. V. (2013). *Land grab: Green neoliberalism, gender and Garifuna Resistance in Honduras.* Tucson: University of Arizona Press.

Brooks, E. (2007). *Unraveling the garment industry: Transnational organization and women's work.* Minneapolis: University of Minnesota Press.

Brown, K. (2013). *Buying into fair trade: Culture, morality and consumption* New York: New York University Press.

Buttel, F. H., and Gould, K. A. (2004). Global social movement(s) at the crossroads: Some observations on the trajectory of the anti-corporate globalization movement. *Journal of World Systems Research* x (i), 37–66.

Chakrabarty, D. (1989). *Rethinking working class history: Bengal 1890–1940.* Princeton, NJ: Princeton University Press.

Chakravarti, U. (1990). "Whatever happened to the Vedic dasi? Orientalism, nationalism and a script for the past." In K Sangari and S Vaid (Eds.). *Recasting Women: Essays in Indian Colonial History,* New Brunswick, NJ: Rutgers University Press.

Chari, S. (2004). *Fraternal capital: Peasant-workers, self-made men, and globalization in provincial India.* Stanford, CA: Stanford University Press.

Chatterjee, Partha. (1989). Colonialism, nationalism and colonized women: The contest in India." *American Ethnologist* 16 (4), 622–33.

Chatterjee, Piya. (1995). Encounters over tea: Labor, gender, and politics on an Indian Plantation. PhD diss., University of Chicago.

Chatterjee, Piya. (2001). *A time for tea: Women, labor, and post/colonial politics on an Indian Plantation.* London: Duke University Press.

Chatterjee, Piya. (2006). Taking blood: Gender, race, and imagining public anthropology in India." *India Review* 5 (3&4), 551–71.

Chatterjee, Piya. (2007). Tea's fortunes and famines: Global capital, Women workers, and survival in Indian plantation country." In A Cabezas (Ed.). *The wages of empire: neoliberal policies, repression and women's poverty.* Boulder, CO: Paradigm Publishers.

Chatterjee, Piya. (2009). "Transforming pedagogies: Imagining internationalist/feminist/antiracist literacies." In J. Sudbury and M. Ozakawa-Ray. (Eds.). *Activist scholarship: Antiracism, feminism and social change* (pp, 131–48). Boulder, CO: Paradigm Publishers.

Chhetri, V. (2004). Chastity belt for Darjeeling tea: Central move to protect India's unique produce against fake onslaught. *The Telegraph,* Calcutta, November 3. Accessed January 21, 2005. http://www.telegraphindia. com/1041103/asp/frontpage/story_3959015.asp.

Cho, S., Crenshaw, K. W., and McCall, L. (2013). Toward a field theory of Intersectionality: Theory, applications, praxis. *Signs* 38 (4), 785–810.

Chowdhury, E. H. (2011). *Transnationalism reversed: Women organizing against gendered violence in Bangladesh.* Albany, NY: SUNY Press.

Collins, J. L. (2002). Deterritorialization and workplace culture. *American Ethnologist* 29 (1), 151–71.

Cornwall, A., Harrison, E., and Whitehead, A. (2007). Gender myths and feminist fables: The struggle for interpretive power in gender and development. *Development and Change* 38 (1), 1–20.

Creswell, J. (2013). *Research design: Qualitative, quantitative, and mixed method approaches, 4th edition.* Thousand Oaks, CA: SAGE Publications.

Cruz Torres, M. L. and McElwee, P. (Eds). (2012). *Gender and sustainability: Lessons from Asia and Latin America.* Tucson: University of Arizona Press.

Darjeeling LaDenla Road Prerana. (2003a). *Area and issue profile of Darjeeling and Sikkim.* Report prepared by Mashqura Fareedi and Pasang Dorjee Lepcha. Darjeeling: Regional Community Development Center Hayden Hall.

Darjeeling LaDenla Road Prerana. (2003b). Small farmers organic tea and Sanjukta Vikas Cooperative: A case study from Darjeeling Hills." Conference paper for Regional Community Development Center by Navin Tamang. Darjeeling: Regional Community Development Center Hayden Hall.

Das, N. K. (2003). "Geographical Indications: The Experience of Indian Tea Producers." Paper prepared for the Worldwide Symposium of GIs, San Francisco, July 9–11.

Das, V., and Addlakha, R. (2001). Disability and domestic citizenship: Voice, gender and the making of the subject. *Public Culture* 13 (3), 511–31.

Dash, A. (1947). *Bengal district gazetteers: Darjeeling*. Alipore: Bengal Government Press.

Davis, D. (2013). Border crossings: Intimacy and feminist activist ethnography in the age of neoliberalism. In C. Craven and D. Davis. (Eds.). *Feminist Activist Ethnography: Counterpoints to Neoliberalism in North America* (pp. 1038). London: Lexington Books.

de Certeau, M. (1984). *The practice of everyday life*. Berkeley: University of California Press.

Derne, S. (2000). Men's sexuality and women's subordination in Indian nationalisms." In T Mayer (Ed.), *Gender ironies of nationalism: Sexing the nation*, London: Routledge.

Doane, M. (2010). "Relationship coffees: Structure and agency within the fair trade system." In S. Lyon and M. Moberg (Eds.). *Fair Trade and Social Justice: Global Ethnographies.* (pp. 229–57). New York: New York University Press.

Dolan, C. S. (2001). The 'good' wife: Struggles over resources in Kenyan horticultural sector." *Journal of Development Studies* 37 (3), 39–70.

Dolan, C. S. (2008). In the mists of development: Fairtrade in Kenyan tea fields. *Globalizations* 5 (2), 305–18.

Dolan, C. S. (2010). Virtual moralities: The mainstreaming of fair trade in Kenyan tea fields. *Geoforum* 41, 33–43.

Elliston, D. A. (2004). A passion for the nation: Masculinity, modernity and nationalist struggle." *American Ethnologist* 31 (4), 606–30.

Elson, D., and Pearson, R. (1981). Nimble fingers make cheap workers: An analysis of women's employment in third world export manufacturing." *Feminist Review* 7: 87–107.

Elyachar, J. (2005). *Markets of Dispossession*. Durham, NC: Duke University Press.

Escobar, Arturo. (1995). *Encountering Development*. Princeton, NJ: Princeton University Press.

Fair Trade Advocacy Office. (2013). "Equal Harvest: Report on the Gender Gap in Smallholder Agriculture." Accessed June 27, 2015. http://www.fairtrade-advocacy.org/ftao-publications/newsletters/157-newsletters-articles/809-equal-harvest-report-on-the-gender-gap-in-smallholder-agriculture#sthash.sfahZjMp.dpuf.

Fair Trade USA. (2015). "What is Fair Trade?" Accessed June 29, 2015. http://fairtradeusa.org/WHAT-IS-FAIR-TRADE/IMPACT/EMPOWERING-WOMEN.

Fairtrade International. (2013). "Welcome to Fairtrade India." Last modified November 22. Accessed June 29, 2015. http://www.fairtrade.net/single-view+M5316f2e262e.html.

Fair Trade Labelling Organizations International (FLO). (2011). Fair trade standards for tea for hired labor. Bonn, Germany: FLO. Accessed April 2011.

Falk-Moore, S. (1987). Explaining the present: Theoretical dilemmas in Processual ethnography." *American Ethnologist* 14 (4): 727–36.

Ferguson, J. (1990). *The anti-politics machine: Development, decentralization and bureaucratic power in Lesotho*. Minneapolis: University of Minnesota Press.

Fernândez-Kelly, M. (1983). *For we are sold, I and my people: Women and industry in Mexico's frontier*. Albany, NY: SUNY Press.

Fernandes, L. (1997). *Producing workers: The politics of gender, class and caste in the Calcutta jute mills*. Philadelphia: University of Pennsylvania Press.

Fernandes, L. (2013). *Transnational feminism in the US: Knowledge, power, ethics*. New York: New York University Press.

Foucault, M. (1979). *Discipline and punish: The birth of the prison*. New York: Vintage.

Foucault, M. (1994). The Subject and Power. In P. Rabinow and N. Rose (Eds.) *The Essential Foucault*, London: The New Press.

Fraser, N. (1997). *Justice interruptus: Critical reflections on the post-socialist condition*. New York: Routledge.

Fraser, N. (2000). Rethinking recognition. *New Left Review* 3 (May–June): 107–20.

Fraser, N. (2013). *Fortunes of feminism: From state-managed capitalism to neoliberal crisis*. New York: Verso.

Freeman, C. (2000). *High tech and high heels in the global economy: Women, work, and pink collar identities in the Caribbean*. Durham, NC: Duke University Press.

Freeman, C. (2014). *Entrepreneurial selves: Neoliberal respectability and the making of a Caribbean middle class*. Durham, NC: Duke University Press.

Freidberg, S. (2004). *French beans and food scares*. New York: Oxford University Press.

Friedmann, H., and McNair, A. (2008). Whose rule rules? Contested projects to certify 'local production for distant consumers.' *Journal of Agrarian Change* 8 (2–3), 408–34.

Gajjala, R. 2014. *Cyberculture and the subaltern*. New York: Lexington Books.

George, G. (2005). Feminist questions, grassroots movements: An overview. *Voices* 7 (1), 1–14.

Gershon, I. (2011). "Neoliberal agency." *Current Anthropology* 52 (4), 537–55.

Getz, C., and Shreck, A. (2006). What organic and fair trade labels do not tell us: Towards a place-based understanding of certification. *International Journal of Consumer Studies* 30 (5), 490–501.

Gezon, L. L. (2002). Marriage, kin and compensation: A socio-political ecology of gender in Ankarana, Madagascar. *Anthropological Quarterly* 75 (4), 675–706.

Gezon, L. L. (2012). Why gender matters, why women matter. In M. L. Cruz-Torres and P. McElwee (Eds.). *Gender and sustainability: Lessons from Asia and Latin America* (pp, 231–43). Tucson: University of Arizona Press.

Gidwani, V. (2008). *Capital interrupted: Agrarian development and politics of work in India*. Minneapolis: University of Minnesota Press.

Goodale, M., and Merry, S. E. (Eds). (2007). *The practice of Human Rights: Tracking law between the global and the local*. Cambridge, UK: Cambridge University Press.

Goodman, D., and Watts, M. (1997). *Globalizing food: Agrarian questions and global restructuring*. London: Routledge.

Goodman, M. K. (2004). Reading fair trade: Political ecological imaginary and the moral economy of fair trade foods. *Political Geography* 23, 891–915.

Goodman, M. K. (2010). The mirror of consumption: Celebritization, developmental consumption and the shifting cultural politics of fair trade. *Geoforum* 41 (1), 104–16.

Government of India. (2011). Census of India.

Grewal, I., and Kaplan, C. (Eds). (1994). *Scattered hegemonies: Postmodernity and transnational feminist practices*. Minneapolis: University of Minnesota Press.

Griffiths, P. (1967). *The history of the British tea industry*. London: Weidenfield and Nicolson.

Gunewardena, N., and Kingsolver, A. (2008). Introduction. In N. Gunewardena and A. Kingsolver (Eds). *The gender of globalization: Women navigating cultural and economic marginalities*. Santa Fe, NM: SAR Press.

Gupta. A. (1992). The song of the nonaligned world: Transnational identities and the reinscription of space in late capitalism. *Cultural Anthropology* 7 (1): 63–79.

Gupta, A. (1998). *Postcolonial developments: Agriculture in the making of modern India*. Durham, NC: Duke University Press.

Gururani, S. (2002a). Construction of third world women's knowledge in the development discourse. *International Social Science Journal* 54 (173), 313–23.

Gururani, S. (2002b). Forests of pleasure and pain: Gendered practices of labor and livelihood in the forests of the Kumaon Himalayas, India. *Gender, Place & Culture: A Journal of Feminist Geography* 9 (3), 229–43.

Guthman, J. (2004). *Agrarian dreams: The paradox of organic farming in California*. Berkeley: University of California Press.

Guthman, J. (2007). The Polyanian way? Voluntary food labels as neoliberal governance. *Antipode* 39, 456–78.

Harcourt, W., and Nelson, I. L. (2015). *Practicing feminist ecologies: Moving beyond the 'green economy.'* London: Zed Books.

Hardt, M., and Negri, A. (2001). *Empire*. Boston: Harvard University Press.

Harrison, F. V. (2007). "Feminist methodology as a tool for ethnographic inquiry on globalization." In *Gender of globalization: Women navigating cultural and economic marginalities*, edited by Nandini Gunewardena and Ann Kingsolver, Santa Fe, NM: School of Advanced Research, 23–31.

Harrison, F. V. (2008). *Outsider within: Reworking anthropology in the global age*. Urbana: University of Illinois Press.

Harris-White, Barbara. (2003). *India working: Essays on society and economy*. New York: Cambridge University Press.

Hart, Gillian. (1992). "Household production reconsidered: Gender, labor conflict, and technological change in Malaysia's Muda Region." *World Development* 20 (6): 809–23.

Harvey, D. (2000). *Spaces of hope*. Berkeley: University of California Press.

Harvey, D. (2014). *Seventeen contradictions and the end of Capitalism*. Oxford: Oxford University Press.

Hodgson, D. L., and McCurdy, S. (2001). Introduction: "Wicked" women and the reconfiguration of gender in Africa." In D. L. Hodgson and S. A. McCurdy (Eds.). *Wicked women and the reconfiguration of gender in Africa* (pp, 1–27). Cape Town: David Philip.

Hyndman, J. (2004). Mind the gap: Bridging feminist and political geography through geopolitics." *Political Geography* 23: 307–22.

Iversen, V. (2003). Intra-household inequality: A challenge for the capability approach? *Feminist Economics* 9 (2–3), 93–115.

Jaffee, D. (2007). *Brewing justice: Fair trade coffee, sustainability and survival*. Berkley: University of California Press.

Jha, Nitish. (2004). "Gender and decision making in Balinese agriculture." *American Ethnologist* 31 (4): 552–72.

Jhabvala, R., Sudarshan, R. M., and Unni, J. 2003. *Informal economy center stage: New structures of employment*. New Delhi: Sage.

Kabeer, N. (1994). *Reversed realities: Gender hierarchies in development thought*. London: Verso.

Kabeer, N. (1999). "Resources, agency, achievements: Reflections on the measure of women's empowerment." *Development and Change* 30:435–64.

Kabeer, N. (2000). *The power to choose: Bangladeshi women and labor market decisions in London and Dhaka*. London: Verso.

Kabeer, N. (2001). Conflicts over credit: Re-evaluating the empowerment potential of loans to women in rural Bangladesh. *World Development* 29 (1), 63–84.

Kabeer, N. (2004). Labor standards, women's rights, basic needs: Challenges to collective action in a globalizing world." In L. Beneria and S. Bisnath (Eds.). *Global tensions: Challenges and opportunities in the world economy*. London: Routledge.

Kandiyoti, D. (1994). Identity and its discontents: Women and the nation. In P. Williams and L. Calismon (Eds.). *Colonial Discourse and Post-Colonial Theory*. (pp, 376–91). New York: Columbia University Press.

Kapadia, K. (2002). "Translocal modernities and transformations of gender and caste." In K. Kapadia (Ed.). *The Violence of development: The politics of identity, gender, and social inequalities in India*. London: Zed Books.

Karim, L. (2011). *Microfinance and its discontents: Women and debt in Bangladesh.* Minneapolis: University of Minnesota Press.

Kascak, L, with Dasgupta, S. (2014). #Instagrammingafrica: The narcissism of global voluntourism.*The Society Pages*, December 29. Accessed July 2, 2015. http://thesocietypages.org/socimages/2014/12/29/instragramming africa-the-narcissism-of-global-voluntourism/.

Katz, C. (2001). On the grounds of global capital: A topography for feminist political engagement." *Signs* 26 (4), 1213–34.

Katz, C. (2001). "Vagabond capitalism and the necessity of social reproduction." *Anitpode* 33 (4), 709–28.

Klenk, R. M. (2004). "Who is a Developed Woman?": Women as category of development discourse, Kumaon, India. *Development and Change* 35; 57–78.

Klenk, R. M. (2010). *Education activists: Development and gender in the making of modern Gandhians.* Lanham, MD: Lexington Books.

Koehler, J. (2015). *Darjeeling: A history of the world's greatest tea.* New Delhi: Bloomsbury.

Kudva, N., and Misra. K. (2008). Gender quotas, the politics of presence and the feminist project: What does the Indian experience tell us?" *Signs* 34 (1), 49–73.

Lama, M. P. (1996). *Gorkhaland movement: Quest for an identity.* Darjeeling: Nathu Press.

Lazreg, M. (2002). Development Feminist Theory's Cul-De-Sac. In K. Saunders (Ed.). *Feminist post-development thought: Rethinking modernity, postcolonialism and representation.* (pp, 123–45) London: Zed Books.

Li, T. M. (2000). "Articulating indigenous identity in Indonesia: Resource politics and the tribal slot." *Comparative Studies in Society and History* 42 (1): 149–79.

Li, T. M. (2001). "Masyarakat Adat, difference, and the limits of recognition in Indonesia's forest zone" *Modern Asian Studies* 35 (3): 645–76.

Li, T. M. (2002). "Local histories, global markets: Cocoa and class in Upland Sulawesi." *Development and Change* 33 (3): 415–37.

Loomba, Ania, and Ritty, Lukose. (2012). *South Asian Feminisms.* Durham, NC: Duke University Press.

Lucas, Linda E. (Ed.). (2007). *Unpacking globalization: Markets, gender and work.* Lanham, MD: Lexington Books.

Lahiri-Dutt, K. (2014). *Experiencing and coping with change: Women-headed farming households in the Eastern Gangetic Plains.* Canberra: Australian Centre for International Agricultural Research. Accessed June 30, 2015. http://aciar.gov.au/files/tr_83_web.pdf.

Lahiri-Dutt, K., and Samanta, G. (2006). Constructing social capital: Self-help groups and rural women's development in India. *Geographical Research* 44 (3): 285–95.

Lynch, C. (2007). *Juki girls, good girls: gender and cultural politics in Sri Lanka's global garment industry.* Ithaca, NY: Cornell University Press.

Lyon, S. (2008). Fair Trade coffee and Human Rights in Guatemala. *Journal of Consumer Policy* 30, 241–61.

March, K. S., and Taqqu, R. (1984). *Women's informal associations in developing countries: Catalysts for change (Women in Cross-cultural Perspective)*. Boulder, CO: Westview Press.

Majumder, S. (2012). "Who wants to marry a farmer?" Neoliberal industrialization and the politics of land and work in rural West Bengal. *Focal* 64, 84–98.

Majumder, S. (Forthcoming) *Landed longing: Farm, factory, protest and development in globalizing India*. New York: Fordham University Press.

Makita, R., and Tsuruta, T. (2017). *Fair Trade and organic initiatives in Asian agriculture: The hidden realities*. London: Routledge.

Massey, D. (1991). A Global sense of place. *Marxism Today* 35 (6), 24–29.

Mayoux, L. (2001). Tackling the down side: Social capital, women's empowerment and micro-finance in Cameroon." *Development and Change* 32 (3), 435–64.

McLaurin, I. (Ed.). (2001). *Black feminist anthropology: Theory, politics, praxis and poetics*. New Brunswick, NJ: Rutgers University Press.

Merry, S. E. (2006). *Human rights and gender violence*. Chicago: University of Chicago Press.

Middleton, T. (2015). The demands of recognition: State anthropology and ethnopolotics in Darjeeling. Stanford, CA: Stanford University Press.

Mies, M. (1982). *The lace makers of Narsapur: Indian housewives produce for the world market*. London: Zed Press.

Mills, M. B. (2002). *Thai women in a global labor force: Consuming desires, contested selves*. New Brunswick, NJ: Rutgers University Press.

Mills, M. B. (2005). From nimble fingers to raised fists: Women and labor organizing in globalizing Thailand. *Signs* 31 (1), 117–44.

Moberg, M, and Lyon, S. (2010). "What's fair? The paradox of seeking justice through markets." In S. Lyon and M. Moberg (Eds.), *Fair trade and social justice: Global ethnographies* (pp, 1–27). New York: New York University Press.

Mohanty, C. T. (1991). "Under Western Eyes: Feminist Scholarship and Colonial Discourses." In C. Mohanty, A. Russo, and L. Torres. (Eds.), *Third World women and the politics of feminism*. Bloomington: Indiana University Press.

Moodie, M. (2008). Enter microcredit: A new culture of women's empowerment in Rajasthan?" *American Ethnologist* 35 (3), 454–65.

Moodie, M. (2013). Microfinance and the gender of risk: The case of Kiva.org. *Signs: Journal of Women in Culture & Society* 38 (2), 279–302.

Mutersbaugh, T. (2002). The number is the beast: A political economy of organic-coffee certification and producer unionism. *Environment and Planning* A 34 (7), 1165–84.

Mutersbaugh, T. (2005). Just-in-space: Certified rural products, labor of quality, and regulatory spaces. *Journal of Rural Studies* 21 (4), 389–402.

Mutersbaugh, T. and Lyon, S. (2010). Transparency and democracy in certified ethical commodity networks. *Geoforum* 41 (January), 27–32.

Mutersbaugh, T., Klooster, D., Renard, M., and Taylor, P. (2005). Certifying rural spaces: quality-certified products and rural governance, *Journal of Rural Studies* 21 (4), 381–88.

Nagar, R., and Swarr, A. L. (2010). Introduction: Theorizing transnational feminist praxis. In R. Nagar and A. L. Swarr (Eds.), Critical transnational feminist praxis. Albany, NY: SUNY Press.

Naples, N. (2003). *Feminism and method: Ethnography, discourse analysis and activist research*. London: Routledge.

Naples, N., and Desai, M. (Eds.). (2002). *Women's activism and globalization: Linking local struggles and transnational politics*. New York: Routledge.

Narayan, K. (1993). How native is a "Native" anthropologist? *American Anthropologist* 95 (3), 671–86.

Narayan, U. (2010). Women: Rights-bearers, economic assets, or stranded starfish? Review of *Half the sky: Turning oppression into opportunity for women worldwide*, by Nicholas D. Kristof and Shirley WuDunn. *Perspectives on Politics* 8, (1).

Nussbaum, M. (2011). *Creating capabilities: The human development approach*. 1st ed. Cambridge, MA: Belknap Press.

Oberhauser, A. M., and Pratt, A. (2005). Women's collective economic strategies and political transformation in rural South Africa. *Gender, Place and Culture* 11 (2), 209–28.

Ong, A. (1987). *Spirits of resistance and capitalist discipline: Factory women in Malaysia*. Albany, NY: SUNY Press.

Ong, A. (1991). Gender and the labor politics of postmodernity. *Annual Review of Anthropology* 20, 279–309.

Ong, A. (2006). *Neoliberalism as exception: Mutations in citizenship and sovereignty*. Durham, NC: Duke University Press.

Ortner, S. (2005). Subjectivity and cultural critique. *Anthropological Theory* 5 (1), 31–52.

Peet, R., and Watts, M. (1993). Introduction: Development theory and environment in an age of market triumphalism. *Economic Geography* 69 (3), 227–53.

Prugl, Elizabeth. (1999). *The global construction of gender: home-based work in the political economy of the 20th Century*. New York: Columbia University Press.

Pulido, L. (1996). *Environmental and economic justice: Two Chicano struggles in the Southwest*. Tucson: The University of Arizona Press.

Purkayastha, B., and Subramaniam, M. (Eds.). (2004). *The power of women's informal networks: lessons in social change from South Asia and West Africa*. Lanham, MD: Lexington Books.

Rai, R. B. (2000). *Hamro Basbhumima Chiyabari Majdur Andolanko Pahilo Charan: Pheri Naya Charan*. Darjeeling: Compuset Center.

Rai, S. M., C. Hoskyns, and D. Thomas. (2013). "Depletion: The cost of social reproduction." *International Feminist Journal of Politics* 16 (1), 86–105.

Ramamurthy, P. (2003). Material consumers, fabricating subjects: Perplexity, global connectivity discourses, and transnational feminist research. *Cultural Anthropology* 18 (4), 524–50.

Ramamurthy, P. (2010). "Why are men doing floral sex work? Gender, cultural reproduction, and the feminization of agriculture." *Signs* 35 (2), 397–424.

Ramamurthy, P. (2011). "Rearticulating caste: The global cottonseed commodity chain and the paradox of smallholder capitalism in South India." *Environment and Planning A* 43 (5), 1035–56.

Rankin, K. N. (2001). Governing development: Neoliberalism, microcredit, and rational economic woman. *Economy & Society* 30 (1), 18–37.

Rankin, K. N. (2004). *The cultural politics of markets: Economic liberalization and social change in Nepal.* Toronto: University of Toronto Press.

Ravi Raman, K. (2010). *Global capital and peripheral labor: The history and political economy of plantation workers in India.* London: Routledge.

Raynolds, L. T. (2002). "Wages for wives: Renegotiating gender and production relations in contract farming in the Dominican Republic." *World Development* 30 (5), 783–98.

Raynolds, L. T. (2009). "Mainstreaming Fair Trade coffee: From partnership to traceability." *World Development* 37 (6), 1083–93.

Raynolds, L. T, Murray, D., and Wilkinson, J., (Eds). (2007). *Fair Trade: The challenges of transforming globalization.* London: Routledge.

Redclift, M (1997). "Sustainability and theory: An agenda for action." In *Globalizing food: Agrarian questions and global restructuring.* Eds. David Goodman and Michael Watts, pp. 333–43. London: Routledge.

Rocheleau, D., and Thomas-Slayter, B. (1996). Feminist political ecology: Global issues and local experiences. New York: Routledge.

Rocheleau, D. (1995). "Gendered resource mapping." In *Power, process and participation: tools for change.* Eds. Rachel Slocum et al. London: Intermediate Technology Publication.

Rocheleau, D., and Edmunds, D. (1997). Women, men and trees: Gender, power and property in forest agrarian landscapes. *World Development* 25 (8), 1351–71.

Roseberry, W. (1989). *Anthropologies and histories: Essays in culture, history, and political economy.* New Brunswick, NJ: Rutgers University Press.

Roseberry, W. (1996). "The rise of yuppie coffees and the reimagination of class in the United States." *American Anthropologist* 98 (4): 762–75.

Roy, T. (2005). *Rethinking economic change in India: Labor and livelihood.* London: Routledge.

Safa, H. I. (1995). *The myth of the male breadwinner: Women and industrialization in the Caribbean.* Boulder, CO: Westview Press.

Samanta, A. K. (1996). *Gorkhaland: A study in ethnic separatism.* Delhi: Khama Publishers.

Sandoval, C. (2000). *Methodology of the oppressed.* Twin Cities, MN: University of Minnesota Press.

Sanyal, K. (2007). *Rethinking capitalist development: Primitive accumulation, governmentality and post-colonial capitalism.* New Delhi: Routledge.

Schroeder, R. (1999). *Shady practices: Agroforestry and gender politics in the Gambia.* Berkeley: University of California Press.

Seligmann, L. (2004). *Peruvian street lives: Culture, power and economy among market women in Cuzco.* Urbana: University of Illinois Press.

Sen, A. (2000). *Development as freedom.* New York: Anchor Books.

Sen, D., and Majumder, S. (2011). Fair Trade and Fair Trade certification of agricultural commodities: Promises, pitfalls and possibilities. *Environment and Society: Advances in Research* 2 (2011), 29–47.

Sen, D. (2012). "Illusive justice: Subnationalism and gendered labor politics in Darjeeling plantations," In S. Roy (Ed.), *New South Asian feminisms: Paradoxes and possibilities* (pp. 131–50). London: Zed Books.

Sen, D. (2014). Fair trade vs. *swaccha vyāpār*: Women's activism and transnational justice regimes in Darjeeling, India. *Feminist Studies* 40 (2), 444–72.

Sen, D., and Majumder, S. (2015). Narratives of risk and poor rural women's (dis)-engagements with microcredit-based development in eastern India. *Critique of Anthropology* 35 (2), 121–41.

Sen, S. (2002). Towards a feminist politics? The Indian Women's Movement in historical perspective. In K. Kapadia (Ed.), *The violence of development: The politics of identity, gender, and social inequalities in India,* (pp, 419–435). London: Zed Books.

Sengupta, H. (2014). *Recasting India: How entrepreneurship is revolutionizing the world's largest democracy.* New York: Palgrave McMillan.

Serageldin, I. (1998). Culture and development in the World Bank. Washington, DC: World Bank.

Sexsmith, K. (2012). Toward gender equality in global sustainable consumption and production agreements." In W. Harcourt (Ed.), *Women reclaiming sustainable livelihoods: Spaces lost spaces gained.* New York: Palgrave McMillian.

Sharma, A. (2008). *Logics of empowerment: Development, gender and governance in neoliberal India.* Minneapolis: University of Minnesota Press.

Sharma, J. (2011). *Empire's garden: Assam and the making of India.* Durham, NC: Duke University Press.

Sharma, K. R., and T. C. Das. (2009). *Globalization and plantation workers in North East India.* New Delhi: Kalpaz Publications.

Sharma, K. R., and T. C. Das. (2011). *Marginalization of Gorkhas in India: A community in quest of Indian identity.* New Delhi: Abhijeet Publications.

Siddiqi, D. (2009). Do Bangladeshi factory workers need saving? Sisterhood in the post-sweatshop era. *Feminist Review* 91, 154–74.

Sivarmakrishnan, K., and Agrawal, A. (2003). "Regional Modernities in Stories and Practices of Development." In *Regional modernities: The cultural politics of development in India.* Stanford, CA: Stanford University Press.

Smith, S. (2015). Fair Trade and women's empowerment. In L. T. Raynolds and E. A. Bennett (Eds.), *Handbook of research on Fair Trade,* (pp. 405–21). Cheltenham, UK: Edward Elgar Publishing Limited.

Spivak, G. C. (1990). Post-structuralism, marginality, postcoloniality and value," In P. Collier and H. Geyer-Ryan (Eds.), *Literary theory today*. Ithaca, NY: Cornell University Press.

Spivak, G. C. (1993) "Scattered speculations in the question of cultural studies." In *Outside in the teaching machine*, pp. 255–84. New York: Routledge.

Spivak, G. C. (2002 [1992]). Thinking academic freedom in gendered postcoloniality." In J. Vincent (Ed.) *Anthropology of politics*, (pp, 452–460). Oxford: Blackwell.

Springer, K. (2005). *Living for a revolution: Black feminist organizations*. Durham, NC: Duke University Press.

Stephen, L. (1993). Challenging gender inequality: Grassroots organizing among women rural workers in Brazil and Chile. *Critique of Anthropology* 13 (1), 33–55.

Stephen, L. (2005). Women's weaving cooperatives in Oaxaca: An indigenous response to neoliberalism." *Critique of Anthropology* 25 (3), 253–78.

Stoler, A. L. (1995). *Capitalism and Confrontation in Sumatra's Plantation Belt, 1870–1979*. Ann Arbor: University of Michigan Press.

Strathern, Marilyn. (1987). "An awkward relationship: The Case of feminism and anthropology." *Signs* 12 (2): 276–92.

Subramaniam, M. (2006). *The power of women's informal organizing: Gender, caste and class in India*. Lanham, MD: Lexington Books.

Subramaniam, M, and Purakayastha, B. (2004). *The power of women's informal networks: Lessons in social change from South Asia and West Africa*. Lanham, MD: Lexington Books.

Sunder Rajan, R., and Park, Y. (2000). "Postcolonial feminism/postcolonialism and feminism" In H. Schwarz and S. Ray (Eds.), *A Companion to postcolonial studies*, (pp. 53–71). Oxford: Blackwell.

Taylor, C. (1992). *Multiculturalism and "the politics of recognition": An essay by Charles Taylor*. Princeton, NJ: Princeton University Press.

Terstappen, V., Hanson, L., and McLaughlin, D. (2013). Gender, health, labor, and inequities: A review of the fair and alternative trade literature." *Agriculture and Human Values* 30 (1), 21–39.

Thapa, N. (2012). Employment status and human development of tea plantation workers in West Bengal. NRPPD Discussion Paper 11, pp. 41–42. Accessed March 11, 2013. http://www.cds.edu/wpcontent/uploads/2012/11/NRPPD11.pdf.

Tsing, Ana. L. (2000). Inside the economy of appearances. *Public Culture* 12 (1), 115–44.

Tsing, Ana. L. (2003). Agrarian allegory and global futures. In P. Greenough and A. L. Tsing (Eds.), *Nature in the Global South: Environmental projects in South and South East Asia* (pp. 124–169). London: Duke University Press.

Visweswaran, K. (1994). *Fictions of feminist ethnography*. Twin Cities, MN: University of Minnesota Press.

Visweswaran, K. (1997). "Histories of feminist ethnography." *Annual Review of Anthropology* 26, 591–621.

Vrasti, W. (2013). *Volunteer tourism in the Global South: Giving back in neoliberal times.* London: Routledge.

Watts, M., and Goodman, D. (1997). Agrarian questions: Global appetite, local metabolism: nature, culture, and industry in fin-de-siecle agro-food systems. In M. Watts and D. Goodman (Eds.), *Globalizing food: Agrarian questions and global restructuring* (pp. 1–34). London: Routledge.

Welker, M. A. (2009). "Corporate security begins in the community": Mining, the corporate social responsibility industry, and environmental advocacy in Indonesia. *Cultural Anthropology* 24 (1), 142–79.

West, P. (2010). Making the market: Specialty coffee, generational pitches, and Papua New Guinea." *Antipode* 42 (3), 690–718.

West, P. (2012). *From modern production to imagined primitive: The social world of coffee from Papua New Guinea.* Durham, NC: Duke University Press.

Williams, R. (1977). *Marxism and literature.* Oxford: Oxford University Press.

Wilson, B. R., and Curnow, J. (2013). Solidarity™: Student activism, affective labor and the Fair Trade Campaign in the United States. *Antipode* 45 (3): 565–83.

Wright, G. (2011). *The Darjeeling tea book.* New York: Penguin.

Wright, M. W. (2006). *Disposable women and other myths of global capitalism.* New York: Routledge.

Index

Note: Page numbers in italics indicate illustrations; those with a *t* indicate tables.

245